AMERICA'S SAFEST CITY

America's Safest City

Delinquency and Modernity in Suburbia

Simon I. Singer

NEW YORK UNIVERSITY PRESS
New York and London

NEW YORK UNIVERSITY PRESS
New York and London
www.nyupress.org

© 2014 by New York University
All rights reserved

References to Internet websites (URLs) were accurate at the time of writing.
Neither the author nor New York University Press is responsible for URLs
that may have expired or changed since the manuscript was prepared.

ISBN: 978-0-8147-6053-6 (hardback)
ISBN: 978-0-8147-6080-2 (paperback)

For Library of Congress Cataloging-in-Publication data, please contact
the Library of Congress.

New York University Press books are printed on acid-free paper,
and their binding materials are chosen for strength and durability.
We strive to use environmentally responsible suppliers and materials
to the greatest extent possible in publishing our books.

Manufactured in the United States of America

10 9 8 7 6 5 4 3 2 1

Also available as an ebook

To my wife, Elena Brachtel Singer, whose love made this book and a lot more that is good in our lives possible.

If indeed we could never establish a wholly unreserved relationship between us, surely the inextinguishable memory of that breach of trust was in part responsible for it. The father had broken a bond with his son that could never be wholly repaired.
—Peter Gay, *Schnitzler's Century: The Making of Middle-Class Culture, 1815–1914*

Your piety is brutality itself. Remember what I told you: Forbid the young people what is permitted and they will, in the end, do it anyhow and also that which is prohibited. Remember!
—Chaim Grade, *The Sacred and the Profane: Three Novellas*

She remembered leaving home with him, books and records and brown bleeding bags of food piled up in the backseat, sleeping bags, kitchen things, the only home she'd known for three-quarters of her life receding in the rearview mirror, and then her mother raging barefoot down the street shouting out for the world to hear that she was throwing her life away. Her mother's face hung there in the window after they'd reached the end of the block, and she could see it now the wet sheen of her eyes and all the gouges and wrinkles of a long day and a long week mobilized in grief—Paulette! You're throwing your life away, your life away!—but she was calm that day too. She'd made up her mind to go, and that was it.
—T. C. Boyle, *Drop City*

There are places I'll remember
All my life though some have changed
Some forever not for better
Some have gone and some remain.
—John Lennon and Paul McCartney, "In My Life"

CONTENTS

ACKNOWLEDGMENTS

Space precludes me from acknowledging all who have contributed to the ideas and data contained in this book. I can only mention a few. I would like to first acknowledge the support of Amherst's Youth Board director, Joseph Bachovchin, and his staff of dedicated professionals. Joe initially contacted the University of Buffalo's Center for the Study of Children and Youth and its co-director Murray Levine about the possibility of a youth needs assessment study. Murray knew of my interest in delinquency and asked if I would take a senior role in working with town officials to develop the requested study. Murray co-authored the reports we produced for the Amherst Youth Board and reviewed subsequent drafts of this book. He has assisted me in producing this book in more ways than I can acknowledge. Thanks as well to Detective Mike Torrillo who headed the Amherst police department youth division during the many years of my Amherst youth studies.

Many graduate students assisted in the data collection and tabulating stages. At the University of Buffalo, Susyan Jou and Tim McCorry worked on the survey and personal interview data. Andrew Pollard made sure every variable was correctly coded and that multiple sources of data were precisely merged. Following my move to Northeastern University, Adam Stearn assisted me further in the data analytical parts of the book. Other students at Northeastern assisted me as well, especially Michelle Comeau and Michael Rocque. My colleagues, Donna Bishop and Peter Manning, listened and generously commented on many of the ideas presented in this book. David McDowall contributed substantially to my statistical analysis of the data. Deans Chet Britt and Jack McDevitt created an academic atmosphere conducive to scholarly research.

The book was also shaped by my long-standing friendship and discussions with Sharon Edelman, Howard Levine, Lionel Lewis, Frank

Munger, and David Pastrich. My children (Miriam, Max, and Rebecca) contributed immensely to my knowledge about the contemporary world of adolescence and young adulthood. Pre- and post-contract reviewers for New York University Press provided the basis for subsequent revisions. Ilene Kalish, the press's executive editor, efficiently facilitated the process of seeing the book from the beginning to end. I am grateful to Caelyn Cobb and Ri Regina for their dedicated administrative assistance. I am especially pleased that this book could appear under the series editorship of John Hagan.

AMERICA'S SAFEST CITY

University of Buffalo's main campus is no longer in the city of Buffalo, New York. It has moved to suburban Amherst, New York.

Introduction

A Personal Journey from Inner to Outer City

I was raised in the South Bronx, several blocks from Yankee Stadium. My parents settled there in August of 1951, impoverished after spending their post-war years in Germany's displaced persons camps. They survived the war, concentration camps, and the death of nearly all their close family members. The trauma of their war-time lives, the inability to properly speak the English language, and a lack of marketable skills made their early years in America terribly difficult. Like so many struggling parents in my neighborhood, they spent much of their time, days and evenings, trying to find work or at work. They seemed too busy to know about the details of my daily activities or the kind of friends with whom I was "hanging out."

Fortunately, the kids I spent time with were generally well behaved. We avoided the street-corner gangs along Ogden and Woodycrest avenues, although we participated in occasional fights and petty acts of theft and property damage. We thought nothing of our bruises and broken noses and viewed our minor acts of delinquency as just acts of mischief rather than serious acts of crime. A few times we were questioned or warned by the police, but never arrested. In retrospect, several of those police warnings made considerable sense since we could have drowned teaching ourselves how to swim in the Harlem River. A police officer's stern threat of arrest for reselling tickets at Yankee Stadium was enough to cause me to desist from this rather lucrative neighborhood activity.

As is the case today, children raised in impoverished inner-city neighborhoods face all sorts of risks. Many youth face not only the risk of assault but also the risk of being humiliated to the point where they withdraw or seek the protection of others who are all too willing to fight. They face the risk of parents who are abusive or too troubled to care for them, and thus the risk of being too often on their own, disconnected from a world of secure, confident, and capable adults. Just as important is the risk of not liking school because of their inability to follow the words of those in positions of authority.

Through no fault of their own, a few of my friends had a difficult time following the rules at Public School 73, and, in turn, they had a lot of trouble finding their way. They found it hard to sit still in our classrooms, where teachers struggled to maintain order. Several of my friends had to make numerous trips to the principal's office and spent time in school detention. My close friend since early childhood, Chester Solinsky, had an especially difficult time. It seemed that the teachers did not like him, and he certainly did not like them. His school-related difficulties continued until he was no longer required to attend. He not only resisted the rules of our school but also the many other rules of society, such as those that would lead to stable employment.

Chester wandered far to find his place. For a while, he found it in Taiwan, where he married and started a business of his own. But the business was not totally legitimate, and he had to leave Taiwan for reasons that he was not yet ready to tell me when we last met. He returned to New York City where his parents lived and where he could renew his license to drive a cab. But with a wife who spoke little English, two young children to support, and considerable debts to repay, he worked long, late-night shifts, and he was all too willing to pick up just about anyone who might pay his fare.

It was not long after his return to New York that Chester's hope of starting his adult life over again ended abruptly. During the summer of 1983, the violence of New York City's impoverished population finally caught up with him. He was shot and killed by four young passengers who demanded his night's earnings. The ages of the passengers were between sixteen and twenty-one. The oldest in the group wielded the gun that ended Chester's life at the young age of thirty-two. Chester's wife became widowed, his children fatherless, and I lost a dear friend.

The newspapers reported that the youth who shot Chester lived in a section of Queens not unlike the South Bronx neighborhood where Chester and I were raised.[1] They speculated that he may have resisted his young robbers. Nobody could know for sure, but I knew Chester was not one to give in easily. He was tougher than I when it came to holding on to our stickball bats, basketballs, or what little money we had in our pockets. Although I never knew him to start a fight, he was quick to defend himself even if it meant holding his ground when threatened. I could picture Chester when confronting his robbers' demands saying, "This is my night's earnings, and I worked much too hard for these precious bucks to give them to you young punks even with that gun." Chester would have surely included an obscenity or two in his declaration to reinforce the point that he could not easily be intimidated.

Chester had learned to resist more than just the threat or authority of a young man holding a gun; he had learned to resist modern-day society's many places of authority. He had trouble conforming to their stated rules in our public school, and then later in his various occupational pursuits. The reasons for Chester's resistance cannot be easily summarized in an introduction to a book about delinquency and control—but perhaps it can be told through the struggles that many youth face in finding their place in a complex modern-day world.

So I begin by wondering in this introduction how different life might have been for Chester if he had been raised in one of society's safer, more affluent places. Would he still be alive if he had been brought up in a wealthy suburb by upper-middle-class parents? Would he have led a more cautious life because caution would have been all around him? There would have been gated suburban subdivisions, burglar alarms, private mall security guards, school resource officers, and the safety of all those large sports utility vehicles. He would have been exposed to adult-supervised after-school activities instead of the school-yard fights that PS 73 was known for. His daily activities would have been supervised as car pools ferried him and his friends from one suburban activity after another. He might even have been more engaged with his parents, and have led a more secure life.

Yet my image of this good suburban life for Chester could be overly idealized. Chester might have been just as rebellious, and he might have had just as many difficulties in his good suburban school as he did at PS 73. Perhaps he had a learning disability that would have placed him among similarly learning-disabled youth, thereby disengaging him even further from the mainstream. Chester might have even become resentful and angry because he could hardly meet the high expectations of his affluent parents. In a more competitive suburban place, he might have felt terribly envious of the kid next door, who was heading off to a prestigious university. Who knows whether his jealousy would have led him to become even more rebellious, and to find comfort in a drug culture of similarly troubled suburban youth?

I was more fortunate than Chester, first in adolescence and then later in adulthood. One broken nose was more than enough for me. Perhaps I was lucky to have been able to leave the South Bronx at the beginning of my high-school years. My parents decided to move right after an elderly woman was robbed and murdered in the lobby of our apartment building. Our neighborhood, they realized, was becoming even more impoverished and less safe. They joined others who were fleeing the South Bronx for New York City's less crime-ridden neighborhoods.

My parents eventually found an apartment in a lower- to middle-income neighborhood in Queens. They openly worried about how they could afford to pay rent three times higher than our rent-controlled Bronx apartment. But the move to a less crime-ridden neighborhood was a good one. With a safer neighborhood came a more competitive high school and friends who valued their education. Not only did these newly discovered friends care about school; their parents cared as well. Together, they seemed less troubled than the families I had known in the Bronx. A few teachers at Forest Hills High School also seemed to make a difference in my life, encouraging my educational pursuits and enabling me to graduate and subsequently to attend college. One academic degree led to another, and I was on my way to leading a more secure life—one that was far removed from my high-crime, impoverished, inner-city neighborhood in the Bronx.

Discovering the Safe City

The idea of a safe place to live always seemed to make sense to me. But it was not until I interviewed for my first academic position that I realized that more than just families were in search of safer places to reside. Businesses and educational institutions were also leaving the inner cities for the outer suburbs. Many of the universities where I interviewed were located in places far removed from the inner-city areas with which their university names were associated.

One of my first job interviews was at the State University of New York at Buffalo, which I learned was not in the city of Buffalo. It had moved, like many of Buffalo's residents, to a suburb that bordered the northeastern part of the city. University officials had decided to expand their campus by relocating to a bordering suburb that had plenty of land to offer. They claimed that they needed a larger geographical area to expand the university into the largest campus of the State University of New York system.

But a less often stated reason for the move is the fact that the older campus bordered an impoverished section of Buffalo. When I started my tenure-track job as an assistant professor in the Sociology Department, I soon learned that several of my colleagues had bitterly protested the university administrators' decision to relocate its main campus and had spent a considerable amount of time campaigning for the university to stay within the city of Buffalo. These colleagues lived in the city and believed—for good sociological reasons—that the future of a good society resided in the diversity of the city. They felt that the university, businesses, and developers were eroding Buffalo's economic base and its racial diversity. They saw the university's move as creating an even more isolated and segregated society.

Despite their protests, the University of Buffalo continued to develop its suburban campus. As millions of Americans fled the inner cities for affluent, less densely populated, and more homogenous suburbs, so too did the University of Buffalo's main campus, along with many other universities and high-tech industries throughout the country. The reasons for this movement cannot be summarized merely by the term "white flight." Other reasons should be considered, such as those that relate to the fact that the centrally located city would be less relevant to the way many Americans needed or wished to live and work. And in the process the inner city was becoming more impoverished and its outer suburbs more affluent.

Of course, I, like many others, prefer to live on the side of the affluent. My late wife and I wanted our young children to attend good, well-funded public schools, close to lots of well-organized recreational activities, in a community with quality housing and friendly neighbors. We preferred the open, less congested, safer residential spaces of suburbia, and we bought into the "American Dream" of a newly built house where each of our kids could have his or her own room. This suburb was not only safe, but also had good shopping, lots of recreational places, youth programs, and roadways that made for an easy commute to just about anywhere. Basically, I liked living in suburbia, especially with the conveniences of an attached garage with its remote opener and my first in-sink garbage disposal.

Why This Book?

My motivation for writing this book is not just personal. I was trained as a sociologically oriented criminologist and have long been curious about how delinquency is related to the kinds of places where people live. My previous writings focused on serious acts of juvenile violence and the geography of juvenile justice. One aspect of my research led me into a maximum security prison for juveniles where I became acquainted with youth who had committed serious acts of violence. The vast majority of these incarcerated juveniles were minority youth raised in impoverished, inner-city neighborhoods; a few came from my South Bronx neighborhood. But there was also a smaller group of adolescents who were raised in middle-class suburbs. The reasons for their frequent and serious offending seemed to relate to more than just one singular cause, such as bad parenting or bad neighborhood. They seemed to have missed out not only on how parents are supposed to parent, but also how schools are supposed to teach, recreational programs engage, and juvenile justice rehabilitate at the first sign of serious trouble.

Still, the fact that is obvious to anyone who has visited a maximum security prison for juveniles is that the vast majority of its inmates were raised in poverty-stricken neighborhoods. The small proportion of middle-class youth remains small because of the support and opportunities that they have received when faced with personal difficulties. In contrast, impoverished youth lack opportunities for prevention, treatment, or diversion from the punishing hard end of criminal justice. The impoverished not only face a harsher life, but also more arrests, most recently prompted by policing that advocates for strictly enforcing civility.[2] But this kind of zero-tolerance policing is less likely to be present among middle-class youth in affluent communities. Rather, there appears to be not only more tolerance for the minor offending of youth in affluent communities, but also more programs to prevent their adolescents from becoming high offending delinquents.

But not all is well in these middle-class families and communities. Otherwise the middle-class, white suburban youth whom I met would not have been incarcerated. Some parents, no matter what their social class, are too deeply troubled themselves to care for their children. Treatment programs and providers are not always that good. Sometimes the good schools are not the right schools for a particular youth's unique learning style or disabilities. Suburban safety nets may not work for a proportion of youth who require more intense treatment and more care than parents are able or willing to provide.

The idea that some cities are safer and better places than others for youth to transition into adulthood is reinforced in the published list of a popular consumer magazine. *Money Magazine* happened to name the suburb where I had lived as "America's safest city"; hence, one part of the title of this book.

Modernity Defined

The other part of the title includes the words "modernity" and "delinquency." These terms are not mutually exclusive. The concept of delinquency as an age-specific category did not exist prior to the social and legal extension of childhood dependency into the teenage years. For example, in pre-modern times, my childhood friends who had trouble in school would not have had to continue to attend, especially during their early high-school years. They would most likely have been working alongside their parents and extended family members. Obviously, this kind of pre-modern world was a lot narrower; there was less of a gap between childhood and adulthood.

The delinquent as legally distinct from the criminal emerged in the nineteenth century along with industrialization and urbanization. Industrialization required vast numbers of people to leave their rural villages for centrally located cities. Although many found work in factories that were close to their inner-city homes, their lives became more divided as they adapted to more than one division of labor. The industrial shape of modernity not only produced a wealth of products, but also an unprecedented level of societal dependency. Parents were required to work farther away from their homes, often long hours on an assembly line. They needed assistance most often in the shape of public schools, community centers, recreational programs, and if all was not going well, a system of juvenile justice. In other words, adolescence had to be better regulated, and one method for doing so was through child welfare and juvenile justice legislation, including such laws as those that required adolescents to attend school even if they did not wish to. By the end of the nineteenth century, juvenile justice officials, probation officers, teachers, guidance counselors, and social workers were all playing a role in the life of adolescents. For many adolescents, the juvenile court became a first- as well as a last-resort response to many of their problems of adjusting to society's demands, like attending school.

Modernity not only impacted how my friends were raised; it also defined their troubling behaviors from truancy to serious acts of delinquency. For instance, in pre-modern times, several of the teenagers who participated in the killing of my friend Chester would not have been subject to youthful offender status. Their adolescence would not have been recognized, and they most likely would have been punished as adult criminals, since there was no system of juvenile justice to define a sixteen-year-old as a youthful offender. That changed with the onset of modernity and its system of distinguishing juveniles from adults.

But in more recent times the definition of delinquent has become less encompassing. The status of delinquent began to split into diverse sets of legal categories at a time when more than one system of juvenile justice was emerging. In New York, youthful offender status could be granted by an adult criminal court. It became another legal label within an increasingly complex system—one that created a range of legal avenues from status offender to juvenile offender and from juvenile delinquent to youthful offender. All these legal labels are produced by a society on the move—one in which the juvenile court and its definition of delinquent no longer served as the sole determinant of who is a delinquent.

Today, there are more definitions of delinquent to consider, including those that have emerged from social science. There are more opportunities for parents and their adolescents to learn about and to reflect on the reasons for delinquency. This is a more recent kind of modernity—one that I refer to as not only self-reflexive, but also "post-industrial."

The beginnings of a post-industrial form of modernity emerged soon after World War II. It not only decentered juvenile justice, but it also decentered the city. It transformed the urbanized and industrialized city into a suburbanized, deindustrialized city. The difficulties my South Bronx friends had in finding work cannot be separated from the fact that the factories where their parents had once worked were gone, moved overseas into less developed countries where labor was considerably cheaper. Meanwhile, job opportunities in the service and information-generating sectors of the economy grew, and while residents of the inner city were becoming even more impoverished, those who could afford to move into safer neighborhoods did so, often into newly developed suburbs.

So the relevance of a book on delinquency and modernity relates to the simple fact that at the beginning of the twenty-first century, the majority of Americans resided in areas defined as suburban. They had moved from their city neighborhoods to suburban subdivisions, and their centrally located downtown department stores and offices relocated to dispersed shopping malls and suburban office parks. As mentioned, universities moved as well to the greener pastures of suburbia. And thanks to an expanding network of highways and suburban roadways, the outskirts of cities became more accessible, especially for those who could afford to purchase a house in a newly built suburban development. This post-industrial form of modernity not only created the places where most Americans lived, but also dictated how they would live. It enabled the expert advice that advocated certain techniques of parenting, as well as specific reasons for the sort of education, recreation, and counseling believed to be important to "normal" adolescent development.

In the chapters that follow, I will highlight how specific features of the post-industrial, safe suburban city have enabled its adolescents to avoid becoming high-offending delinquents. I argue that the residents of a safe city are able to do so through parenting techniques that are distinctly modern and through a whole host of adults in positions of assisting youth and their parents. This is the relational part of living in a post-industrial society, and why there are fewer middle-class and upper-class youth among today's high number of incarcerated juvenile offenders.

It is the thesis of this book that affluent youth have more opportunities to be relationally modern, and therefore are better able to avoid the potentially devastating consequences of frequent and serious delinquencies. Of course, this is not the case for all youth. Some adolescents struggle more than others and have a more difficult time finding their place in the modern-day world, as noted in the chapters that follow.

A Roadmap to Delinquency and Modernity

The journey begins in chapter 1 where I draw on the concept of safety to formulate a modern-day society's definition of crime and delinquency. I initially ground the concept of safety in *Money Magazine*'s list of safest cities, and then expand its definition of safety to include more than the risk of officially recorded crime. A variety of safety indicators should be considered, such as the quality of a community's school and recreational programs for its youth. In the second part of the chapter, I illustrate how a newly built suburban city is different from the older centrally located city. Among the demographics that I cite is the fact that most Americans today live in areas classified as suburban.[3] Suburbia has become a popular place to reside for good reason: It is perceived as a better place to raise children into healthy, law abiding adults. Another way to frame this point is by stating that the affluent suburban city affords opportunities to its youth that are less available to those in the inner city, such as good public schools and recreational facilities in a largely middle-class community.

The deeper reasons for identifying the suburban city as one kind of city within a larger metropolitan area is further related to *Money Magazine*'s definition of a city, based exclusively on population size. The city has become decentered; common definitions of "urban" and "suburban" no longer matter. A larger metropolitan area contains affluent suburban cities and impoverished inner cities. I show that a large suburban city has its proportion of poverty stricken residents, and that today the centrally located city still has its middle-class. The proportion varies from one metropolitan area to the next. The important point is that in a post-industrial era, urban and suburban can no longer clearly be defined. Although both the urbanized and suburbanized city have become decentered, I show that it is more so the case in suburbia where residential subdivisions, shopping malls, office parks, and light indus-trial zones are dispersed along non-hierarchically arranged roadways. In the post-industrial mix of high-tech, information-age economies, there is no easily identifiable structure demarcating inner and outer city zones. A kind of complexity, isolation, and rationality reproduces the way that adolescents are expected to find their place in the mod-ern world—first in their smaller suburban setting, and then in their larger society.

The latter part of chapter one describes how the resources of the affluent safe city can support adolescents. Another way to make this point is to state that money, good schools, and good recreational pro-grams make a difference not only in adolescents' educational and occu-pational pursuits, but also in how they are able to avoid the official des-ignation of delinquent.

Chapter 2, which extends my initial discussion of suburban cities, begins with several stories of famous and not-so-famous individuals. Most of the stories have good outcomes, but a few are terribly tragic. I then proceed to provide a definition of modernity that is closely linked to the concept of adolescence. Both modernity and adolescence are complex and transitional periods of time. Modernity provides the familial, educational, and legal settings that allow adolescents to transi-tion into adulthood. There is a structure to this kind of modernity and its many divisions. The school is one division; the family and the juve-nile justice system another. In each of these settings, I argue, adoles-cents are expected to think on their own, reflecting rationally about the rules of their many complex social settings. The good stories that I tell are stories of youth who, thanks to the adults in their lives, ultimately had the capacity to grasp societal demands for complexity, autonomy, and rationality.

While chapter 2 focuses on the structure of a post-industrial soci-ety and its safe cities, chapter 3 considers the social and psychological mechanisms that lead adolescents to find their place in the modern-day world. The term "relational modernity" is offered to describe expecta-tions for modern-day relationships. Stories of adolescents who were seriously discontented and who committed serious crimes are told to illustrate the difficulties that they had in becoming relationally modern. They were not able to attain that required level of trust, empathy, and identification that might have enabled them to avoid serious troubles. They lacked the adult support that could have prevented them from committing serious acts of crime. I highlight the adolescent development literature to show the importance of adult shared understandings, and how those understandings are not merely the exclusive product of one singular setting. Although parents and extended family members are considered critically important, the enabling features of modernity are encountered in a range of educational, recreational, and occupational pursuits.

Chapter 4 draws on several classic ethnographic accounts of street-corner delinquency and crime. They are still relevant because they illustrate the problems that a small segment of youth has in conforming to the demands of the larger, law-abiding society. I describe street-corner youth as being too attached to their local street corners and unable to move into the larger world. Street corners are their only source of status and identity in a world that has essentially passed them by. The several historically significant ethnographies that I review all emphasize the corner in a neighborhood street—one that is largely absent in affluent suburbs. Then, in moving beyond a street-corner view of delinquency, I emphasize the importance of relational modernity in allowing for more than one enabling source of control.

My detailed analysis of delinquency in America's safest city begins in chapter 5 and concludes in chapter 7. In chapters 5 and 6, I draw on personal interviews conducted with twenty-six young adults who were initially surveyed during their high-school years. I match their personal interviews as adults with those earlier surveys, as well as with surveys of their parents. Their stories as gathered in a personal interview situation allow me to identify sources of trouble that I further relate to a general list of discontents. In discussing the means by which these young adults have been able to transition successfully from adolescence, I address their need for trust and empathetic identification. In chapter 5, I contrast low- and high-offending youth with one another. In chapter 6, I then consider a middle category of adolescents and their several sources of discontent.

In chapter 7, I analyze several years of survey data. I present statistical models of delinquencies based on familial, educational, peer-group, and neighborhood settings. I draw on multivariate techniques of analysis to present a picture of the reasons relationships matter in their familial, educational, and peer-group settings. I present the incidence of delinquency, the range and types of offenses, and how these offenses can be categorized on a scale of offending. Most importantly, I show the range of diversionary programs and how parents and their youth evaluate various recreational activities. The relational reasons for frequent offending are related to the results of structural equation modeling techniques.

My concluding chapter states why modernity matters. It restates a relational theory that takes into account the struggles of a large segment of adolescents. I repeat the point that these struggles are different from those of impoverished inner-city youth. Any theory of delinquency must take into account both the upside and the downside of modernity, and the reasons why a safe city can never be entirely safe. I hope the pages that follow can be viewed as relevant to those interested in the reasons for delinquency and its control in all the world's inner and outer cities.

Amherst, New York's Boulevard Mall could be located in any car-dependent suburb.

1

America's Safest Cities

America's safest city is located on the northeast border of Buffalo, New York. In 1996 *Money Magazine* published its safest city list and named Amherst, New York, the safest of all American cities.[1] Amherst is still considered relatively safe. Although *Money Magazine* no longer publishes its safest city list, its initial ranking of cities still receives plenty of circulation on the web and in print. More recently (2010), the list's current publisher, Congressional Quarterly Press, designated Amherst as the safest of all American cities.[2] In 2012, *Money Magazine* produced its list of *America's Best Places to Live*, and in that list Amherst ranked number 50 of the top 100 cities with populations of 50,000 or more.[3]

In assessing safety, *Money Magazine* relied on the FBI's index category of crimes—defined as acts of murder, rape, aggravated assault, robbery, burglary, and auto theft.[4] Non-index offenses such as acts of violence without a weapon or fraud were not included. The magazine initially confined its ranking to municipalities of more than 100,000 residents. Defining a city based exclusively on population size means that many municipalities on *Money Magazine*'s list are commonly viewed as suburbs, but since their populations have grown rapidly, they have been included as cities. A half a century earlier, the population of Amherst was much smaller, and too few people resided within its borders to qualify for the FBI's Uniform Crime Reporting (UCR) publication of city crime rates.

On the bottom of *Money Magazine*'s list of safe cities are older, more densely populated cities with large segments of impoverished neighborhoods. The same year that the magazine named Amherst the safest city, it named Newark, New Jersey, America's most dangerous city. The chances of being the victim of a violent crime or theft is substantially greater in Newark, as well as other impoverished inner-city neighborhoods, with their dilapidated buildings, littered streets, bars, and residents hanging out with little work to occupy their time. The point has been repeated many times: Some cities and neighborhoods are more dangerous than others.

The editors of *Money Magazine* limited their definition of safety to officially recorded rates of crime, although crime rates are not the only determinants of safety. A city's safety can be defined by its quality of housing, air, places of labor, and, for the purpose of this book, its educational and recreational programs. These additional indicators of safety are considered quality of life indicators, and I will suggest they make a difference on a city's crime and delinquency rates. Inner cities with a high proportion of impoverished neighborhoods would score low based on a range of quality of life safety measures. Affluent suburbs throughout the developed world score high because of their good schools, spacious neighborhoods, and well- organized local governments. Few parents would deny the importance of sending their child to a good, well-funded public school in a community that has plenty of before- and after-school activities to choose from. But there are other layers of safety to consider that have made the suburbs popular places to live. For instance, newer houses built to current housing codes provide a higher level of physical safety than older dilapidated housing.

In part, this chapter is about layers of safety as they relate to rates of crime. The notion of a safe place to live is not far removed from the idea that good families, good schools, and good neighborhoods are the best places to raise a child. Not only are good parents necessary to maintain a safe city; so, too, are caring teachers, coaches, and youth-service professionals. In a good community, they enable safety by means of their capacity to regulate. This modern-day regulative component demands civility, expert knowledge, and parents willing to assist in confronting a range of adolescent difficulties. However, regulative safety depends not only on the personal resources of families, but also on the public resources of a city. To regulate is to prevent minor acts of deviance from becoming major ones. It presumes that children and adolescents perform their best when they are raised with knowing adults. To ignore an adolescent's troubles, such as bullying, depression, or drug use, can produce more serious troubling behavior.

The regulative and relational side of safety cannot easily be separated. If adolescents are frequently assaulted in their neighborhoods or
in their homes, trust in others will be shaken. Repeated victimization
from an early age can lead to feelings of terrible insecurity in adulthood. A secure environment requires more than minimizing the risk of
physical victimization; it also involves conditions that allow individuals
to gain enough confidence to move about from one social setting to the
next. To face family members, peers, teachers, and others without the
fear of being humiliated depends on the existence of a basic level of
trust—trust not only in one's parents and extended family members,
but also in teachers, coaches, and a range of professionals. Such trust,
which contributes to relational safety, is also crucial to the effectiveness
of the regulative controls that are deemed essential to producing low
rates of delinquency.

My next point relates to the safety of place. Why not just refer to
Amherst as one big safe neighborhood? Neighborhoods are parts of cities. They lack their own government and are generally in closer proximity to one another. But the cities of today are not the cities of an earlier era. Suburban cities are within larger metropolitan areas and often
separated from them by natural barriers, highways, or large boulevards.
They tend to be less densely populated places, and often far from impoverished sections of an inner city. The middle-class neighborhoods of
older cities were in closer proximity to the less affluent ones. Suburban
cities tend to lack downtowns, and their residents are less likely to rely
on public transportation.

The shape of the suburban city should be considered further. *Money
Magazine*'s image of a city is a more modern one, because it is based
exclusively on population size rather than urbanization along with
industrialization. The suburban city exists because the economy of
developed countries like the United States is post-industrial, thereby
allowing more of its residents to live in dispersed places. More rapid
forms of transportation and intricate forms of electronic communication have facilitated this shift. To pursue many middle-class and upper-
class professions, it is no longer necessary to live close to a manufactur-
ing plant or to commute to a centrally located downtown. The suburban
office park has become a newly built place to meet and to work. For
many in a post-industrial world, it is more important to own a car and

This Amherst, New York, office building is part of an office park, and is representative of the newly built businesses in suburban cities.

to live in proximity to the nearest airport than to have easy access to a downtown bus or train terminal. In other words, the centrality and density of a city have given way to suburbia's decentered, more sparsely populated spaces.

There is another component to safety embedded in *Money Magazine*'s list. The safe city is an affluent city. The residents of Amherst have higher income-producing jobs, providing them with the money to purchase spacious houses in both newly built and older suburban subdivisions. There is a sharp contrast between the suburban city of Amherst and the most dangerous city on *Money Magazine*'s list, Newark, New Jersey. The density and affluence of these two cities should be considered. Although many suburban cities have become substantially wealthier than their older inner cities, there are exceptions. For instance, Manhattan has become increasingly a city for the very rich who can afford multimillion-dollar condos. But the Buffalos and Newarks of America are at the opposite end of the spectrum, and I suggest, more typical of urban America than the zones of inner-city wealth that exist in a few of America's largest and most desirable cities. Those who can afford to live in affluent suburbs have the good paying jobs and the hard cash to afford not only higher priced houses, but also the high property taxes that support good schools, youth recreational programs, and a juvenile justice system that is slow to label its offending youth as delinquents.

Before proceeding with definitions of safety, cities, and affluence, I consider *Money Magazine*'s bottom-line indicator of safety—crime rates.

Crime and the Safe City

The authors of *Money Magazine*'s 1996 safest city list write:

> To arrive at our safety rankings, we adjusted the FBI's 1995 crime sta-
> tistics for 202 cities with populations of at least 100,000 to give greater
> emphasis to the crimes you consider to be the most threatening. The
> safest place of all: Amherst, N.Y., a bucolic suburb of 107,000 residents
> just outside Buffalo that posted the lowest rates for both overall violent
> crime and burglary. Indeed, its 79 violent crimes and 201 burglaries per
> 100,000 residents are 88 percent and 80 percent below the national aver-
> age, respectively. In Amherst, just one in 1,259 people was a victim of
> violent crime last year. Amherst ranked fifth safest in the U.S. for auto
> thefts, as just one in 505 people suffered a car theft in '95.[5]

In announcing that Amherst, New York, is America's safest city, *Money Magazine* focused on the risk of victimization—an issue not far removed from how criminologists think about crime. The magazine's assessment seems straightforward: the total number of index offenses divided by the total population and multiplied by a constant.

But the validity of that formula should be considered in greater detail. A city's crime rate consists of more than just its indexed category of offenses; there are also non-indexed offenses to consider. Police-recorded crimes (albeit serious ones) represent only a small propor-tion of the total amount of actual crime. The reasons for this are related to both the objective and the perceived seriousness of crime. Serious injuries require hospitalization and for medical officials to report the incident to the police. Generally, victims and witnesses wish to see offenders punished for their crimes and are quick to call the police.

But others may not wish to involve the police because of the offender's age, or because they might know them or their parents. Some victims may not wish to see an adolescent arrested, adjudicated as a criminal or delinquent, and possibly sent to a prison or reformatory. In these and other cases, offense seriousness is influenced by familiarity and by a belief that justice is more appropriately served through less formal means. Thus fights between classmates in a public school yard or between sports team members often do not come to the attention of the police. Petty property damage by a neighbor's adolescent may be settled without calling the police. In other words, offenses can remain unrecorded acts of crime because they are considered too trivial to report or the victims prefer an informal approach.

Particularly relevant are the characteristics of the offender. Age matters for legal as well as practical reasons. Many parents believe that their law-violating youth are deserving of another chance, and should not be convicted of a crime. They support the idea of juvenile justice, especially for their own adolescents. Presumably, parents know their own children better than others' and are more inclined to see their kids (or kids who look like their own) as more deserving of a second and even third chance. Alternative methods for resolving disputes may be sought through organizational settings that do not officially record offenses, such as school disciplinary committees or youth courts operated by teens under adult supervision. These informal means of administering juvenile justice fall under the rubric of juvenile diversion—a form of justice that is more likely to prevail in the safe city. Safe cities have an advantage in that locally sponsored treatment programs are often facilitated by their youth boards. Youth boards for the prevention and control of delinquency were advocated by President's Johnson's 1968 Crime Commission, and have remained in communities that could sustain their funded programs.[6]

Violence and personal theft form a narrow band of index offenses, and one that is made even narrower by *Money Magazine*'s exclusion of larceny as an index offense—although it is technically an index offense. The justification for this narrow band is its fear of crime—not just any crime but crime resulting in serious injuries or theft. Surveys of the population and harsh legislative penalties for violent index crimes confirm their seriousness.[7] Still, there is a larger spectrum of non-index crimes that can create considerable harm, such as acts of fraud or the devastating harm that can result from an adolescent's early addiction to drugs. These non-index offenses are not included in the calculated crime rates leading *Money Magazine* to rank Amherst as especially safe.

The narrow band of index offenses becomes even tighter when considering that citizen-reporting and police-recording behaviors are often influenced by location. This is especially the case for adolescents. The police make more arrests in impoverished inner-city neighborhoods than in affluent suburban cities. The impoverished inner city has less in the way of the diversionary roads for confronting the illegal conduct of its youth. In the more dangerous cities of America, less *official* tolerance for offenses produces higher arrests. For instance, in 2011 about 12,000 youth were arrested in New York City for possessing small amounts of marijuana.[8] The vast majority of these youth were black and Hispanic; about half had never been arrested before. In contrast, few white adolescents are arrested for the possession of pot in safe city suburbs like Amherst.

The editors of *Money Magazine* are not in the business of elaborating the problems with a safe-city list based on police-recorded crime. That is the task of criminologists who have developed self-report and observational techniques to understand the broader spectrum of recorded as well as unrecorded offenses. How this larger population of offenses is uncovered depends on the types of questions asked and to whom those questions are directed. In surveys of victimization, a general population is asked about their experiences as victims of crime and only a small proportion of those offenses are reported to the police. The more serious the crime, the more likely it is to be reported.

Delinquency Rates

When the focus is on offenders instead of offenses, surveys reveal that offending among both affluent and non-affluent adolescents is quite common. Occasional acts of delinquency rarely result in an arrest and the adjudication of an adolescent in juvenile or criminal court. Apparently, this is not the case for inner-city black youth, whose rates of arrest far exceed those of white suburban youth. The difference between affluent and non-affluent youth would seem obvious based on any visit to a police station, juvenile courtroom, or reformatory. Or, as Travis Hirschi has stated in his highly acclaimed 1969 book, the *Causes of Delinquency*,[9] "there is little doubt that the lower-class boy is more likely to end up in a reformatory than to go to college." But based on his survey data, Hirschi found that parents' occupational, educational, and welfare status made no significant difference in youth offending rates. Hirschi concluded that "social class differences with respect to self-reported delinquency are very small."[10] Hirschi attributes the reasons for more lower-class youth ending up in reformatories to their lack of familial, educational, and general societal attachments. Hirschi reports what others have reported before him and continue to report in countless journal articles: The adolescents who end up arrested are more often those detached from the larger society; they do not get along with their parents or they dislike school, frequently because they perform poorly in school and have low verbal scores. Middle-class and upper-class youth are fortunate because they are raised in more verbal households and in public as well as in private schools where their educational needs are most likely met.

Hirschi is not the only distinguished criminologist to consider the nature of the relationship between delinquency and social class. The late twentieth-century delinquency literature includes a few studies of middle-class and upper-class delinquency.[11] For instance, William Chambliss observed a lower-class group of youth and a middle-class group of youth in their respective neighborhoods.[12] His widely cited 1973 ethnographic study provided evidence of a middle-class advantage. Chambliss referred to the lower-class youth he observed as "Roughnecks" and the middle-class ones as "Saints." Although the Saints committed just as many offenses as the Roughnecks, the Roughnecks experienced numerous arrests, and one member of the group was incarcerated. Despite the reportedly equal rate of offending, the Saints were able to avoid any arrests, and as a consequence their delinquency was officially ignored.

Chambliss cited several reasons for the Saints' so successfully avoiding official identification as delinquents. First, the police were less likely to refer to their acts of delinquency as acts of crime. Instead, the police viewed the middle-class and upper-class Saints as mischievous or as "boys just being boys." These youths were also more articulate than the Roughnecks and could talk their way out of an arrest. Moreover, with their stronger verbal abilities, the Saints performed better in school, and several of them were also actively engaged in their school government. Thus, they appeared to be not only in the right class in society, but also in the right class in school. Another critical factor was their ability to show deference to authority when it mattered the most.

In contrast to the Saints, the Roughnecks were less verbal and less gracious in their dealings with the police.[13] They also committed more serious offenses than the Saints. Although both groups committed acts of theft, the Roughnecks were more likely to assault one another. Chambliss tells us that their acts of fighting were not just interrupted by the police, but also led to more arrests and detentions, with the reason cited being concern for the adolescents' safety and the safety of others in the neighborhood. Thus the kind of offenses deemed serious enough to warrant arrest depended on official beliefs about how to prevent further harm.

The contemporary criminological literature continues to show how the poor are overrepresented in official statistics. Of particular concern is the effect of race on their disproportionate confinement. Impoverished inner-city minority youth are disproportionately represented in the juvenile justice system. The difference between the likelihood of black versus white arrests reflects more than just the seriousness of offense. Of critical importance are the perceptions of officials, particularly how the police and other legal officials view the capacities of youth to avoid repeating their delinquent behaviors or graduating to committing more serious adult-like crimes.

The class-based story of delinquency and control has become a familiar one: Middle-class youth indeed commit delinquent acts but in ways that are less likely to lead to their adjudication as delinquent in juvenile court. As mentioned, the first reason for this is the severity of the offending action. Middle-class youth are less likely to commit index offenses; in affluent suburbs there are few if any identifiable youth gangs. Safe cities are safe because they contain fewer high-offending youth who beat and rob others. The second reason for the difference has to do with the resources of middle-class parents and their communities, which can help prevent adolescents' minor acts of offending from becoming major ones. There are more such resources in a safe city, which in turn contribute to what I refer to as the regulative end of safety.

Regulative Safety

A safe city is a well regulated city. It depends on inclusionary sources of control. Essentially, the residents of a safe city believe in juvenile justice. They support their youth board and its various delinquency prevention programs. They are against exclusionary forms of control that tend to stigmatize, label, and isolate their adolescents from the mainstream of society.[14] Parents, neighbors, youth professionals, police, and other legal officials see more harm than good coming from zero-tolerance policies. Instead, the police are more inclined to warn than to arrest, and in that sense they become regulatory agents for maintaining the safety of their community. Parents and school officials are equally important to this endeavor, and their joint efforts also extend further to creating special classes, tutoring opportunities, and even different kinds of schools. If adolescents are smoking too many ounces of marijuana or consuming too much alcohol or using too many illicit substances, efforts to prevent their serious addiction to harder drugs may take precedence. Thus, the communities of middle-class and upper-class youth appear to be not only kinder, but also smarter in the way that they regulate minor offending to prevent youth from becoming high offending serious criminals.

This ability to regulate offending takes on a more or less complex organizational form depending on the social class of the community. In more affluent communities, more formal organizational settings are at work. In less affluent communities, safety is regulated by means of familial and territorial controls. For instance, Gerald Suttles's 1968 ethnography of an inner-city Chicago slum neighborhood remains a classic for its illustration of how those living in impoverished inner cities are able to regulate their lives through their ethnic and familial ties. These ties tend to be territorial in shape, leading to the emergence of youth gangs to protect their local neighborhood turf. Suttles describes the inner city as creating a highly localized sense of place. In the absence of other formal organizational structures, residents have difficulties responding to one another in ways that move beyond their local neighborhood affiliations.

In contrast, Suttles indicates that the middle-class and upper-class residents of suburbia are less inclined to deal with their disputes based on neighborhood affiliations. They may disagree with their neighbors, but those disagreements rarely relate to their ethnicity or familial ties. According to Suttles, "people who live in the suburbs or more impersonal residential areas seem relatively indifferent to the location of their enemies." He further states that in the suburbs, "old and bitter enemies may pass each other without even knowing it. Persons in these areas often carry out their antagonism by proxy through a series of voluntary and formal organizations and seldom meet their opponents face-to-face."[15]

So the regulative is more formal and less physically in your face in more affluent suburbs. A more controlled, rational response is characteristic of the middle-class. For instance, Mary Baumgartner observed disputes among suburbanites whom she classified as either blue collar/ working class or white collar/professional class. In contrast to the more blue-collar suburbanites, those in the professional class have "an aversion to confrontation and conflict and a preference for spare, even weak strategies of social control." They tended "to tolerate or do nothing at all about behavior they find disturbing." Moreover, the more affluent suburbanite neighborhood approached disputes in a "conciliatory fashion." Baumgartner concluded her analysis by stating the suburban life of the more affluent revolves around a culture of avoidance, a kind of "moral minimalism" that leads them to rarely call the police.[16] The term "moral minimalism" may be misleading if it suggests the complete avoidance of doing something. Rather, in affluent places, a complex regulative way of approaching disputes emerges, based on a negotiated order—one that is complex.

A rational, negotiated order is also pursued when adolescents are brought into juvenile court. The juvenile justice literature is filled with numerous examples of how affluent youth are advantaged. Aaron Cicourel's classic 1968 study of the social organization of juvenile justice shows how the capacities of middle-class parents and their adolescents to negotiate influence each stage of the juvenile justice process—from arrest to judicial decision-making. Cicourel relates cases in which middle-class youth who had been arrested several times were able to avoid the harsh penalties of the juvenile court. In one instance,

> The court hearing was described as an amiable setting with the family seriously attentive to the judge, and the offender neatly dressed [and] displaying the "proper" demeanor and deference. To the [police] chief, the families almost always appeared as a kind of ideal of the "good family." The judge's actions were described as those of a kind but serious disciplinarian who scolded the offender and reminded the family of their responsibility to the child. The disposition was said to be a stern warning and some trivial punishment like six months of mowing the huge lawn surrounding the family house.[17]

The juvenile justice officials Cicourel cites are being true to the principles of the juvenile court. They are acting as an administrative court and not a criminal court. They are taking into account the familial and individual characteristics of the adolescent—that he comes from a good family, is well dressed, and shows deference to authority. The judge looks to a less severe punishment as being in the best interest of the adolescent as well as of the state. The regulatory force of the juvenile court emerges through a shared class-based understanding of how best to punish or treat. This is the visible shape of a system of delinquency control that was created by the middle-class to provide its youth with more than one set of options, choices believed to be critical to allowing a delinquent youth to learn by their mistakes and to develop into a normal adult.

A more visible aspect of regulative safety involves prevention. Jonathan Simon relates America's late twentieth-century criminal justice reforms to middle-class anxieties, observing that these anxieties have led to the compromising of important civil liberties, and to prevention strategies that have created more security for some. He writes: "Compared with how we lived a generation ago, the lives of virtually all Americans are today more embedded in security technology such as locks of all sorts, alarms, private security and procedures of stopping, questioning, and searching. But all too often, these technologies, like giant SUVs, increase the security of some only by reducing the security of others."[18] Techniques for regulating safety are visible, and they provide an advantage to those who can afford the giant SUVs, the gated suburban communities, and a range of security devices.

There is also a less visible shape to the way that middle-class parents regulate the behavior of their youth. Educated middle-class parents are increasingly involved in the lives of their adolescents. Some have referred to this involvement as over-parenting—too much control. It occurs in the wake of a larger set of personal and societal anxieties. Margaret Nelson relates how middle-class parents attempt to secure their children's future. In comparing parents who have graduate degrees with those who have bachelor's degrees or less, Nelson found that graduate degree parents expressed more protective beliefs about their adolescent and young adult children. They were more concerned about their children growing up too quickly.[19] They believed that their children should remain in school as long as possible, with some insisting that they attend graduate school. The more professionally oriented parents not only were more involved in their children's activities; they also assisted and guided them in their various educational and occupational pursuits.

Highly educated parents are not just developing their ideas on how best to raise children from their parents. They know that their children are living in a technically developed society, and that to stay in the middle class they must develop the skills that will allow them to earn a decent living. They know that the family farm or good union job is no longer there to provide for their adolescent, at least for the majority of those in society's post-industrial suburbs. Parents know that they cannot regulate their adolescent's behavior on their own. They look to the expertise of others, encountering the subject matter of adolescent development in their college courses and in parenting magazines and best-selling books. A part of this expert advice can be illustrated in advertisements directed at parents with adolescents.

The first advertisement I draw on was sponsored by the federal government's office of National Drug Control Policy. It makes the point that parents should talk to their children about drugs. The advertisement (www.theantidrug.com) appeared in the *New York Times* (a paper that requires more than an elementary grade school level of reading comprehension). The advertisement asks, *"How far should you go?"*

Suggesting that parents first talk to their children about the risks of a range of delinquent acts, then focus on the illicit use of drugs and alcohol, the ad states:

> Let them know just where you stand on risk-taking and its consequences. And spell things out, because it's the contract both you and your teen will be living by. Set clear rules with your teen for safety and guidance. That's right, getting them to agree to the rules and understand the consequences gives them more responsibility and every teen wants that. And yes, do keep close tabs on your teens. Know where they are and who they're with. Cell phones make it easier than ever to just "check in." It's not saying you don't trust your teen, it's saying you care. Get on the Internet, too. Familiarize yourself with the kind of content they might be exposed to. Above all else, one of the most powerful things you can do for your teenager is to set a good example when it comes to drug, tobacco and alcohol use. Respect them, be honest with them, be clear with them and they'll do the same. Everyone wins.[20]

The message is clear: talk to your child, negotiate order, come to an agreement, and watch closely. You can win this battle by recognizing your adolescent's need for respect and honesty. In turn, they will recognize you and your concerns, especially if you are straightforward with them about their safety.

Here is another advertisement that provides parents with advice on how best to prevent their depressed child from becoming enmeshed in the criminal justice system. It appears on the U.S. National Institute of Health website where parents can learn how depression may relate to delinquency:

> Depressed teens who act out may also become involved with the criminal justice system. Parents are often advised not to intervene, but to "let them experience consequences." Unfortunately, this can also harm teens through exposure to more deviant peers and reduction in educational opportunities. A better solution is to get the best possible legal advice and search for treatment on your own, which gives parents more control over techniques used and options.[21]

This is a real concern. It makes sense that a depressed child would have a heightened risk of becoming delinquent. Although the research literature may be less than clear on this point, the advice for parents focuses on an opportunity for them to make a difference in the lives of their adolescent children. As announced in the advertisement, the risks involved when parents allow their children to manage on their own are considerable. In other words, the worst course of action for parents is to do nothing and thereby leave their children to become embroiled in a formal justice system. To avoid this possibility, the National Institute of Health website states parents should obtain the "best possible legal advice" and "search for treatment." The purpose is clear: parents can regulate the behavior of their adolescents.

Yet who but the affluent are in a position to search for treatment, and at the same time to obtain the best possible legal advice? These are not simple tasks. They involve more than just buying an infant car seat or the safest new car. A combination of personal and social resources is required—resources that may be summarized by the term "capital," as in personal, cultural, and social capital. Personal capital comes into play with regard to the capacities of individuals to understand the language of expert advice. Intelligence matters along with the ability to comprehend the vocabulary of newspapers like the *New York Times*, which is where the first cited advertisement was placed. Cultural capital matters in that there is an identifiable set of middle-class value orientations that exemplifies how parents believe they can protect their children late into adolescence and early adulthood. The social capital relates the connections that parents develop through their networks of friends, neighbors, therapists, good attorneys, and educational programs to assist them in confronting their adolescent's troubles.

Clearly a lot is expected of parents today. Parental abilities to regulate the safety of their adolescents depend on their knowledge, which is enabled through their intellectual and financial resources. This leads to the third advertisement. At times more is required than just late night discussions about the potential harm of illicit drugs. The regulatory force of safety is enhanced by twenty-first century technologies. Drug testing, cell phone location indicators, and Internet monitoring technologies enable forms of control under the guise of keeping adolescents safe. There is money to be made from an advertisement that states how best to control your youth's drug use. The advertisement by *at home Drug Test*, promises to "confirm instantly that your children are free of the drugs most commonly offered to kids aged 11 to 18." The advertisement further states that "The *at home Drug Test* gives you peace of mind. And simply knowing you have it gives your kids a power weapon to fight peer pressure and avoid substance abuse. More importantly, the *at home Drug Test* can help you talk honestly about drugs with your child."[22] These drug testing kits are not freely available. They are not cheap. On the contrary, they are beyond the budgets of those who are struggling to pay their monthly rent.

Drug testing is not the only twenty-first century tool that parents have for monitoring their children. Cell phones can be used to find the location of their child, and a range of Internet tracking devices can monitor the activities of adolescents.

Relational Safety

Few would deny the importance of good and healthy relationships to normal adolescent development. Children should feel secure in their homes and neighborhoods. They should not have to fear physical or emotional abuse. A child's emotional well-being is critical. Otherwise, there is the risk of all sorts of adolescent as well as adult troubles. In other words, people need a good dose of relational safety as they move about from one stage of their life to the next.

A good dose of relational safety begins in the home. Although the relationship between parent and child is critically important, there are other relationships to consider as well, particularly as children move into adolescence and then adulthood. Relationships with teachers, coaches, neighbors, youth service providers may be less intense than parental relationships, but they are still important. And then there are peer-group relationships that become especially critical in adolescence, particularly as highly emotional romantic interests develop. The key point is that in a modern-day society, relationships emerge in more than one particular social and psychological setting.

Relationships can be near and far as well as thin and thick. A student relationship with a teacher may be defined as more or less intense depending on the size of the classroom. There is an assumption that student and teacher will wish to please one another and proceed with a degree of confidence that is considered enabling. Parents trust that their child's teacher will not humiliate their child and that teachers will create an emotionally safe school setting in which to learn. There is more to safety in how other adults are expected to provide a secure environment for those entrusted to their care. Athletes must trust their coaches, and coaches must trust their athletes. When this basic level of trust evaporates into the thin air of modernity, one too many conflicts can arise. The adolescent may begin to feel less safe in his or her relationship, and in turn more troubled by encounters with the next set of teachers or coaches.

Unlike those of earlier, pre-modern times, modern relationships are less often dictated by the intensity of a locally defined place. People move about in places that are far removed from their grandparents' homes. Parents expect their children to move for educational and occupational pursuits, and in each of these pursuits there is an organizational setting where relationships can emerge in a more or less intense form. For many in the technically developed world, there is a faceless quality to relationships that make them even more indirect. While people are able to stay more in touch, they are doing so at a greater distance. The telephone, email, instant messaging, and the Internet are enabling relationships albeit from a distance.

All these technological devices become mediums for thick as well as thin relationships, and they require an on-going level of trust. If that often faceless form of trust is violated, relational safety is threatened. But this faceless form of trust that is often from the distance is critical to normal human development. If it is not there early on in the life of the individual, it can create serious problems. In writing about how this potential lack of trust can further exacerbate the anxieties of living in a post-industrial society, Anthony Giddens observes that "If basic trust is not developed or its inherent ambivalence not contained, the outcome is persistent existential anxiety. In its most profound sense, the antithesis of trust is thus a state of mind which could best be summed up as existential angst or dread."[23] The angst is the dread of having to confront the future without the confidence in the relational safety of a multitude of social settings.

To proceed with confidence in the modern-day world of relationships, it is critical to recognize not only the personal in relationships, but also the positional—the roles that people play in relation to others, such as parent, teacher, coach, or therapist. Although a thick layer of trust is expected in the personal relationships that children have with their parents, the positional role of other adults must be trusted as well, especially as the child transitions into adolescence. Normally, adolescents are expected to be less dependent on their parents and more involved with their peers and other adults. The role of teachers, clergy, camp counselors, and coaches in a range of activities is positional and should contribute to the child's relational safety. These professionals are in positional roles that are more fleeting and more embedded in larger bureaucratic structures, such as a school system or town's youth recreational department.

Relational safety also enables adolescents to learn that they can rely on the larger modern-day world of adults to develop their own identities, independent of their parents. Adam Phillips presents a psychoanalytical point of view of adolescence as "a period of transition and transgression." Adolescence is when "parents as the primary source of well-being is gradually given up as one becomes both more self-reliant and more or less able to entrust oneself to people outside the family."[24] Relationships are not just contingent on parents or, for that matter, peers. Extra-familial adult as well as adolescent relationships are considered critical to enable a successful transition into adulthood. Many of these relationships develop through activities that take place within and outside of the school. Thus teachers, coaches, or neighbors are sources of extra-familial adult relationships.

In a safe neighborhood or city, an extended network of neighbors and professionals enables adolescents to become emotionally secure. This extended network of caring and law-abiding adults creates a consensus of values. There is collective efficacy in the way that a community is able to maintain low rates of crime through personal and positional relationships with its youth. In his recently published *Great American City*, Robert Sampson provides ample evidence that some neighborhoods are more able to control their rates of crime than others. They are more collectively adept at enabling their residents to control troubling behaviors so that the likelihood of serious crime is reduced. Sampson found the residents of low-crime neighborhoods are more inclined to assist one another than those in high-crime neighborhoods.[25] They are more willing to trust one another as well as to civically engage with each other by participating in various community organizations. In these more collectively efficacious neighborhoods, residents produce thick layers of trust that enable them to feel secure in how disputes and life's many difficulties are confronted. Sampson provides numerous examples, and detailed analyses of both survey and observational data support his points about neighborhoods making a difference in rates of crime. For instance, in lower crime neighborhoods, those who have the misfortune of losing a stamped letter are more likely to find it picked up and then posted; they are also more likely to receive assistance if they should happen to have a heart attack.[26]

So, low rates of crime are correlated with high levels of trust. High-crime neighborhoods are those where neighbors are less likely to trust one another; they are unable to depend on one another to deal with each other's disputes and misfortunes. This is one level of trust; there are others to consider, such as the trust between parent and child and the trust between teacher and student. Children who are physically and emotionally abused by teachers or clergy are at risk because that deep-seated sense of trust that is essential has been violated. This loss of relational trust can produce on-going states of anxiety. Children who are unable to trust parental figures of authority may become fearful of their neighbors, school officials, and peers. They lack the essential trust that would allow them to proceed from one set of relationships to the next.

Children who lack relational safety as defined by this element of trust lack the ontological security that distinguished child psychologists such as Eric Erikson deem essential.[27] Reports of clergy and teachers who sexually abuse are not confined to impoverished neighborhoods. The post-traumatic stress that emerges from a physically or emotionally abusive relationship knows no geographical or temporal boundaries in the life-course of individuals. The idea of a safe city is that there, the likelihood of encountering an adult who would sexually abuse a child is less since schools and professionals are well regulated.

Cities

Here is *Money Magazine*'s 1996 list of America's ten safest cities, beginning with its safest: Amherst, New York; Thousand Oaks, California; Irvine, California; Simi Valley, California; Sunnyvale, California; Virginia Beach, Virginia; Livonia, Michigan; Plano, Texas; Madison, Wisconsin; and Mesquite, Texas. On the bottom of its list are America's ten most dangerous cities: Newark, New Jersey; Atlanta, Georgia; St. Louis, Missouri; New Orleans, Louisiana; Detroit, Michigan; Baltimore, Maryland; Miami, Florida; Washington, D.C.; Flint, Michigan; and Birmingham, Alabama. Since 1996 Amherst has occasionally moved into second, third, and as low as sixth place. Of the four hundred cities that are ranked, Amherst is consistently listed as one of America's safest cities.

Money Magazine's list of safest cities is not a list of centrally located, densely populated cities. Most residents of the greater Buffalo area would refer to Amherst as a suburb of the city of Buffalo. According to the U.S. Census Bureau, Amherst is classified as a township, presumably because of its own local government. Townships are defined as cities in the most general sense. Suburban cities not only have their own government, but also have defined geographical boundaries. To call the suburb of a larger city a city is to suggest that the centrality and the density of a city matters less today then in earlier times.

So were the editors of *Money Magazine* neglecting the common definition of a city for the convenience of producing its safest city list? A singular measure of a city based simply on population size may actually reflect how cities have developed. Most of the U.S. population now resides in areas that are classified as suburban. Could *Money Magazine*'s definition of a city be that of a suburban city, one where the centrality of a city matters less?

The New American City Is a Suburban City

Safe-city suburbs have grown rapidly. They are now qualified to be listed in numerous city lists, including *Money Magazine*'s list of safest cities. But the definition of a city was never based exclusively on city size. In 1790 when the United States had its first Bureau of Census count, the most populous city was New York with a total population

Amherst, New York, was not only named the safest city in America
by *Money Magazine* in 1996, but also identified as one of the fifty best
places to live in 2012.

of just 31,131, which is substantially less than the 122,366 residents that
Amherst recorded in 2010.[28] The definition of a city could never be
based exclusively on population size. Rather, it depends on having their
own municipal governments and being self-contained places of commercial and residential activity. Based on those criteria, Amherst and
the other affluent suburbs qualify as cities.

So by the end of the twentieth century suburban cities became the
preferred cities. In contrast, at the beginning of the twentieth century,
most Americans moved from their rural villages to densely populated
inner cities, like Buffalo and Newark. Within less than a century, the

suburban city increased in size so that older cities began to lose populations to their neighboring newer cities. This shift occurred throughout
much of the United States, and as Claude Fisher, Michael Hout, and
Jon Stiles further observe, "The late nineteenth century and the twentieth century were both eras of rural depopulation, but in the nineteenth
century Americans became city people and in the twentieth century
they became suburban people."[29] Furthermore in 2000, "only one-fifth
of Americans lived outside metropolitan areas and most of the remaining great majority lived in suburbs."[30]

A closer look at population trends in the last century in America's
safest city and its more dangerous neighboring city of Buffalo reveals
the twentieth-century trend toward suburbia. In 1900, Amherst was
described as consisting of quaint villages surrounded largely by farmland. According to U.S. Census figures for that year, Amherst recorded
a population of only 4,223. That same year Buffalo's population was
83 times bigger at 352,387. By 1950, both Amherst and Buffalo became
more populated; their respective populations grew to 33,744 in Amherst
and to 580,132 in Buffalo. Thus in 1950, Buffalo's population was 17 times
that of Amherst. By the 2000 census the population of Amherst dramatically increased, while Buffalo's sharply declined. According to the
2000 census, Amherst's population of 127,748 residents quadrupled
from its 1950 population of 33,744 residents, while Buffalo's dropped by
nearly 50 percent to only 292,648 residents. From the city of Buffalo
being 83 times larger than Amherst at the beginning of century to only
twice as large at the end of the century corresponds with trends in the
entire nation.[31] Similarly, *Money Magazine*'s most dangerous city (Newark, New Jersey) lost about one-third of its population between 1950
and 2000, from 438,776 down to 273,546.

The Newly Built Suburban City as a Good Place to Live

So why have suburban cities like Amherst become desirable places to
reside in the later part of the twentieth century? One obvious reason is
that modern technology makes suburban living possible. Technological
innovations have made it possible for people to travel and communicate
farther and faster than before. Technology quickened the pace of travel
to a level that could not be imagined in earlier times. For instance, in

1840, horse drawn carriages and steamships traveled at a peak speed of 10 miles per hour. To live more than several miles from work could significantly extend a long and arduous day. Most people lived in villages where they walked to where they worked. People began to move further from their villages when in the latter part of the nineteenth century the steam-driven locomotive train became a popular form of travel. Still, the top speed of travel was only 65 miles per hour. Trains made it possible to travel farther and street-car suburbs began to appear, extending the municipal boundaries of many cities.[32]

A second reason is that suburban living became more affordable. It was not until the middle of the twentieth century that people really could afford to move about at unprecedented rates. Mass-produced automobiles became cheaper and home ownership more affordable. Real estate developers and auto industry executives supported an expansion of highways and roadways, creating consumer demand for automobiles and newly built suburban subdivision homes. During the post–World War II years, the United States became more prosperous, and the proportion of the population in the middle-class increased dramatically. Perhaps one of the largest incentives for suburban developers was the availability of government-sponsored low-cost mortgages to returning veterans. The car-dependent suburbs became the newly built places for residential and commercial development.[33]

A third reason is that inner and outer cities became less distinguishable. With farmland and pastures being turned into suburban subdivision homes, shopping malls, and office parks, the metropolitan area became the greater city area. Most importantly large suburban cities became economic entities of their own, no longer dependent on a centrally located, inner-city downtown. Instead, a larger network of decentered suburban cities arose, and the places where people worked expanded to a larger metropolitan area. Like the spokes on a wheel, the suburban city emerged as the newly built, multi-nucleated city of the modern world.[34]

A fourth reason for the growth of the suburban city is the desire to live in less densely populated places. In the less densely packed suburbs, individuals can enjoy the privacy of their own places and indeed the privacy of their own rooms. The typical suburban house may be described as a home demarcated by a front yard and often a fenced-in backyard. Privacy is maintained by having enough bedrooms, living rooms, and recreation rooms so that each member of the family has the opportunity to be on his or her own. Suburbanites are able to enjoy not only bigger homes, but also privacy in their modes of transportation, with an automobile as opposed to public transportation being the primary means for getting around.

Last but not least, many families prefer the suburbs because they believe that they are better places to raise their kids. They are seen as better because their schools are perceived as better. Suburban cities may indeed be better because they have their own school districts with their own sources of funding. There is less of a mix of impoverished kids in affluent suburban districts because they are exempt from the school busing that inner-city youth face.[35] Not only are the schools perceived to be better, but there are also more before- and after-school activities to occupy the minds and bodies of youth. Many of these are town-sponsored recreational and youth board programs which can provide youth with the competency, confidence, and character believed to be critical to healthy adolescent development.

The low rate of crime coupled with the luxury of homeownership, privacy, physical space, fresh air and good to excellent public schools make the suburbs a desirable place to live. Commutes need not involve lengthy journeys into the inner city. Instead, a car ride to a suburban office park or high-tech industrial zone is all that is often required. One other aspect of suburban cities that make them into attractive places to live is the suburban shopping mall as a fun and safe place to shop.

The Risk of Living in Suburbia

An early generation of distinguished urban scholars considered the growth of suburbia as highly undesirable. Richard Sennett, Lewis Mumford, and Jane Jacobs saw suburban living as isolating, segregating its residents from the full diversity of human kind. The suburbs, they believed, could make it hard for residents to reach their full human potential.[36] Instead, it was within the more densely populated inner city where diversity could be found. As Sennett writes, "The great promise of city life is a new kind of confusion possible within its borders, an anarchy that will not destroy men, but make them richer and more

An Amherst, New York, office park building.

mature."[37] Autonomy could not be achieved through the group-think of suburbia. For Sennett, Mumford, and Jacobs, racial and ethnic groups living in close proximity to one another and having to negotiate order enabled a good society.

The beauty, the wonders, and the enabling features of inner-city life also appear in numerous novels. For instance, the Nobel Prize winning novelist Saul Bellow writes:

> On Broadway it was still bright afternoon and the gassy air was almost motionless under the leaden spokes of sunlight, and sawdust footprints lay about the doorways of butcher shops and fruit stores. And the great, great crowd, the inexhaustible current of millions of every race and kind pouring out, pressing round, of every age, of every genius, possessors of every human secret, antique and future, in every face the refinement of one particular motive or essence—I labor, I spend, I strive, I design, I love, I cling, I uphold, I give way, I envy, I long, I scorn, I die, I hide, I want.[38]

The repeated "I" conveys a feeling of a free, autonomous self, who can choose his or her own destiny. The light in the fire of city life is the ability to see oneself as uniquely situated in a larger world—not the smaller world of a village. Old-world traditions could be left behind, and new traditions developed—ones that recognized the proximity of others who are different in their ethnic and racial origins.

In contrast to this glorified vision of city life, suburbia is pictured as being too isolated by its miles of highway. Its residents are living too far from one another, segregated by their social class. To the glorifiers of the city, suburbanites left their city roots for the wrong reason. They left because they were too exclusionary and inward-looking, taking a them-against-us perspective and creating a new kind of village mentality that could not recognize the other who might look and act differently.

But the cities of Saul Bellow and that of Philip Roth are not the cities of today. The Newark, New Jersey, that Philip Roth described in his novels is not the same Newark that led *Money Magazine* to name it as America's most dangerous city. Not only are the outer suburban cities homogenous; so are inner cities, which have lost much of their middle-class. Bellow's words about Broadway are less true today: The butcher shops and fruit stores have been replaced by supermarkets often located far from the center of the city; Manhattan's neighborhoods have become places for the wealthy who can afford million-dollar co-ops and condos. In smaller cities like Buffalo and throughout the United States, the economic and racial divide is between an affluent suburban city like Amherst and the impoverished inner city.

The divide that I have identified between inner and outer cities is mainly an American story. As I noted there are exceptions, such as in Manhattan where the impoverished have been moved into the city's boroughs. In many parts of the world, the impoverished live in outer cities (e.g., the *banlieues* of Paris and the *favelas* of many cities in the global south).

Safe Cities Are Affluent Cities

Today's suburban cities are not just bedroom communities to commute to and from. They have become places of commercial and residential activity. They are places of employment, places of education, and places to shop and to be entertained. The chances of finding well-carved butchered meat and freshly procured fish are greater in affluent suburbs than in impoverished inner-city neighborhoods. The ubiquitous shopping mall has become a place of entertainment. Sociability has emerged in the way that suburbanites arrange to meet each other at the local mall's sparkling fountains, artificial gardens, or food courts. There are recreational parks, sports facilities, and places of entertainment. The University of Buffalo and other colleges in the city of suburban Amherst provide residents with concerts, theatrical performances, and public lectures.

The range of educational, occupational, recreational, and cultural pursuits defines Amherst not only as a city but also as a place of affluence. There is an admission fee for residing in high-priced suburbs. The price of admission is the ability to afford home ownership or rents that are substantially higher than those in the inner city. To be able to afford to live in a safe city is in itself an indication of affluence. The affluent can consider the best places to live and to vacation as well as the best automobiles to buy and the best colleges to send their children. The impoverished have little reason to consult *Money Magazine*'s list or for that matter any other popular consumer magazine's list.

Relative Affluence

Affluence has its absolute and relative forms. Not everyone in a safe city is equally affluent. Absolute affluence reflects the fact that a higher proportion of affluent residents reside in safe suburban cities. The safest and most dangerous cities are distinguishable from one another not only by their crime rates but also by their poverty rates. Although a small segment of Amherst's population lives in government subsidized low income residential subdivisions, Amherst is a largely affluent suburb.

Affluent cities are safe cities as illustrated by their rates of employment, income, and wealth. Indications of affluence are readily visible to anyone who has visited Amherst; the opposite is equally true of Newark. Census figures reveal how affluence is directly related to rates of official crime. Amherst residents are more likely than Newark residents to have completed high school, have graduated from college, to be employed, and to own their own homes. Race is linked to states of affluence, and this is also the case in that the population of Amherst contains only a small proportion of non-whites.

In terms of education, 92 percent of Amherst residents graduated from high school compared to 58 percent of Newark's residents. Only 9 percent of Newark's adult residents completed a bachelor's degree compared to 47 percent of Amherst residents. In terms of employment, the reported unemployment rate for Newark is 15 percent, while it is only 4 percent for Amherst. The difference may even be larger in that many Newark residents may have simply given up looking or were never employable to begin with. In terms of income, the median family income of Amherst residents was $69,000, while it was only $31,000 for Newark's residents. Moreover, 20 percent of Newark's families were impoverished based on earnings of less than $10,000 a year, compared to only 4 percent of Amherst residents. More than 5 percent of Amherst families reported incomes of over $150,000 while this was the case in less than .2 percent in Newark. Another indication of income is having accumulated enough money to buy a home. Here again Amherst scored high with 76 percent of its residents owning their own homes compared to only 23 percent of Newark's.

As indicated, there are few minorities in America's safest city. The vast majority (90 percent) of Amherst is white compared to 43 percent in Newark. Moreover, only 1 percent of Amherst residents identify themselves as Hispanic and 9 percent as foreign-born compared to 29 percent Hispanic and 24 percent foreign-born in Newark.

Not Everyone in an Affluent Suburb Is Affluent

In a large suburban city, there are more or less expensive housing developments directed to a range of potential middle- and high-income buyers. Those who moved from a more expensive residential housing market to another suburban city may wish to purchase a home that is nearer to the value of the house they left behind. The range of new versus old subdivision homes and the cost of those homes vary significantly.

In Amherst, the less affluent subdivisions are close to the shopping malls and busy boulevards. They also border the city of Buffalo and contain the town's government-subsidized housing programs. To live in these affordable housing units, residents must report that their income is relatively low. Bureau of Census data confirm observed differences.[39] A comparison of the highest and lowest census tracks indicates substantial differences in levels of affluence. For example, in the highest income census track, 21 percent earned over $150,000, while in the lowest earning census track, 16 percent reported family incomes of less than $10,000. Similarly, those high-income family income tracks had a home ownership rate of 97 percent compared to 34 percent in the lowest income tracks. The percent with college degrees (31 percent), employed in white-collar occupations (87 percent), and living in low density areas was also relative to these income differences. The population density of Amherst's wealthiest census tracks was 2,309 residents per square mile compared to 7,159 in the least affluent track.

Conclusion: The Safe City as a Place of Modernity and Control

A safe, affluent suburban city like Amherst has a low official rate of personal crime because its residents are better able to regulate safety. They are able to do so because of their own personal resources and their willingness to abide by expert knowledge on how best to prevent their adolescents' delinquency. They can draw not only on their own resources, but also on the collective resources of their larger community. An affluent suburban city like Amherst can afford good schools with good teachers, guidance counselors, coaches, and others who can influence the lives of adolescents. Parents, youth service providers, and other officials are more on the same page in regards to regulating the safety of their community's adolescents. They are in sync about the need for regulating their city's youth to avoid delinquency. A successful transition from adolescence to adulthood is more likely because adolescents arc living in one relationally safe setting after another.

A suburban city is not like the inner-city neighborhoods of the past. It is a less public, more car-dependent place. It lacks a centralized downtown so that commercial activities are dispersed along a beltway of office parks, light industrial zones, and shopping malls. Similarly, the control of delinquency is less visible and centrally observable. There is not only more privacy in suburbia but more of an informal system of juvenile justice. Although informality in the juvenile justice system exists for impoverished youth, they are less in a position to negotiate justice.

There are implications to *Money Magazine*'s list of safest and most dangerous cities. By understanding more of the dynamics in how delinquency is controlled among middle-class families, we can also better understand why there has been a dramatic increase in the rate of incarceration among black juveniles. Since 1985, the incarceration rates have steadily increased partially because of law enforcement's focus on crack cocaine in largely black inner-city neighborhoods.[40] Bruce Western has found that during this same period, the rate of serious drug use based on self-reported emergency visits among whites and blacks remained virtually the same.[41] John Hagan reviews these and other sources of data to conclude that a combination of class and place created the conditions for the more disproportionate arrest of black inner-city youth:

> The arrival of the cheaper and more powerfully addictive crack cocaine in the mid-1980s was obviously economically attractive in impoverished black communities, while the more expensive and less addictive powder cocaine remained a party drug of choice for more advantaged college and business-class users. The limited private spaces in poor black neighborhoods pushed the crack drug trade into the public "open air" market spaces of the street corners, while college and business-class users of powder cocaine were able to take advantage of the private spaces provided, for example, by college residences and hotel suites.[42]

The limited private spaces and the public street corners of impoverished inner-city youth define the dangerous city. In contrast, suburban cities have less visible public space. Adolescents can avoid public street corners as the places for their drug and alcohol use. The privacy of their suburban rooms, backyards, wooded parks, and automobile provide them with opportunities to be more on their own and delinquent in a variety of pursuits. The difference is that the safe city is an affluent place where the rate and seriousness of delinquency is better controlled.

I close this chapter by referring to a commonly cited reason for why a safe city is particularly safe. It repeats many of my earlier points. It comes from a report on a topic of substantial policy concern—the disproportionate confinement of minority youth in the juvenile justice system. The U.S. government's Office of Juvenile Justice and Delinquency Prevention sponsored the report in New York State and in other states as well. It compared juvenile justice in suburban cities that included

America's safest city with juvenile justice in the inner city of Buffalo, which *Money Magazine* rated as one of America's most dangerous cities. The report states that differences in the race of youth locked in juvenile facilities can be partially attributed to "the greater availability of diversion programs in suburban areas" and that this availability, "coupled with the greater affluence of suburban families and their ability to access services for their children and compensate victims, leads to over-representation [of minorities] in the juvenile justice system."[43]

A variation on this observation can be found in nearly all federally mandated state studies of the disproportionate confinement of juveniles. It basically states that in more affluent suburban communities, there are more options for youth to avoid the formal system of juvenile justice, which includes adjudication as a delinquent in juvenile court and possible placement in a state-operated facility for delinquents. The youth of affluent suburbs are fortunate to live in the kind of city where they have more of a second and even third chance to avoid the delinquent label. Amherst youth live in a place of diversionary programs, making them less likely to face arrest and incarceration for their offenses. Subsequent chapters should explain why the adults in these newly created cities are so willing to expend the resources to make their treatment-oriented programs possible. Any explanation of why some youth are more likely than others to benefit from these services must take into account modernity and its post-industrial cities.

One of Amherst, New York's modern looking high schools.

2

Confronting Modernity and Adolescence

In contrast to the youth of America's most dangerous inner cities, safe-city youth are less often arrested, and as a consequence less likely to be adjudicated delinquent. Without having been officially designated delinquent, they are more likely to successfully transition into adulthood. But success means more than just avoiding being brought into juvenile court. In an affluent suburb, it means meeting the expectations of a society composed of parents, teachers, coaches, clergy members, friends, and a range of youth service professionals. The pressure to succeed exists not in a pre-modern, village-like community where status is often determined at the time of birth, but in a society that is distinctly modern—one that expects its adolescents to achieve status in one social setting after another.

For many adolescents, the suburban roadway to meeting societal expectations can be readily adjusted to their capacities. Caring parents, teachers, coaches, and friends can take into account the unique capabilities of an adolescent. If parents are particularly troubled by their child's behavior, they can obtain expert advice, usually from a mental health professional. But parents, teachers and a whole host of youth service professionals are often unable or too busy to provide the support that youth require as they adjust to their adolescence. Their adolescent peers may also be sources of support, but at times friends can be just as competitive and status conscious. Relationships can become awfully superficial, making it terribly difficult to navigate from one social setting to the next.

So, a segment of adolescents may have a particularly difficult time grasping all that is required of them as they move about their familial, educational, and peer-group settings. Their parents, teachers, coaches, and friends are not necessarily all on the same page. There may be disagreement as to how best to proceed. Conflict over a middle-class value like attending college may require recognition that not every youth has the ability or personal desire to attend college. Learning difficulties may be too severe; they may have suffered all sorts of traumas that make it difficult to concentrate. They might also have trouble thinking independently in their educational pursuits. A more structured, directed environment is desired. Last but not least, they may have difficulty buying into the rationality of the school setting and the teacher as a source of authority. Instead, they may look for an alternative route that enables their most basic desires.

This chapter is about the struggles of youth, and how their adolescence is influenced by a society on the move. It attempts to show that for a large segment of youth, societal demands are not easily met. They require a multitude of modern-day communities. Their parents may be a major resource, but then again, parents cannot operate on their own. They depend on the schools their children attend, and if their children are significantly troubled, they depend on a mental health system as well. In a worst case scenario, parents and their adolescents must figure out how to navigate the juvenile justice system.

All these systems are there for a purpose. Their general goal is to enable adolescents to transition successfully into adulthood in a society that is not simply structured. The sociologists of the late nineteenth century associated urbanization and industrialization with complex divisions of labor. The simplicity of village and rural life was replaced by increasingly specialized ways of laboring. In the de-industrialized, suburban life of a safe city, the office park has replaced the factory, and complexity has taken on a less visible form. A lot of decisions are being made inside offices or through computer programs that are not easily understood.

An awareness of suburbanization is critical. As Michael Kruse and Thomas Sugrue state, "suburbanization has come to affect all aspects of post-war life. Any effort to understand modern America must put suburbs at the center. The two are inseparable."[1] If adolescents are to transition successfully into adulthood, they must learn to grasp their newly created suburbanized world, which involves navigating within and among familial, educational, and peer-group settings. In each of these settings, there is a normal level of responsibility that is gradually assigned to adolescents; they are expected to think more and more for themselves. Adolescents should be able to make their own rational decisions. They must confront not only the complexities of modernity, but also the responsibilities and rationalities of a post-industrial society.

In this chapter, the capacities of youth to confront modernity and their own adolescence are first illustrated by the stories of five adolescents. These are the stories of the famous and not-so-famous. They include the stories of youth raised in terribly troubling circumstances, too often leading them to commit horrible acts of violence. They are also the more typically good stories of youth raised in safe and affluent cities by middle-class and upper-class parents. They are not necessarily the stories of youth living in America's safest city; I reserve those stories for chapters 5 and 6. Here, I start with a good story of a youth from an affluent suburb whom I euphemistically name "Terribly Young."

Stories of Trouble in Adolescence

Terribly Young

As stated in the report sponsored by the Office of Juvenile Justice and Delinquency Prevention, the suburban youth of the greater Buffalo area are less often adjudicated delinquent; the youth of Buffalo's urban center are more likely to be arrested for the same kinds of offenses. This disparity between impoverished and affluent youth, as noted in the previously cited observational study of Chambliss and Cicourel, partially explains the overrepresentation of minorities in the juvenile justice system. The reasons for these disparities in the official identification of adolescents as delinquents relate to disparities in the opportunities for a range of diversionary programs. These programs attempt to produce an informal inclusionary form of juvenile justice which avoids officially labeling adolescents as delinquents.

The story of Terribly Young is the not-so-uncommon story of an upper-middle-class youth. While driving home from a late-night weekend party, Terribly Young was stopped by the police, who searched his car and found several ounces of marijuana, pipes, and other drug-related paraphernalia; the quantity indicated that Terribly Young was dealing in drugs. He was charged with a felony and subsequently released to his parents. At the time of his arrest, he was sixteen years of age. With the assistance of a private attorney whom his family hired, Terribly Young was deemed eligible for the town's diversion program.

He was subsequently discharged, and in appreciation Terribly Young wrote the following unedited letter:

> Dear Chief Probation Officer Riley:
> I would like to point out how thankful I am for being granted the opportunity to make right of what I have done wrong. The pre-trial diversion program gave me a chance to realize how serious and real breaking the law is. Along with being granted the pre-trial program I was obligated to pay all fees to the court, finish the JDP [Juvenile Diversion Program], visit a personal counselor, finish twenty hours community service, and take random drug tests. Because my record was so important to a successful future for me, I completed all the tasks I was allotted to accomplish within six months. In doing so I learned not to get in trouble. I do not plan on ever having to show up to court for anything again. I think every kid with a first offense deserves the pre-trial diversion program. Because one's record is so important, a clean one is important for their future. I am very grateful for the opportunity I was given.
> Sincerely,
> Terribly Young, an arrested youth in one of America's safest cities

Perhaps these are not exactly the youth's own words. Perhaps his attorney or parents prodded him to produce this letter of gratitude. In either case, the letter expresses appreciation for diversion and the fact that he felt fortunate to have a chance to avoid a criminal record.

His diversion might not have been possible if his parents had been unable to afford the cost of a private attorney and the time they both needed to spend in court. If they lacked the money and health insurance to afford private counseling, professional therapy, and extra-school tutoring, Terribly Young might not have been so fortunate. Officials made a difference as well. They could identify with Terribly Young's parents, who were indirectly paying (through their tax dollars) the salaries of those who were operating the local court. They could also recognize Terribly Young's potential—seeing him more as one of their own and thus being more willing to give him a chance to avoid conviction in criminal court. Terribly Young himself knows this to be the case, as he notes that he wishes all kids could have the same second chance that he received.

No one single factor led to Terribly Young's successful diversion. His parents lived in a community where the public schools were considered excellent and where there were plenty of town services. They realized after Terribly Young's arrest that they needed more assistance to deal with the issues that led to his frequent drug use. They hired a skilled therapist who noted Terribly Young's poor school performance. The therapist recommended that a privately paid educational psychologist conduct an evaluation. The ten-page report by the educational psychologist pointed to Terribly Young's significant strengths and weaknesses on various intelligence tests. A professional tutor was recommended to assist Terribly Young in his weakest subjects. Medication was also recommended to deal with his diagnosed Attention Deficit Disorder.

Terribly Young and his parents related that their conversations with a skilled therapist were highly beneficial. They gained insight into some of their complex family dynamics that might have led to his extensive smoking and dealing pot. They also realized that they had to place more restrictions on his activities; they established a curfew and other rules. Last but not least, tutoring along with medication seemed to make a difference because his grades improved.

So in Terribly Young's letter, we find evidence of a family that has not only the means to support diversion, but also the personal financial and emotional resources to confront his troubles. Terribly Young and his parents trusted the expert advice of professionals. They consulted the National Institute of Health website that I mentioned in the previous chapter. Terribly Young's parents continued to educate themselves on the reasons for adolescent drug use. He passed his regularly administered drug tests.

A less happy story would undoubtedly emerge for adolescents who were not as well supported. Terribly Young benefited from 1) parents who cared; 2) the money and health insurance to obtain professional advice, which included therapy, medication, and programmed activities; and last but not least, 3) a safe city's system of informal and formal juvenile justice—one that provided him with the opportunity to avoid the official status of delinquent or criminal.

Terribly Young's diversion as an adult was ultimately a successful one on several counts. He was able to attend a business college and then graduate within the recommended four years. He now works as a buyer for a large retail chain.

Willie Bosket

Willie Bosket was not nearly as fortunate as Terribly Young. He had far fewer chances. He lacked caring parents. He was raised in one of New York City's most impoverished inner-city neighborhoods. He never had the opportunity for a normal childhood. He lacked the essential safety of place that would have enabled him to develop into a normal adolescent. As a young child, he was sexually abused by his grandfather. Equally troubling, his childhood traumas were repeatedly ignored by a juvenile justice system that lacked the resources and commitment to confront Willie's life-threatening troubles.

While Terribly Young's name is a pseudonym designed to protect his true identity, Willie Bosket's name is well known. At the young age of fifteen, he became infamous for the murder of two New York City subway passengers in two separate incidents that occurred a week apart from one another. He was a chronic violent offender. Despite a known pattern of childhood violence, prevention and control programs were not there for young Willie. He never received the intense therapy, security, and safety that he desperately needed. Instead, he was subject to all sorts of well-known risks that fall under the general category of childhood neglect and abuse.

Several facts about Willie's life are presented by Fox Butterfield in his book on the Bosket family[2] and in my own 1996 book on *Recriminalizing Delinquency*.[3] He lived in a dangerous neighborhood. He never met his father, who was incarcerated for murder from the time of his birth. His mother worked long hours to pay the month's rent and to feed Willie and his siblings; as a consequence, he received little or no adult supervision. Not surprisingly, he had problems in school despite his extraordinarily high IQ.

New York City's juvenile justice system could have intervened early in the life of Willie Bosket. He was only nine years of age when his mother asked the juvenile court to assist her in dealing with Willie's disruptive behavior. She brought him to Manhattan's Juvenile Court (technically referred to as New York's Family Court), as many impoverished families look to the juvenile justice system to provide the psychological services that would assist them in raising their youth. Bosket's mother hoped that officials would help her son. Unfortunately, she was virtually ignored, and as a consequence, Willie was ignored as well. The reason might be that he was a difficult juvenile not only to his mother and their neighbors, but also to officials who dreaded Bosket's violent outbursts.

Despite repeated referrals to juvenile court and his known acts of violence, Bosket's stay in various residential placements was always relatively short. He required an intensely therapeutic setting, and instead received punishment in detention centers where older youth residents would victimize younger ones.

Butterfield's story about Bosket is not only that of a highly disturbed youth, but also about a highly disturbed family, destroyed by a history of violence. It is also about a system of juvenile justice that failed to recognize the reasons for a youth's violent behavior, and the need for an intensely therapeutic setting far from his impoverished inner-city neighborhood and family members. It is the story of a small number of inner-city youth and their families, who are too impoverished to address their children's troubles. They are unable to confront not only their children's troubles, but their own troubles as these may occur through illness, unemployment, and crime. They lack the health insurance, investment accounts, and capacities to hire attorneys and therapists. In other words, they lack the resources of those who live in affluent suburban cities.

The story of inner-city youth that is more typical is that of Willie Bosket rather than that of Terribly Young. Impoverished inner-city families depend on the government to assist them in dealing with their troubled youth. At the time that Willie Bosket was being repeatedly referred to juvenile court, New York City seemed to lack those resources. The juvenile justice system became less focused on providing the treatment-oriented services that might have made a difference in Willie's life. The system was losing control of its seriously troubled youth—those who needed more supervision, perhaps in an expensive therapeutic school. Butterfield describes the sad shape of New York City's juvenile court and how it lost control of its delinquent youth in these terms:

> In Manhattan, the Family Court in the early 1970s was so starved for funds that all the judges had to share one legal assistant to research their cases. The prosecutors, pleasantly misnamed corporation counsels, were badly paid, dispirited, and often fly-by-night lawyers who could not get jobs elsewhere. They had no clerk, no typist to help draw up briefs, no

secretary to answer the phone, and seldom more than five minutes to prepare a case. Then there was the problem of witnesses. The prosecutors had no way to serve a summons except through the mail. Half to three-quarters of their cases were dismissed because witnesses failed to appear. Even the police treated the Family Court as a joke and often did not show up when needed to testify. By one estimate, young people appearing in the Manhattan Family Court were sent away as PINS [Person in Need of Supervision] or delinquents less than 10 percent of the time.[4]

Still, officials who read Bosket's psychological reports knew that he was too emotionally disturbed to return to his home and neighborhood. One report stated:

> After his father was convicted and imprisoned prior to his birth, his mother rejected him and expected him to act out in a violent fashion because of the similarities she had drawn between father and son. The trauma of her husband's violent actions and her subsequent feelings of rage and abandonment in the face of a newborn child may have caused her to associate these attributes with the expected child. In any case, she has constantly drawn attention to his physical similarity to his father and therefore remarks about their comparison, particularly to Willie. This comparison is usually negative. It is believed she has conveyed to Willie this negative feeling and the image of inadequacy, violence and worthlessness to him. Willie, apparently feeling rejected, incorporated these qualities into his personality in order to gain his mother's love and approval. Unfortunately, it did not.[5]

The upshot of this part of the report is that Bosket was a repeatedly rejected child. His father was not there to love him, and his mother's love was not there for him either. He was emotionally damaged at a young age; neighbors, his mother, and officials could see that damage in his pattern of repeated acts of violence. There are more disturbing details to his life that Butterfield notes. He reports that young Bosket's grandfather taught him about sex by sleeping with him in the same bed. "'I'm going to teach you about sex,' James told his grandson. . . . Then James lay on the bed and told Willie to penetrate him with his penis. He used Vaseline as a lubricant."[6]

So in the sad story of Bosket we have a large part of the story of why we have dangerous cities. Willie Bosket is currently serving multiple life sentences not only for the acts of murder that he committed at the age of fifteen, but also for the subsequent attempt to murder a prison guard. He is considered too dangerous to be in a regular prisoner population and has lived his adult life virtually in isolation.

To state simply that he is sociopathic or psychopathic is to ignore the reasons for his having become emotionally disturbed. These reasons are far from obvious. But they should not be viewed as independent of 1) a city's juvenile justice system that lacked the funds to provide treatment and lost sight of its rehabilitative mission; 2) a family that lacked the capacity, understanding, time, money, and energy to address Willie's troubling childhood behaviors; and 3) a deeply troubled child who was repeatedly abused.

The Case of David O

The case of David O is an equally sad story. It illustrates the point that a safe city is no guarantee against extreme violence. Extreme acts of violence occasionally occur among middle-class and upper-class youth. Seriously troubled youth reside in good families and in good communities. Every large safe city has its recorded adolescent cases of suicide and murder. I have been asked by David O not to use his real name, because he does not wish to draw attention to his family and to his victim's family as well. Like Terribly Young, his anonymity is reflected in the pseudonym that I have assigned to him.

David O falls into that small percentage of middle-class and upper-class adolescents whose first act of crime is a brutal act of violence. At the age of fifteen, David O was arrested for the murder of an eight-year-old boy who lived nearby in the suburban wooded subdivision where both of their families resided. Acts of extreme violence like that of David O have occurred in safe cities like Amherst as well. As is the case with Willie Bosket, there were deep-seated troubles in David O's life that led him to commit his lethal act of violence.

But unlike Willie Bosket, David O was raised in an affluent household by college-educated parents. His father was a trained engineer who spent most of his career in the upper echelons of corporate management. Although the reason for David O's act of murder cannot be attributed to monetary impoverishment, he suffered from a kind of impoverishment that is often independent of social class—that is, the impoverishment of being raised in a family that lacked the love and the emotional support that would have enabled him to deal with a range of troubles, including those that revolved around his relationship with his parents and step-parents.

The reasons why David O brutally murdered his next door neighbor's young child cannot be fully described in these limited pages. Instead, I present a snippet of the reasons that David presented to me in his own words in the course of the many years that I have known him. I should note that I first met David when he was incarcerated at a maximum security prison for juveniles where I worked as a summer school teacher. He was just starting his life sentence for a crime he committed at the age of fifteen. He is now forty-eight and still serving his life sentence after being repeatedly rejected by the parole board because of the severity of his offense. The reasons that I summarize are based on numerous visits to prison, phone calls, and letters over the course of many years.

First, David attributed his early childhood troubles to his parents' bitter divorce when he was only eight. His mother remarried soon after, and no longer wished to parent David. She insisted that her young son live with his father. His father also subsequently remarried, continued to work long hours in the corporate world, and had little time for his rejected son. David not only felt neglected and unloved, but also jealous of the attention that his younger half-siblings received. David felt rejected not only by his natural mother, but also by his step-mother with whom he lived at the time of his offense. He described her as emotionally abusive. He recalled how she would tease him and parade around the house half-naked when his father was not around. Naturally, he had to come to terms with his sexual desires, which he could not easily express. In fact, David had to repress a lot that was going on. He was isolated, without friends. He was performing poorly in school. He had moved many times. The only family member he felt close to was his grandfather, who had just passed away six months before David committed his crime.

His father believed in physical punishment for any act of misconduct, including those resulting from problems at school. This is how
David described his father's method of punishment: "Discipline was
generally handed out with a belt, extension cord or a 1 × 2 board across
the legs or back side." David's father is a very large man. I recently met
with him and could imagine how scary it must have been for a young
child or adolescent to be beaten by a father who towered over him. Yet
David said he felt then that he deserved to be punished. He felt isolated,
alienated, and deeply troubled. He wrote, "At age eight I was already an
introvert. I had no friends, isolated myself and acted out aggressively
toward authority and others." Now as a middle-aged adult in prison,
he can reflect on the emotions that led to his act of violence. The reasons are deep, and despite the fact that he has not had the luxury of
intense therapy, he recognizes how troubling his family situation was
at the time of his offense. He wrote, "To feel as if my mother didn't love
me or want me in her life is debilitating at best. It's just not natural for a
mother to not love her son. I felt rejection, betrayal, alone and unloved."

The year that he committed his crime, the only adult who seemed
to really care about him had passed away. No matter how far away
David happened to live, his grandfather would find time to visit him.
"My grandfather at age 65 drove up to wherever we lived, to spend time
with me once a month. The trips were hundreds of miles, and at that
time, I never realized the significance of the sacrifice he made for me."
When his grandfather died suddenly, an important part of David died.
His parents were insensitive about his loss, and David was subsequently
depressed. He stated:

> This was the point I totally lost it. My grandfather was my last friend.
> After this I progressively got worse. I shut down as a feeling person. I gave
> up. When I misbehaved, I allowed myself to think it was ok. . . . I didn't
> do school work, was disruptive, skipped school, was expelled for fighting.

And then that tragic day that dramatically changed the course of David
O's life arrived—a day that he has regretted every day and night of his
life. He first described it to me when he was seventeen as a nightmare
that turned out to be real. It started in the morning with a fight at school:

> I got into trouble and the principal called my father. I was getting ex-
> pelled again for fighting. . . . I was sent home from school early and spent
> the day restlessly watching TV and my father's pornography.

He had relied on his father's pornography in the past as an escape from
the reality of his troubled life. But on this tragic day, it was not enough
to just masturbate. He was terribly frightened by the brutal beating he
expected from his father for having been suspended earlier in the day
from school.

So he turned off the television and went to meet his young neighbor
who was returning by bus from school. Tommy was happy to see David,
and as he had many times before, looked forward to playing Cowboys
and Indians with David in the wooded area that was in back of their
houses. Tommy's parents liked David and previously had trusted him
to watch their son. But lately they were concerned about David playing
with Tommy alone in the woods. A week earlier, Tommy's mother told
David that he could no longer take her son where they had previously
played. David knew he was disobeying Tommy's mother as he walked
with Tommy into the woods where he initially intended to play the
games that they had played so many times before.

Yet this time as they walked, David was overwhelmed by the most
terrible of thoughts: He pictured himself strangling his young friend.
No sooner had that thought occurred, it passed into action, and David
realized that he had just strangled his young neighbor to death. Tommy
was lying next to him, dead.

Soon, he was arrested, detained, charged, convicted, and sentenced
to life. Since then, he has been repeatedly denied parole because of the
severity of his offense—an offense that he has thought about endlessly
as he wonders about the life and adolescence that he could have had if
not for the evil thought that had entered his mind. The murder was an
act of mutual destruction: While his childhood and adolescence had
been destroyed, he could not stand the thought that his young neighbor
and his family had a happy life, and in killing Tommy, he cut off any
chance to live a normal life himself.

Living in an affluent suburb and having a high-income earning father could not save David O. Nor could his potential to perform well in
school and score high on a number of standardized intelligence tests.

Like Willie Bosket, David O lacked the security, love, and other emotional bonds that would have enabled him to confront his troubles. Child protective services might have made a difference in their lives. A more protective and secure environment might have prevented their troubles from escalating into serious crime.

But a treatment-oriented system of juvenile justice was not there for them. A couple of years before David O committed his act of murder, New York State legislators mandated that juveniles as young as thirteen who committed violent crimes be sentenced in criminal court. The passage of automatic waiver legislation because of youth like Willie Bosket produced the life sentence that David O currently serves. If David O had committed his crime several years earlier, he would have been adjudicated in juvenile court and given a disposition that recognized his adolescence. Instead, he was interrogated, convicted, and sentenced as if he were an adult. Though a fifteen-year-old, his age hardly mattered.

There are more sad stories that I could relate about violent juvenile offenders who have been sentenced in criminal court. They tend to be stories of impoverished black youth rather than stories of white affluent youth. Willie Bosket is more typical of juveniles sentenced in criminal court. Like Bosket they suffer from the cumulative disadvantages of their states of impoverishment. They often have not had good legal representation or parents who know how to prevent their children from admitting to crimes they may not have committed.[7]

Stories of the Rich and Famous

For now I return to more typical stories of delinquency. After all, this book is mainly about delinquency and control in safe, affluent suburbs. So I return to stories like that of Terribly Young, whose story is not unlike some of the published stories about the adolescence of the rich and famous. Among the many stories to draw on, I focus on two in which individuals have admitted their adolescent misconduct.

There are others that I would like to include in all their details, such as the story of Mitt Romney's late adolescent act of bullying another prep school student. His alleged bullying received extensive media coverage in the midst of the 2012 presidential race. As reported, Mitt Romney and several other students assaulted another student at their elite boarding school. Although candidate Romney never admitted to the offense, which was initially reported in the *Washington Post*, the incident was confirmed by four of his classmates who said they participated in the assault.[8] As reported, Romney forcefully cut another student's bleached hair while several of his friends held him down. If eighteen-year-old Romney had been charged in criminal court for assault with a dangerous weapon (a sharp scissor can produce serious injuries), he might have been convicted of assault. But that did not occur, perhaps because upper-class youth are sheltered by their elite private schools and high-status parents. As is the case for many middle-class and upper-class youth, there were ways to deal with misconduct that avoided criminal punishment.

Bill Gates

All that I know about Bill Gates, founder of Microsoft, has already been published. The part of his biography that is most relevant to this book involves his father's revelation that Bill was not a well behaved child. The evidence of Bill's childhood difficulties may appear to many to be trivial —not worthy of the term "delinquency." Indeed, there are no reports of uncontrollable violent outbursts as was the case with young Willie Bosket. Instead, Bill's early adolescent difficulties may be viewed within the boundaries of normal adolescent troubles. But they were serious enough for Bill's parents to look for counseling by a professional therapist.

According to interviews conducted with Bill and his father by Robert Guth for a lengthy *Wall Street Journal* profile, young Bill appeared to lack self-control. He could have been diagnosed as suffering from childhood conduct disorder.[9] The story that Bill and his father tell is of a rambunctious, ill-mannered child, whose disruptive behavior produced terrible family fights. In one reported incident, his father became so angry at young Bill's dinnertime antics that he threw a glass of water into his son's face. This kind of physical response would not normally constitute an act of child abuse, but today's experts in childhood development caution parents against any sort of physical confrontation.

But there is another part of the story that the Gates family likes to tell—one that concerns highly educated parents who had the good judgment to recognize early Bill's troubling behavior. They did not wait for dinnertime troubles to degenerate into more serious behavioral problems. They sought the advice of a professional therapist, who met not only with young Bill, but also with his parents, and then developed a treatment plan. The recommendation that followed altered Bill's life. The therapist said that Bill should be allowed to be more independent. She felt he needed to be more on his own. His father reflected on his own route to independence and agreed that it would be best to allow young Bill more freedom to explore Seattle. Bill's parents also learned that his public school was not the best place for their highly intelligent son.

The Gates family had the money to afford private school, and it is in that setting where Bill first learned about the personal computer. He benefited from his private school and the freedom that he had to wander about Seattle into places such as the University of Washington's computing center. The rest of Bill Gates's story is well known.

We can credit young Bill's success not only to his innate intelligence, but also to his parents' ability to recognize 1) the need for a professional therapist to delve into the complexities of their family situation, such as why he might be misbehaving at the dinner table; and 2) young Bill's desire to pursue his own (autonomous) interests that could be rationally accepted by all.

Barack Obama

The stories that Barack Obama tells of his adolescence did not prevent him from becoming the first African American president. As a young black male, he could have easily been subject to the hard end of the justice system. Impoverished inner-city youth are at risk not only because of their race, but also because their parents are more often single and generally less able to provide for their adolescent child or children. Officials calculate the implicit risks of single parenthood. Absent a suitable parental figure to provide the extra controls that they believe a youth requires, officials will tend to intervene to provide an extra level of supervision, often in the shape of detention.[10] So the fact that Obama was an African American youth being raised by a single parent might not have boded well for him if he had been arrested for virtually any type of offense.

This is how President Obama reflected on his adolescent acts of delinquency in his published memoir: "I blew a few smoke rings, remembering those years. Pot had helped, and booze; maybe a little blow when you could afford it."[11] "A little blow" refers to the sniffing of cocaine, the possession of which is a felony. Clearly Obama's adolescent acts of alcohol and drug use were not a liability in his political campaigns. Although he escaped official detection, his mother was alert to his troubling behavior. Despite her single parent status and the fact that she was not always there for him, she acted on her concerns. He quotes her as saying to him:

"Don't you think you're being a little casual about your future? . . . One of your friends was just arrested for drug possession. Your grades are slipping. You haven't even started on your college applications. Whenever I try to talk to you about it you act like I'm just this great big bother."[12]

The conversation that Obama recalls might seem typical of the difficult conversation that at times many parents have with their adolescent children. For Obama drugs were not only common in his circle of adolescents, but also a way of coming to terms with his identity. Obama devotes a considerable number of pages to describing his confused identity; his mother is white and his father is black. He feels further confused because he looks black and was raised primarily by grandparents who are white. But to his mother, this search for identity was no justification for his continued drug use. His friend's drug arrest was an ominous sign of what could be in store for her son. Obama's mother could not accept this lost sense of self: She could not provide that sense of self, and she herself had wandered far in search of her own identity.

Obama was fortunate to have not only a mother who believed in his capacities to succeed in his educational and occupational pursuits, but also grandparents who provided him with the love, emotional support, and care that allowed him to transcend his mediocre high-school grades and occasional drug use. But at the time, he had to enter into a dialogue with his mother. Such a dialogue between parent and child is never perfectly even, as Obama's recollection of their conversation indicates:

I started to tell her how I'd been thinking about maybe not going away for college, how I could stay in Hawaii and take some classes and work part-time. She cut me off before I could finish. I could get into any school in the country, she said, if I just put in a little effort.

"Remember what that's like? Effort? Damn it, Bar, you can't just sit around like some good-time Charlie, waiting for luck to see you through . . ."

"A good-time what?" . . .

"A good-time Charlie. A loafer." . . .

I looked at her sitting there, so earnest, so certain of her son's destiny. The idea that my survival depended on luck remained a heresy to her; she insisted on assigning responsibility somewhere—to herself, to Gramps and Toot, to me. I suddenly felt like puncturing that certainty of hers, letting her know that her experiment with me had failed. Instead of shouting, I laughed. "A good-time Charlie, huh? Well, why not? Maybe that's what I want out of life. I mean, look at Gramps. He didn't even go to college."[13]

So a crisis in adolescence for Obama related not only to his own struggles to come to terms with his multiracial identity, as he details in his book, but also to resistance to parental demands that he become a college-educated adult. Obama had the good fortune to attend an elite private high school where his intelligence was nurtured, and he had a choice of paths to pursue. He could choose: 1) the preferred parental identity of his mother, pursuing the straight and narrow path of becoming a college-educated adult; 2) the good-time Charlie identity, which meant the life of a slacker living for today and not thinking about long-term objectives; or 3) the identity of his grandfather who managed without a college education, working jobs that, though decent, lacked the occupational prestige of those that required a college degree.

Of course, Obama, like many capable adolescents, confronted the possibility of a multitude of identities. Obama's story of crisis is especially relevant because it is a modern-day story. He moved around a lot. He lived in the larger global world. His mother's pursuit of a doctoral degree and her second marriage had taken him in childhood to Indonesia. He could draw not only on his multiracial identity, but also on the multiethnic lives and stories of family members—his father from Kenya, his mother from Kansas, his step-father from Indonesia—along with living with grandparents in Hawaii. Yet despite his movement from place to place, he was secure in having a mother and grandparents who were there for him and who provided him with the love and care that propelled him into his distinguished career as an adult. His capacities as an adult were enhanced by the fact of his good fortune to gain admission into elite private and Ivy League schools where he excelled.

I conclude from each of the snippets of seriously and not-so-seriously troubled youth that parents, therapists, teachers, and other caring individuals can make a difference in how well adolescents are able to confront their troubles. These troubles include an arrest (Terribly Young), trauma because of abuse (Willie Bosket and David O), disruptive behavior (Bill Gates) and underachieving school performance along with drug use (Barack Obama).

Adolescence

I now shift from the stories of adolescents to definitions of adolescence. Among the possibilities, I prefer the definition given by Elizabeth Scott and Laurence Steinberg, who see adolescence as "a complex mixture of the transitional and the formative."[14] By "the transitional," they mean the "rapid and dramatic change within the individual in the realms of biology, cognition, emotion, and interpersonal relationships, and by equally important transformations in major social contexts—family, peer group, and school." By "the formative," they refer to "events and experiences" that place adolescents on a particular course in life. There may be positive experiences, like a teacher who encouraged higher education. There may be negative experiences that make it difficult to transcend adolescence.[15]

In the developmental literature, the view of adolescence as a distinct period in the life course of individuals is widely recognized. Developmental psychologists, neuroscientists, and legal scholars have repeatedly stated why adolescents should not be prosecuted and sentenced as adults, and judicial authorities have come to concur. Recently, for example, the U.S. Supreme Court has acknowledged the fact that adolescents are not yet ready to think like adults, stating that "developments in psychology and brain science continue to show fundamental differences between juvenile and adult minds" and in "parts of the brain involved in behavior control."[16] This majority opinion reflects what many parents have long known: Teenagers are not ready to take on adult responsibilities because they are susceptible to the influences of others and unable to realistically think about the potential consequences of their delinquent behaviors.

Modernity

Although a segment of adults also may have considerable trouble thinking rationally about the consequences of their behavior, adolescents deserve special consideration because they live in a society that has limited their adult-like responsibilities. In childhood, they are required to spend long hours with their peers in compulsory school settings. They cannot work, get married, or have children. They are supposed to wait until they achieve the technical skills that would allow them to become a fully responsible adult. This was not always the case. In pre-modern times, adolescents did not transition into adulthood since they were generally already there.

The psychological move into adulthood is usually coupled with physical moves as well. Parents move and their children are expected to move for educational and occupational pursuits. This, too, was not always the case. The pre-modern world is one of limited movement; only a few were able to travel beyond their local villages. As previously noted, it was not until locomotive and motorized travel that vast distances could be traversed in ways that exposed larger segments of the population to diverse ways of thinking and acting. Technological innovations of the nineteenth and early twentieth century produced a modern industrial society that began to get people to move rapidly.

But it was the impoverished and the persecuted who had to move more during periods of industrial modernity. They moved from their countries of origin to escape famine, war, and all sorts of natural disasters. Past and current waves of uneducated as well as educated immigrants have moved because of promise of a better life. Today's families, parents, and young adult children are encouraged to move for their educational and occupational pursuits. Vacations are also times when people like to move; as tourists, they can become self-fulfilled and enlightened by the larger world.

A late modern-day world is also a world of the Internet and instant communication. It is one where information travels fast and everyone can know everyone else's business no matter how far they happen to be at the time. Being in Dubai, London, New York, or Tokyo matters little to the frequent-flyer parent who can still manage nearly every night to Skype with their children and give them a kiss goodnight. Being local is increasingly irrelevant as numerous commentators have noted in the world of late modernity.

The writings of Anthony Giddens are relevant in distinguishing how the social and psychological are less influenced by a local sense of place. He states that

> "Place" is best conceptualized by means of the idea of locale, which refers to the physical settings of social activity as situated geographically. In pre-modern societies, space and place largely coincide, since the spatial dimensions of social life are, for most of the population, and in most respects, dominated by "presence"—by localized activities. The advent of modernity increasingly tears space away from place by fostering relations between "absent" others, locationally distant from any given situation of face-to-face interaction. In conditions of modernity, place becomes increasingly phantasmagoric: that is to say, locales are thoroughly penetrated by and shaped in terms of social influences quite distant from them.[17]

The point should be repeated—the local in today's contemporary world is increasingly less relevant as sociability depends less on direct physical presence.

The social emerges from the distance—even more so today with the advent of social media as the preferred technique for many adolescents to communicate with one another. Community produced on Facebook and other social media sites makes a traditional image of a face-to-face community something of an ancient past. But this does not mean that today's adolescents are any less social than those of an earlier century. What has changed are the techniques for becoming socially modern. They require adolescents to adapt not only to their biological transitions during puberty, but also to newly created familial, educational, and peer-group requirements. Their ability to reach adult status and create a sense of self independent of a locally defined place requires acknowledging that they, their parents, and society are on the move.

Relos Are Modern-Day Families

There are plenty of examples to draw on to illustrate how the middle class is less attached to a localized place. Corporate and professional pursuits require a substantial proportion of safe-city parents to move, and they move knowing that their past place of residence will be similar to the next. The housing, schools, town services, and recreational pursuits should be equally good. This point is illustrated in a *New York Times* series on social class, in which one article focuses on how suburban parents move about from one affluent suburb to the next. These "Relos"

> move every few years, from St. Louis to Seattle to Singapore, one satellite suburb to another, hopscotching across islands far from the working class and the urban poor. . . . They have traded a home in one place for a job that could be anyplace. Relo children do not know a hometown; their parents do not know where their funerals will be. There is little in the way of small-town ties or big-city amenities—grandparents and cousins, longtime neighbors, vibrant boulevards, homegrown shops—that let roots sink in deep.[18]

Relo families may indeed lack a singular, geographically identifiable place where they can say they were raised and where their children were raised as well. Consequently, they must rely on short-term relationships. They have moved too often to draw on extended family relationships. Long-time neighbors require a long-time presence; this is not the case for those who must relocate every couple of years, when corporate headquarters call.

But Relo children (along with the children of military personnel, diplomats, journalists, and academics who move frequently) are rarely the disturbed youth who end up in juvenile prisons. Many Relo youth are able to adapt quite well to their new neighborhoods, schools, and before- and after-school activities. They are able to manage despite having moved from one place after another. Although there is instability in their lives, they are able to create a modern-day sense of community—a community that may be described as being rather thinly layered. This sort of community contrasts sharply with the thick physical image of a community of a less modern world—one confined to a narrowly defined geographical place. "Community" is now defined instead in terms of a complex set of organizations partially sponsored by government agencies, including those residing far from local townships. For instance, many of the recreational and youth programs that are considered so desirable in affluent suburbs are supported by Youth Board funding, which is generated from state monies granted through the federal government's Office of Juvenile Justice and Delinquency Prevention.

Although Relo family members may occasionally miss the tightly knit communities of their great, great grandparents' villages, there are a multitude of communities that they are able to appreciate in their modern-day suburb. Community is no longer singular. So the hockey rink becomes a source of modern-day community as well as the neighborhood block association and the parent-teacher association. Communities in their miniature are to be found everywhere; subdivisions have their communities, suburban office parks and shopping malls have their communities as well. The term may be deemed vacuous, lacking the real meaning of "community" and referring more to myth than reality. But the term still exists and is routinely used to justify how and where people move.

The essential point is that while a traditional community may be lost, a modern-day loosely structured set of communities has been gained. There is a familiarity to these communities that makes moving easier. They have been homogenized. Risks have been lowered, and safety has been enhanced through security devices and gated subdivisions. The key here is standardization—making everything as familiar in the present as it might have been in the recent past.

So the subdivision homes and neighborhoods remain the same; the shopping malls and office parks remain the same; the schools and their before- and after-school activities remain the same. Families move from one colonial four-bedroom house with two and half baths, finished basement recreational room, and attached two-car garage to another. They are able to maintain the familiarity of place. The kids can be enrolled in the same sport teams and clubs, and in the same equally good schools with advanced placement classes. The shopping malls and the big box stores are still there and remain popular for good reason; they remain the same from one place to the next.

There is a big benefit to all this standardization of modernity's many globalized places. You know what you are getting when you shop, eat, or drink at any chain store. You can count on enjoying the same Starbuck's Grande Latte whether in New York or in Berlin. Moving from one safe city to another allows residents to deal with societal complexity and expectations for their children's educational and occupational pursuits.

Complexity: The De-Localized Sense of Place

A sense of self in the midst of a modern-day world that has de-localized places requires adolescents to confront divisions within their larger and smaller worlds. An understanding of language is essential. Middle-class and upper-class youth are advantaged by their parents' complex use of language with conditional tenses and sub-clauses rather than simple declarative words.[19] The youth of car-dependent suburbs learn language from an early age in places that were unheard of in earlier times. Considerable amounts of time are spent moving children from one activity to the next in an automobile, minivan, or SUV. The conversations that take place between parent driver and child passenger are front-seat/back-seat conversations through the view of a rearview mirror. The back-seat language skills that children learn through mirrored images of their parents reinforce a less face-to-face form of communication.[20] So, too, is that back-seat way of communicating indirectly taking place through computer and smart-phone screens.

These car-dependent and digital forms of communication are not confined to suburbia. They describe modern-day communities that are more or less organized communities in urban as well as suburban cities. Robert Sampson's scholarship has long recognized the importance of organization in community in densely populated cities. Well-organized communities in inner cities have lower crime rates, because their residents are more collectively efficacious. Sampson defines collective efficacy as consisting of "two fundamental mechanisms—social cohesion (the 'collectivity' part of the concept) and shared expectations for control (the 'efficacy' part of the concept)."[21]

The kinds of relationships that would enable people to know and assist one another are not the dense relationships of earlier pre-modern times. In fact, there is no pretext for returning to these pre-modern communities. They are no longer possible. Sampson is critical of the

This newly built Amherst, New York, subdivision lacks the density of an older city.

notion that thick, personal relationships are the essence of a good neighborhood. The social order of a good city depends on thin, neighborly relationships. He states that "When ties are 'thick,' it may even be that outcomes are worse rather than better. More important, there is the mathematical impossibility of relying on friendship or other close personal ties to achieve social order in the contemporary (or any) city—there are simply too many people to know."[22]

But modern-day individuals need to buy into the thin layers of their relationships. When people move, they say good bye not only to their neighbors, but also to a range of professionals. In their new homes, they must obtain a physician, dentist, accountant, and a range of professionals in the service of their children. They develop relationships like the professional ones they experienced in the not-too-distant past. These relationships are important to their well-being, and they require the capacity to trust that professional expertise will be the same. As thin relationships, they work. They assume that people are equally capable of buying into expertise that is not always visible or understandable. This is what it means to be essentially modern.

And it is the expertise that is offered by professionals that essentially advantages the affluent over the impoverished. They have the intelligence, education, and money to afford the expert knowledge that is seen as enabling of their educational and occupational status. Yet all this expertise is barely understandable, and at times, can be conflicting. An earlier century of sociologists noted that the urbanized industrial city is a confusing place to many of its residents. In his 1903 essay on "The Metropolis and Mental Life," George Simmel observed that city life produced a blasé attitude among its residents. He wrote that urbanites were subject to an "uninterrupted fluctuation of external and internal impressions" and were conflicted by too many ways of thinking and acting. Whereas "the slower, more customary, more uniformly flowing rhythm" of small-town life was less dizzying, the city required its residents to confront "the rapidity and contradictory quality" of their everyday impressions.[23]

Another distinguished early twentieth-century sociologist would later write that city dwellers could not escape conflicting beliefs. In his 1923 published study of impoverished inner-city girls, W. I. Thomas described how they faced conflicting social definitions of how best to behave from parents, spouses, and neighbors, as well as officials and professionals:[24]

> The world has become large, alluring, and confusing. Social evolution has been so rapid that no agency has been developed in the larger community of the state for regulating behavior which would replace the failing influence of the community. . . . There is no universally accepted body of doctrines or practices. The churchman, for example, and the scientist, educator, or radical leader are so far apart that they cannot talk together. They are, as the Greeks expressed it, in different "universes of discourse."[25]

The secular world of a large city was not enough to unite its residents, because it lacked the authority and the consistency of the past.

Thomas provided support for his hypothesis based on the results of a government-sponsored survey of medical doctors on the impact of premarital sex. The questions and answers are quite dated but are consistent with Thomas's point that there is inconsistency in modern-day expert knowledge. In response to the question,

May it be taught that under "certain conditions intercourse in the unmarried is harmless or beneficial?" . . . [f]ifty-one replies were received. . . . Twenty-four were, in substance, "not permissible"; fifteen, "permissible"; four, "in doubt"; eight were indefinite, as, for example: "Adults will probably decide this for themselves."[26]

Of course, this is quite a dated example. Few of today's medical doctors would view premarital sex as harmful. The focus in counseling an adolescent would probably be on various birth control options. The important point for Thomas and others is the lack of a central authority in a modern society. Experts are supposed to be that source of authority, but they often disagree. To grasp how best to proceed (or how best to transition into adulthood), adolescents must confront their conflicting messages. Or, as Lewis Mumford observed, they must understand that "the mark of the city is its purposive social complexity."[27]

Angst over how best to proceed is notable among safe-city parents. There is a competitive edge to parenting, which leads some Amherst parents to publicly announce their child's status, and in turn their own status as good parents, through bumper stickers, for example, stating: "My child is an Honor Student at Sweet Home High School." The place of the message is the thing that makes suburban living possible—the automobile. The message shows parental pride and the willingness to announce their child's academic success in a fast-moving, highly superficial setting.

Autonomy: You Are on Your Own in Suburbia

The automobile is a non-public form of transportation. It requires its drivers and passengers to be more on their own than if they were on a bus or subway. Many suburban residential and commercial areas lack sidewalks so people have no choice but to travel from one place of activity to the next without having to confront another. But being on your own in suburbia is desirable. The fact that most Americans now live in suburbs and own cars reflects more than just their desire for the safety of a city. It represents the desire to freely choose where to travel on your own without having to depend on a bus schedule.

A modern-day sense of self is enabled. A sense of self refers to a reflective self, an esteemed self, an efficacious self, or an actualized self. The actualized self is a higher ordered self, according to distinguished psychologist Abraham Maslow. His popular theory of self-actualization is based on the idea that people have a hierarchy of needs. The most basic ones are physiological, such as the need for food and shelter. Then, there is the need for belonging and love. Family, friends, and community are critical in this next rank of needs. Once other needs are satisfied, the final, upper-most need involves self-actualization, which is "a matter of degree and of frequency rather than an all-or-none affair."[28] Maslow defines the self-actualized individual as having experienced

> an episode, or a spurt in which the powers of the person come together in a particularly efficient and intensely enjoyable way, and in which he is more integrated and less split, more open for experience, more idiosyncratic, more perfectly expressive or spontaneous, or fully functioning, more creative, more humorous, more ego-transcending, more independent of his lower needs, etc. He becomes in these episodes more truly himself, more perfectly actualizing his potentialities, closer to the core of his being, more fully human.[29]

But the theory has been popularized beyond Maslow's initial intent. It is a goal that is not easily attainable: Very few can attain this stage of self-actualization. Yet it has entered the popular literature and the corporate world, as illustrated in Lee Bolman and Terrence Deal's best-selling text on *Reframing Organizations*, in which they quote the Manager's Guide at Federal Express as stating:

> Modern behavioral scientists such as Abraham Maslow have shown that virtually every person has a hierarchy of emotional needs, from basic safety, shelter, and sustenance to the desire for respect, satisfaction, and a sense of accomplishment. Slowly these values have appeared as the centerpiece of progressive company policies, always with remarkable results.[30]

Where there is a recognition that a self-actualized worker is a good worker and one who can contribute to a corporation's success, there is

an assumption that basic needs can be, and have been met. The affluence of a safe city and its families is more likely to assure that basic
needs are met, allowing adolescents to pursue their own interests—
often through a wealth of enabling choices.[31]

An autonomous sense of self is generally considered essential and
basic to personal development. Children must learn to express their
desires. Usually toddlers begin to articulate their own feelings when
they learn to say the word "no." Critical to an enlightened society is the
belief that each individual is capable of saying "no" or "yes" to various
pursuits as long as they do not harm others. The modern democratic
nation-state is rooted in the notion of individual responsibility, free
will, and the right to pursue personal happiness.

But an individual's ability to make his or her own decisions can easily be compromised, as all sorts of troubles in a range of social settings
can arise. Legal officials recognize this to be the case for the mentally
ill as well as for adolescents. Age as well as mental defect becomes an
extenuating reason for adjusting the stated penalties associated with an
offense. Generally, adolescents are more often subject to the influence
of their peers; a well-known criminological fact is the group context of
their delinquency.[32]

Naturally individuals prefer to make their own choices. They prefer
to choose the person they wish to marry, the careers they wish to pursue, and the places they wish to live. They resist dictatorial rules. Similarly, adolescents as individuals prefer not only a democratic society,
but also a democratic family where they can express their own point of
view, particularly about the rules of the house. A household where rules
can be negotiated, such as how late to stay out, would seem preferable
to one dictated by an authoritarian style of parenting.

The bright side of this belief in autonomy for adolescents is that it
is enabling of their eventual adult responsibilities. Adolescents need
to learn to negotiate rules and advocate for their own interests. They
need to be self-efficacious in their educational and occupational pursuits. The collective is a place for group rewards not individual ones.
In pre-modern times, the individual's self-interest was to be denied.
Today a more enlightened society is one where a sense of self reigns
supreme, as reflected in such concepts as self-efficacy, self-esteem, and
self-actualization.

This wooded Amherst, New York, subdivision provides its residents plenty of opportunities to be on their own.

An affluent suburb provides plenty of physical space for its residents to develop their sense of self. Suburbanites have more square footage in their houses, more back- and front-yard space, and more areas to just hang out and play. Their typically three- or four-bedroom house usually has a room for each child. In the typical suburban house, there are additional rooms for family members to be on their own. In densely populated cities where families must reside in apartments, it is more likely for rooms to be shared; physical space has to be negotiated. In contrast to house living, apartment living means that family members are more apt to encroach on each other's physical space.

Yet there is a dark side to individual autonomy in a modern-day society, one that Emile Durkheim identified in industrialized Europe at the end of the nineteenth century. His use of the term "social anomie" occurred in the context of the rise of emerging secularized nation-states. He feared the enlightened citizens of Europe's cities were at risk of losing the controls of their earlier village-like communities. The Protestant Reformation loosened the authoritarian control of a centralized church; Jews like himself and other ethnic minorities were obtaining rights of citizenship; and the old ascribed caste system was being replaced by one that depended on individual achievements. A segment of citizens were losing their way, and it so happened that they resided in Northern Europe where various forms of Protestantism began to dominate.

More people began to move both physically and mentally, and all this movement created its own set of risks. For a segment of the population, there was the risk of being too much on one's own—with one's own individual pursuits, desires, and dreams that might be in conflict with the interests of others. For most, these could be adjusted through school experiences, which, Durkheim emphasized, should reinforce the universal values of a secularized nation-state. Children could learn their place in their educational and subsequent occupational pursuits, forming goals that could be attainable, desires that were realistic, and dreams that would be realistically pursued.

But for a segment of the population, their individual hopes could be easily shattered. They could go too far off on their own; their desires could become unattainable. Durkheim wrote:

> All man's pleasure in acting, moving and exerting himself implies the sense that his efforts are not in vain and that by walking he has advanced. However, one does not advance when one walks toward no goal, or— which is the same thing—when his goal is infinity. . . . To pursue a goal which is by definition unattainable is to condemn oneself to a state of perpetual unhappiness.[33]

According to Steven Messner and Richard Rosenfeld, the unattainable in modern-day dreams explains high rates of violence. Crime rates are higher in the United States than in other economically developed countries because the American Dream of wealth by any means necessary dominates the mindset of many Americans. "With few exceptions, everyone is encouraged to aspire to social ascent and everyone is susceptible to valuation on the basis of individual achievement."[34] The belief that every American is capable of going from rags to riches is especially frustrating for the poor and those who lack the capacities to perform well in school and in their place of work. The pressure to succeed for a segment of the population can be unbearable.[35] A sense of self that is law abiding can be easily lost along the way.

Rationality: Late Modern Rules and Adolescence

There is a late-modern way to parent. It involves different universes of parenting discourses. At times Relo parents may turn into so-called "Helicopter," "Velcro," or "Drill Sargent" parents. Undoubtedly, these styles of parenting can be distinguished by those who have authored these terms. What they have in common is a way of parenting that is quite different from pre-modern times. Surely, if the residents of early nineteenth-century rural Amherst were able to see what has become of their quaint farming village, they would be shocked by what modernity has brought. If they focused on the parenting styles of those who inherited their land a hundred years later, they would be surprised to see parents acting as glorified chauffeurs, conveying their kids from one activity to the other. They would also be perplexed by the way adolescents depend on their parents. In place of parents who relied on their teenagers to work the farm, they would see parents who negotiate a range of activities that their adolescents would like to pursue. Since parents from pre-modern times believed in an authoritarian model wherein obedience to family, church, and community reigned supreme, they might wonder why contemporary parents would even bother listening to their youth.

Parents and their adolescents must come to terms with the fact that in the late modern world of safe cities, they are operating with different sets of rationalities. The justifications and universes of discourse are many. Styles of parenting are continually being debated in books, in magazines. Helicopter, Velcro, or Drill Sergeant parents are accused of over-parenting for not allowing their adolescents to develop the autonomy that they need to become independent, self-efficacious adults. But these parents may claim that the modern-day world is tough—that their kids need guidance, supervision, and a push to compete successfully for all that is good in society. They need the stability of a suburban place.

Relo parents are only partially on the move. They have the stability of one good suburban neighborhood after another. Home ownership provides a semblance of stability. In his book documenting the development of American suburbs, Kenneth Jackson quotes Walt Whitman as stating that "A man is not a whole and complete man unless he owns a house and the ground it stands on." Jackson further quotes an *American Builder* article as stating in 1869, "It is strange how contentedly men can go on year after year, living like Arabs a tent life, paying exorbitant rents, with no care or concern for a permanent house."[36] But Relos are indeed able to own their homes; recall that home ownership is substantially greater in suburban Amherst than urban Newark. It is the impoverished who are less likely to own their own home, and they are also less likely to move since they can hardly afford the expense of relocating, particularly to a safe city.

Rules as Rationalities

Late-modern rules are rationalities. They may be divided into those that emphasize their moral, social, and legal components, respectively. Serious offenses draw on all these components; they overlap with one another. It is hard to imagine how any society could maintain its social order for long if it did not prohibit acts of theft and violence. But there are categories of offending that are deemed more or less serious. The less serious offenses have less of an overlap, particularly when they are illegal acts committed by adolescents. For instance, a proportion of Amherst parents and their youth approve of alcohol consumption and the smoking of pot within certain limits. These acts are in violation of legal rules regarding underage drinking and pot smoking, but they are not necessarily violations of moral and social rules.[37]

MORAL RULES

The family is the primary source of moral rules, and generally the first place for inculcating morality into the life of the child. Moral rules are closely associated with moral authorities. But as Durkheim noted, the authority of elders could no longer have the same force as in earlier times. He wrote that "it is in the great cities that the moderating influence of age is at its minimum." This loss of authority means that "Traditions have less sway over minds" and new "ideas, fashions, customs, new needs are elaborated and then spread over the rest of the country."[38] To inculcate moral rules, families require the assistance of schools, clubs, workplaces, and all sorts of civic organizations.

Critical to a conception of modernity is how industrialization produced a middle-class culture and newly shaped moral rules. The middle class was expanding and creating their rules of appropriate behavior.

In *Schnitzler's Century: The Making of Middle-Class Culture, 1815–1914*, Peter Gay identifies newly emerging sources of nineteenth-century morality.[39] One involved the middle-classes' starting to record their personal feelings in the form of private diaries. Gay describes how the subject of his book, Arthur Schnitzler, who became a famous Austrian playwright, was deeply disturbed by his father's violation of an emerging moral rule, which dictated that diaries are private and are not to be read without the expressed permission of their authors.

Perhaps Schnitzler should have known that his diary was at risk of discovery. Just as any father might want to investigate his child's use of the Internet these days, so Arthur's father was curious about his young son's late-night activities. In reading Arthur's diary, he was shocked to learn that his son was indulging in promiscuous sexual encounters that he would describe in full pornographic detail. His father, like any good parent, was naturally upset and subsequently confronted his son.

Arthur was perhaps as upset at his father. His father acted in a way that his son believed he should not. Without the permission or the presence of his son, Arthur's father had opened a personal diary. He had violated Arthur's right to personally reflect in the privacy of his bedroom. He violated the privacy of his personal journal. His father clearly acted consciously in violating this emerging moral rule. Without permission, his father intentionally opened his closed desk drawer and read from his diary detailed descriptions of Schnitzler's late-night sexual escapades.

With Arthur's father being shocked by what he read and had suspected, and Arthur in turn being shocked by his father's reading of his personal diary, each must have perceived the other as violating expressed moral rules of decency. Undoubtedly, both father and son were aware of the risks that they had taken to pursue their just claim to a moral rule. Arthur's father as a parent and physician was well aware of the risks of a sexually transmitted disease. He was concerned as parents are today about the health and safety of their teenage children. His father acted in a way that many parents who restrict or record their child's Internet use would agree.

But to Arthur and many adolescents today, their parents' attempt to monitor and supervise violates an important moral rule—the right to privacy. That is a right to a private sense of self—filled with inner emotional thoughts that are to be released only with permission. Arthur forever distrusted his father—their emotional bond, he wrote, was permanently broken. Son no longer trusted father, despite the good intention of his father's concerns.

In telling the story of Schnitzler's century, Peter Gay relates more than just the culture of nineteenth-century middle-class enlightened Europe. He is relating the emerging rationalities of modernity as they produced conflicting moral rules. The notion that a father must ask his son's permission to look at his personal items is a modern one. It is a product of enlightened times and less authoritarian rule. The pre-modern rules of ancient times and of less technically developed states may be considered patriarchal; fathers do not need to ask permission from their children or their wives for the acts they wish to pursue. The assumption that the family could be a place of negotiating rules of order is a modern-day one.

SOCIAL RULES

Social rules are more general than moral rules. They are the product of the groups and the unique places where people reside or like to hang out. Social rules are less fixed than moral rules. They develop through relationships with others. They function as a consequence of expressed needs. Social rules can be viewed as organizational rules in that they produce a complex set of behaviors that are meant to meet organizational goals. To be social is to be organizationally attuned and to follow the dictates of a group. Sources of ambiguity about social rules reflect the fact that people move from one social setting to the next. The social rules governing the classroom can be viewed as different from the rules governing the school yard, the athletic field, the street corner, or any place where adolescents like to hang out, such as a basement recreational room, where they might drink with friends.

In contrast, Max Weber observed bureaucratic rules as singularly tight in the emerging nation-state of Germany. His often cited phrase about "the iron cage of bureaucracy" suggests a hierarchy of organizational rules governing how people should think and act.[40] A singular mindset defines some groups more than others and is more critical to some organized settings than others. Such groups and settings can include, for example, a football team where players must be tightly coordinated with one another; a military or police team involved in a specific task; or a team of surgeons operating to save an individual's life. All these teams operate with a singular set of rules so that their members are able to coordinate their assigned tasks.

But organizational behavior is less tight in some settings than others. High-tech companies that encourage their employees to speak up and innovate from the bottom-up do not want their high-paying professional staff to all think alike. As the contemporary world of business continues to disperse over the Internet, across suburban office parks, and through home offices, the rules of dress, hours, and place of work continue to be modified. The means by which certain tasks are to be performed become more loosely defined. For example, no one is telling me how to write this book.

In the post-industrial culture of affluent suburbs, there are few rules guiding how youth should view their music, clothes, and sexual orientations. The transitional in modernity and adolescence is the freedom to critically assess past and present rules. The self-reflection required to properly assess these rules requires sense-making capacities, which, as Karl Weick sees, also enable individuals to act in complex organizational settings.[41] Many adolescents lack this critical sense-making ability; they have not arrived at the point where they are sufficiently mindful of their actions when confronting one complex organizational place of action after another.

Still, a minimum degree of sense-making is required of adolescents as they navigate their places of activity. They generally know when and where to smoke weed or to snort cocaine and how to steal that attractive department store bracelet. Most adolescents know to act one way with their parents, another way with their teachers, and still another with their peers. They know that the rules of the house are not the same as those at a house party or playing field. Like good organizational theorists, adolescents are mindful of the social rules that they are subject to and that they subject others to as well. In their contemporary adolescent groups, they have mastered the art of creating their own set of social rules.

LEGAL RULES

Those social rules that can lead an adolescent into a tattoo parlor or into one too many piercings can also cause considerable parental grief.

The music may be too loud and annoying. Some relief can be derived from the fact that their adolescent child is performing well in school and has not (to their knowledge) committed an act of delinquency that could lead to their arrest and prosecution. The bottom line for many safe-city parents is to prevent their child's involvement in the juvenile or criminal justice system. To nip the problem in the bud, as the saying goes, parents must be alert to their child's potential violation of legal rules. Minor acts of offending can lead to major acts of crime.

Arrested adolescents may question the stated validity of legal rules, or more specifically the illegality of their pot or alcohol use. Safe-city youth are lucky because officials are generally slow to arrest and prosecute them, and tend to look instead for alternative routes to sanctioning offending youth. There is some ambivalence in how to respond to minor offending.

Taking into account a youth's adolescence only partially mitigates criminal responsibility. Assumptions about the limited capacities of adolescents to be mindful of the consequences of legal rules overlap with assumptions about their limited rationality. The U.S. Supreme Court ruled in 1960 that competency to stand trial depends on whether an individual "has sufficient present ability to consult with his lawyer with a reasonable degree of rational understanding—and whether he has a rational as well as factual understanding of the proceedings against him."[42] An understanding of legal rules matters if there is to be justice in a criminal justice setting. More recently, the U.S. Supreme Court questioned punishing adolescents as if they were adults, particularly in cases where they are subject to the sentence of life in prison without any possibility of parole.[43]

Today in states like New York, where America's safest city is located, there is considerable ambiguity in a diverse set of legal terms relating to adolescence. "Juvenile delinquent," "restrictive delinquent," "person-in-need of supervision," and "juvenile offender" are just some of the possibilities. To fully understand the meaning of each term requires intimate legal knowledge of the state's juvenile justice system and legal rules. But each term carries with it a separate set of penalties or treatments, reflecting its own unique mix of legislated rationalities.

Confronting Transitions in a Temporary Society

To survive adolescence and to move successfully into adulthood requires that adolescents grasp societal complexity, their own autonomy, and the rationality of a multitude of moral, social, and legal rules. The stories that I have told suggest that adolescents cannot do that on their own, but need parents, officials, and other youth service professionals, who can recognize the unique circumstances of adolescence, as well as the fact that today's adolescents are not living in a pre-modern village.

So the kids will be encouraged to leave for college, to pursue their own occupational desires, and marry whom they choose. Parents will relocate because they no longer need that three- or four-bedroom house; they may wish to downsize or move to a community of retirees. They may use their accumulated frequent flyer miles to become frequent tourists. All these moves as illustrated by the term "Relo" make the local in the post-industrial world of American safe cities seem increasingly irrelevant. At the same time, the rules of the road are far from clear. This kind of society is referenced by Warren Bennis and Philip Slater in the title of their book, *The Temporary Society*. The citizens of this kind of society must learn "to live with ambiguity, to identify with the adaptive process, to make a virtue out of contingency, and to be self-directing."[44]

Yet not everyone is equipped to live in an ambiguous society. Terribly Young, Bill Gates, and Barack Obama managed to confront the ambiguities and conflicts in their adolescence and achieve adult longterm success. Their well-grounded families enabled them. Willie Bosket and David O were not as fortunate. They were seriously disadvantaged. Willie Bosket was exposed not only to the violence of a dangerous neighborhood, but also to the violence of dangerous family members, as well as being subject to a juvenile justice system unwilling to provide intense therapeutic care. Although David O had the safety of a middle-class suburban subdivision, he lacked the secure place of family and friends. He could not confront a school system that was indifferent to the sources of his difficulties. Willie Bosket and David O's problems were ignored, and the price they and their victims paid was terribly high. Like other seriously troubled youth, they lacked the relational in modernity that would have enabled them to confront society's demands.

A child has the helping hand of an adult when entering one of Amherst, New York's public libraries.

3

Relational Modernity

Bill Gates, Barack Obama, and Terribly Young could successfully transition into adulthood because they and their parents could recognize adolescent troubles. Bill Gates had the good fortune of having parents who could afford the assistance of a professional therapist. They also had the money to pay for young Bill's private school tuition. Terribly Young's upper-middle-class parents could afford the hourly fees of a high priced attorney, a neuropsychological evaluation (which was not covered by their health insurance), and private tutoring. Both sets of parents sought the expert advice of professionals. Barack Obama was equally fortunate. He had the opportunity to attend an elite private school and to have grandparents who were there to assist him as he struggled to come to terms with his social as well as racial identity.

Willie Bosket and David O were not as lucky. David O was never in a position to reveal his deeply troubling thoughts and his terrible family situation. His mother rejected him, and his father was too busy to become emotionally engaged. Willie Bosket never met his imprisoned father, and his mother was overwhelmed by her son's violent outbursts. She lacked the personal and social capital of the affluent; she could not afford professional assistance, and the juvenile justice system was unable to provide the secure care that he obviously needed.

The good stories that have been told are enabling stories. They are stories of caring relationships—ones that are not just confined to family members. They are also modern-day stories of more than one social setting. They are the stories of relational modernity—of how trouble in adolescence is recognized not just by the youth themselves but also by the adults in their lives. There is no one-way street in a relationally modern world. Instead, a relationally modern world requires recognition at both ends, with adolescents having attachments to parents, teachers, coaches, and others who represent the values of a law-abiding society, and parents, teachers, coaches, and others being socially and personally engaged with youth. Thus, the good stories of youth involve adults who could recognize adolescent troubles and adolescents who could recognize them as well. They could recognize and be recognized. This chapter begins by telling a few more stories of middle-class youth who became seriously delinquent. They and those around them were unable to recognize their difficulties. In one case of serious violence, there were deep-seated mental disabilities. The misrecognition of those serious disabilities is common in cases of serious violence. In the two other cases of violence and theft, the adolescents were living in a sub-urban bubble where their values were singularly directed toward their own selfish desires.

Although there are plenty of concepts to explain why a small segment of adolescents commits serious acts of crime, they generally ignore the self-reflecting part of being modern. Social bonds are the product of individuals who have the capacity to trust and empathetically identify with one another. They provide opportunities for recognition. So children may appropriately care about their parents, but at times their parents are too troubled to care for them. Parents may have significant difficulties relating to their adolescent children, and similarly be unable to recognize their troubling behaviors. Mental health experts, teachers, extended family members, and neighbors may or may not be there to assist. If they are attuned to adolescent concerns, then they may be in the position to regulate their safety and to gain the trust and empathetic identification that is required for creating critical social bonds.

Modernity's Seriously Discontent

School Shootings

A book on suburban delinquency could not be complete without mention of school shootings and why these serious acts of crime are most often committed in suburban middle-class school districts. Eric Harris and Dylan Klebold are well known names in the annals of deadly school shootings. In 1999 they murdered and injured dozens of students at Columbine High School, before turning their guns on themselves.

The suicide notes they left told a familiar story of anger, resentment, and humiliation. Unfortunately, no one could hear their rage prior to their deadly attack. In *Rampage: The Social Roots of School Shootings*, Katherine Newman concludes that

> It's the boys for whom a range of unfortunate circumstances come to-gether—those who are socially marginal, psychologically vulnerable, fixated on cultural scripts that fuse violence with masculinity, live in areas where firearms are readily available, and attend schools that cannot identify this constellation—who constitute the likely universe of school shooters.[1]

Newman further states that their acts of violence (and the acts of violence of other school shooters) might have been prevented if school officials had identified signs of their mental illness, depression, and rage. Accordingly, the subtitle of her book is "Why Violence Erupts in Close-Knit Communities—and What Can Be Done to Stop It."

Perhaps school officials would have been more proactive had they indeed been living in a close-knit community. But tightly knit communities in modern-day cities are hard to find, and even within those communities, it is difficult to maintain a dense level of scrutiny. By contrast, in a pre-modern village, everyone knows one another and knows of one another's activities. In those contexts, crime is less the responsibility of individuals, and more the responsibility of a group. Group mourning and group retaliation take place when one clan, tribe, or close-knit community is in conflict with another.

So could the parents of Eric Harris and Dylan Klebold be blamed for not properly raising them? The parents were not charged with negligence. They appeared to be good, middle-class, well-educated parents. They were better off than Willie Bosket's mother, and there were no reports of abuse. While Klebold was described as depressed, Harris appeared psychopathic. Both were in and out of the juvenile justice system, and subject to their suburban city's diversionary programs. They had received professional counseling, the extent of which is not clear. This is a case where more was required than occasional therapy and soft-end diversion. Deep-end therapy in a secure therapeutic school might have made a difference. But this can be said only after the fact. That their rage was not recognized and their feelings of resentment and humiliation were not easily confronted are facts of modern-day life.[2]

I can easily picture Harris and Klebold's fifteen-minute weekly visit to a probation office. I can further picture how their parents were overwhelmed by their sons' difficulties and troubling behaviors. They needed a tightly knit community to deal with them. But there was none. Like all of modernity's suburbanized cities, Columbine is a loosely knit place where residents are expected to be very much on their own. Sure, it has the money, the resources, and the potential support of a treatment-oriented juvenile justice system. Despite the affluence of Columbine, there was no easily identifiable way to prevent these and other tragic school shootings.

Suburban Rape

There are other serious acts of middle-class violence to consider, although they are not always as extreme and as well publicized as Columbine. Many group acts of sexual assault remain unreported and their perpetrators never identified. Often the victims are too traumatized or too embarrassed to report their rape. Social class may also contribute to the official reporting or under-reporting of crime. Moreover, the middle class is in a better position to avoid prosecution and conviction, because they are in a better position to informally settle disputes and to afford the high price of an attorney. This seemed to be the case when a mentally handicapped girl was raped by a group of star high-school athletes. There was the usual display of power, and between the status of the boys and the status of their parents, it looked as though the boys could be protected from criminal prosecution.

Nonetheless, the act of group rape that rocked highly affluent Glen Ridge, New Jersey, eventually led to several athletes' conviction in criminal court. They lured their victim into their suburban basement recreational room, and proceeded to force her to perform sexual acts in a group setting. A few of the athletes left in disgust and were never charged. Still, no one tried to prevent those who remained from taking advantage of an intellectually disabled girl and her inability to say no.

In *Our Guys,* Bernard Lefkowitz describes Glen Ridge's schools as excellent. The high-school sports teams and their athletes were held in high esteem. But looking further into the personal histories of the "Jocks," Lefkowitz found that some had a shady history of abusing girls and belittling those who were less fortunate. As Lefkowitz observes, "The Jocks didn't invent the idea of mistreating young women." Rather, he writes,

> The teenagers adhered to a code of behavior that mimicked, distorted, exaggerated the values of the adult world around them. These values extolled "winners"—the rich businessmen, the professionals, the attractive, fashion-conscious wives, the high-achieving children. They denigrated the "losers"—the less affluent breadwinners, the decidedly dowdy wives, the inconspicuous, bashful, ungainly kids. Glen Ridge placed the elite kids—the kids with masculine good looks, the kids who stood out on the playing field—on a pedestal.[3]

Lefkowitz speculates that the Jocks' prior history of abuses was ignored because they lived in a society that valued winners over losers. But this is surely not the case for all members of society, even those in affluent communities. The parents of the disabled girl who was raped surely loved their daughter. The youth who walked out in disgust were not on the same page as their fellow athletes. Those who eventually reported the crime and testified, despite threats, were not buying into a "winner-take-all" set of beliefs.

Lefkowitz further asks:

> Where were the grownups of Glen Ridge while this was going on? The truth was, most of them were on the sidelines. The most common explanation they gave for their passivity was that they didn't know. The Jocks, they said, were sustained by an impenetrable, subterranean youth culture whose members were bound by a code of secrecy.[4]

The fact of the matter is that they were living in a modern-day world where parents are not always there to observe their adolescents. In all probability, the parents were at work, like the vast majority of middle-class parents of adolescents. They most likely believed like many other parents that their adolescent children had the good sense to behave properly when they were away from home. They surely had no idea of their sons' criminal possibilities.

So the question remains, should they have known? The answer is a qualified "yes." The first sign of their adolescents' abuse of girls should have been a warning; their troubling behaviors should have been recognized as troubling. This sort of recognition is not easily possible in the loosely knit suburban subdivisions of a highly affluent community. It requires a high level of relational modernity, not just from the parents in their lives, but also from their teachers, coaches, and peers.

Honor Students Who Burglarize and Cheat

My last highly publicized incident is about a serious act of theft committed by honor students in bucolic, Ivy League Hanover, New Hampshire.[5] Many of its residents might state that Hanover is not a suburb but a small, quaint town of about 10,000 residents. According to *Money Magazine*'s list of small American cities, it ranked as the second best place to live.[6] The schools are excellent, the streets are safe, and the median family income is substantially higher than in most other affluent suburban communities ($121,000 per year in 2012).[7]

Regardless of these ideal circumstances, a group of nine high-school seniors broke into their school's administrative office one night and stole the answers to their final exams. This was not just a typical act of school cheating; there was a breaking and entering felony charge and the possibility of a criminal court conviction. New Hampshire mandates criminal responsibility for youth over the age of seventeen. However, the town was split as to whether the nine seniors who were enrolled in honor classes should be prosecuted in criminal court. The local prosecutor said it was his duty to do so, while the parents lobbied for a less severe, more informal school response. Naturally, they did not want their children to have criminal records. So the parents hired attorneys, and they were able to get the charges dropped. No youth was charged or convicted of the felony burglary that they had committed. Instead, only one student was convicted of a class B misdemeanor.

The parents clearly made the case that their adolescent children deserved another chance. They believed in juvenile justice for their children, despite the fact that New Hampshire says otherwise. When I first ask my students about this case, most state that they should have been prosecuted for their criminal act. When I then follow with a question about what they would want if the act had been committed by their child, most are with the parents.

Yet there is another question that Lefkowitz asks in the Glen Ridge Jocks context that is worth repeating in this academic one: Where were the parents? Did they have any idea that their adolescent children could become big-time cheaters? Or was cheating to be expected—not to be taken seriously and merely administratively resolved? I do not doubt that the parents were shocked, disappointed, and terribly upset about their child's behavior. It can be assumed that the parents, a Dartmouth professor, a corporate president, and a journalist, obtained their upper-middle-class positions through legitimate means and that they have a stake in societal rules. Furthermore, it can be presumed that they hold the ethical values that would counter a by-any-means-necessary view to justify cheating in any form. And indeed, they did respond appropriately by saying that this was a wake-up call; they should have recognized that they and their children were becoming too competitive and too obsessed with scoring well.

But there is more that is involved. Like the Jocks, the charged Hanover youth were living in a bubble—one divorced from the rules of the school and the larger community. They were isolated in a world of equally competitive adolescents. They were acting in pursuit of their interests, which in cases of cheating ignores the interests of others. They may have scored high in parental attachment based on their desire to achieve the upper-middle-class status of their parents. But in pursuit of scoring well on standardized exams, they scored low in recognizing how troubling their behavior could be.

Relational Capacities for Control

The school shooting story refers to seriously troubled youth whose mental illness could not be easily observed. The suburban rape story and Hanover's honor students' act of burglary suggest a disconnection between adolescent and adult worlds. Here, the point is that a socially conditioned world requires a multitude of places where parents in their authoritative positional relationships can understand the world of their adolescents. Adults as well as adolescents must learn to recognize one another as they struggle to manage their routines. For some adults and some adolescents there is more of a struggle to recognize and to be recognized.

The remaining sections of this chapter detail relational capacities for recognizing adolescence. It draws on the previous chapter's definition of modern-day adolescence as a complex transitional and formative period of time. Adolescents must learn to fit into the rationalities of a complex society that emphasizes an autonomous self. The means for doing so involves recognizing on-going sources of identity, empathy, and trust. Recognition of how parents and other adults, as well as the adolescents themselves, are relationally attuned to one another is critical to what it means to be civilized and well mannered.

A Civilizing Effect

Norbert Elias has written extensively on the civilizing effects of modernity, and how individuals are expected to continuously monitor themselves. Describing city traffic, and elaborating its implications metaphorically, Elias shows how modern times produce threats that tend to be internally driven, as opposed to the external, physical threats of premodern times. Thus, as he puts it,

> Traffic on the main big city in the complex society of our time demands a quite different molding of the psychological apparatus. Here the danger of physical attack is minimal. Cars are rushing in all directions; pedestrians and cyclists are trying to thread their way through the melee of cars; policemen stand at the main crossroads to regulate the traffic with varying success. . . . The chief danger that people here represent for others results from someone in this bustle losing his self-control.[8]

So how are parents and others able to create self-control? Parental monitoring and sanctioning of a child from an early age is considered

One of Amherst, New York's older suburban subdivisions.

critical.[9] But parents are not just in the business of controlling their child; their role is not exclusively that of imparting self-control. Parents are not punishing machines; they are supposed to provide the emotional support, love, and affection that enable their children to develop normally. But in the rush of modern-day traffic, too much may be going on in their lives; they might not always be so loving, perfectly attuned to their child's needs, and aware of what might be happening at school and with their child's friends.

But trust and empathetic identification in pursuit of self-control is not limited to the thoughts and actions of parents. Modernity depends on more than parents to raise adolescents. It depends on communities of parents and professionals who can advocate particular forms of adolescent and parental identities.

Identity

In that transitional period of time known as adolescence, identities are hardly fixed. They are on-going, emerging in a web of familial and

non-familial relationships. Gender, race, and ethnicity are static identities, usually fixed from time of birth.[10] They differ from the terms people
use to classify themselves. Social class may be considered a fixed identity in less modern times. The upper class stayed rich, and the lower
class stayed impoverished. In a democratic society, it is not the class or
family that adolescents are born into that ultimately defines their identity, but the class that they are able to achieve.

Evolving adolescent identities are created through a variety of status-
generating places.[11] If an adolescent performs especially well in school,
there is the identity of an honor student. There is also the identity of
an athlete, musician, or any number of characterizations that are most
often associated with extra-curricular activities. Identities can be less
organizationally inspired, as in appearing cool or well dressed.[12] The latest fashions, tastes in music, Internet chat rooms, and Facebook post-
ings are among society's many identity-producing places.

But the search for identity can lead adolescents down the wrong
kind of suburban roadway. Parents may rather casually refer to adolescent's misdeeds as a function of their inability to think beyond the
moment. They are often carried away by a crowd of friends or a friend,
and may fail to see the potential consequences of their group act of
delinquency. This lack of forethought leads some parents to refer to
their adolescents as having "half a brain." Scott and Steinberg relate
this point when they tell of the late night escapade of one of their own
teenage sons:

> When he was fourteen, Ben and several of his friends secretly left the
> house where they were spending the night at 2 A.M. to visit the nearby
> home of the girlfriend of one of the boys. When they arrived at the girl's
> home, they threw pebbles at her window to wake her. Unfortunately for
> the boys, the pebble-throwing set off a burglar alarm, which sounded
> a siren and sent a dispatch to the local police station. Upon hearing
> the siren, the boys ran—right into a patrol car that was racing toward
> the house. Instead of explaining their situation to the police, Ben and
> his friends panicked and scattered. One of the boys was apprehended
> by the police and taken home. The others returned to the house where
> they were spending the night. The next morning, Ben's father received a

phone call from the girl's parents, explaining what had happened. After picking Ben up and lecturing him about the dangers of running, in the dark, from armed police who thought they had interrupted a burglary, his father asked him, rhetorically, "What were you thinking?"

"That's the problem, Dad," Ben said. "I wasn't."[13]

Clearly, distinguished experts on adolescence like Scott and Steinberg know that adolescents are more impulsive than adults. One reason for their impulsivity is biological: They have an underdeveloped prefrontal cortex that prevents them from reigning in their impulses as well as adults can. Another reason is that adolescents are more likely to mimic the thoughts and actions of their friends.

So the modern perception of identity recognizes the biology of adolescence, its impulsivity, and the influence of peers. Puberty will pass; the prefrontal cortex will become more developed; and adolescents will move on to a more adult group of friends. There will be a transition, and how successful it is depends on their ability to think on their own.[14] But as adolescents, they want to make their own decisions, perhaps more often than their parents would like.

As part of their high-school curriculum, Amherst adolescents might have read John Stuart Mill's influential nineteenth-century essay *On Liberty*. When confronted by their parents about one too many piercings and tattoos, they may feel compelled to cite the following passage: "The only purpose for which power can be rightfully exercised over any member of a civilized society against his will is to prevent harm to others. His own good, either physical or moral, is not sufficient warrant." They might also quote Mills when he states that "The only freedom which deserves the name is that of pursuing our own good in our own way, so long as we do not attempt to deprive others of theirs, or impede their efforts to obtain it."[15]

To most parents these kinds of statements are nonsensical; adolescents are not free to behave as they wish. Parents are generally unable to approve their adolescent's libertarian view when it comes to the consumption of illicit drugs. Instead, parents may dust off their introductory criminology textbook and quote a passage from Travis Hirschi's hugely popular book, *The Causes of Delinquency*. Hirschi, like many distinguished criminologists, advocated a theory of social control that emphasized the importance of societal constraints. He quoted the distinguished seventeenth-century philosopher Thomas Hobbes as stating: "Of all passions, that which inclineth men least to break the laws, is fear. Nay, excepting some generous natures, it is the only thing, when there is appearance of profit or pleasure by breaking the laws, that makes men keep them."[16] But Hirschi is not so naïve as to think that the prevention of delinquency is just about state-mandated punishment. Rather just as Durkheim before him, he advocates the constraints of the school and the community which form a social bond that inhibited adolescents from violating the law. Delinquency prevention could emerge in attachments to school, recreational activities, and parents. All legitimate activities are important, although good parenting is most important.[17]

Still, life can be too constraining. An adolescent's identity can be too entwined with that of his or her parents or classmates. Individual autonomy can be lost. A balance is required, and a delicate one at that. According to Charles Tittle's theory of social and psychological control, deviant behavior can be understood as individuals' desire "to escape control exercised against themselves and to extend their own control."[18] Autonomy and control must be in sync with one another. Deviance occurs when the controllers are too controlling, denying an essential sense of self. Higher rates of emotional troubles among girls can be attributed to less freedom to express themselves in their chosen forms. Of course, there is the assumption that the desire to be free to pursue one's own choices, including that of being stupid, is a basic human desire.

The Proper Way to Instill Identity

The distinguished European and American social theorists of the late nineteenth and early twentieth century wrote at a time when identities could no longer be easily ascribed from the time of birth. They noted the competitiveness of an industrialized economy, and the importance of properly educating a child. The tribal, village-like apprentice identities of the past were useless in the operation of a factory, and instead new techniques had to be learned. The place for that to happen was the school. In 1903 Emile Durkheim referred to school as "a small society. It is therefore both natural and necessary that it have its own morality corresponding to its size, the character of its elements, and its function."[19] It is a place where common identities are to be forged. A modern sense of self can be solidified through symbols of school spirit, such as school rings, school alumni associations, and school mascots.

But there is more to identity than school-controlled attachments. Surely, the Columbine school shooters were not buying into these kinds of identity-forming techniques. Moreover, the Jocks at Glen Ridge High School and the honor students who burglarized in Hanover were pursuing sets of identities that placed them beyond the edge of well-known school rules. Identities to early twentieth-century philosophers of education had to be on-going; they could hardly be considered static. Herbert Spencer in his 1911 essay on education expressed this on-going view of identity when he suggested that parents should not just act as enforcers of stated rules. Spencer believed that children should be free to learn by their mistakes. He believed that for youth to develop their competency, they should be granted the freedom to explore. This meant less punishment and more understanding and reflection. Thus, Spencer preferred disobedient English youth to more obedient German youth, because he saw the ability of the English youth to think for themselves as critical to modern-day functioning identities.[20]

Identities Focus on the Self

But in society's many identity forming places, identities shift from the place of the family to school and then to peers. In each of these settings, there is the contemporary expectation that individuals will be able to know how best to proceed in their own best interests. Here, Albert Bandura's theory of self-efficacy is relevant.[21] Self-efficacious people are those who can make friends, resolve interpersonal disputes, take advice, and overcome adversity. This means confronting difficulties, and for the self-efficacious adolescent, it means transcending a possibly troubled childhood. Beliefs in capacities to act are critical: "Beliefs of personal efficacy constitute the key factor of human agency. If people believe they have no power to produce results, they will not attempt to make things happen."[22]

An autonomous, efficacious self is a relatively modern concept. In earlier times, there was less concern about the individual and more attention devoted to familial, ethnic, and neighborhood affiliations. Group affiliations mattered more than those amongst individuals. People cared more about their group responsibilities. The ancients suffered from their community's mistakes, and felt plagued as a group by those who violated the bonds that maintained their group status. Modernity has shifted the tables. The language of "caring for" no longer makes modern-day sense. The way that parents raise a normal adolescent to become an autonomous adult is by caring about them not for them. To achieve this efficacious modern-day self, adolescents must be cared about. The mentally ill, the intellectually disabled, or those who have severe physical disabilities must be cared for. Richard Sennett makes this point when he states that those who are disabled must be cared for;[23] by implication a cared *for* adolescent is one whose autonomy is denied. When parents "helicopter" their adolescent or young adult children they are caring for them, and in turn denying their autonomy. Clearly, young children must be cared for because their ability to manage on their own is limited. Older children must gradually be given the independence to discover their own likes and dislikes and to learn by their mistakes. Parents who supervise their adolescents too closely deny their right to a modern-day enlightened *identity,* one that is distinct from that of their parents. By not allowing adolescents to be on their own, over-protective parents run the risk that their children will never develop the autonomy to manage on their own.

Empathy

The Columbine school shooters, the "Jocks" who raped, and the honor students who burglarized could not feel the pain, the injustice of their actions to others. They failed to prevent one another's acts of serious crime. They could identify with one another through the intensity of their definitions, justifications, and beliefs as to how best to disobey stated rules. They empathized with each other's deviant desires.

In the late modern world, there is a thin as well as a thick quality to this kind of empathy. Adolescent friendships that lead to offending are generally episodic—they can be considered empathetic only for a little while. The thin and thick of empathy is contained in Simon Baron-Cohen's definition of empathy as "setting aside your own current perspective, attributing a mental state (sometimes called an 'attitude') to the other person, and then inferring the likely content of their mental state, given their experience."[24] Baron-Cohen's extensive research shows how autistic individuals are limited in their capacity to empathize with others. They have trouble recognizing facial and verbal expressions. Depending on the extent of their disability, autistic individuals have considerable trouble with the worlds of others. They are generally unable to understand how other people feel and think and, unfortunately, live more in a world of their own. Like other emotions, empathy can be defined on a continuum; normally it is not a feeling that you either always or never have.

The extent of empathy that individuals have can be confused with sympathy, which can lead to the caring for an individual rather than caring about him or her. One is more cognitive, while the other is representative of the emotional, affective side of the mind. Baron-Cohen defines sympathy as occurring when "you feel both an emotional response to someone else's distress and a desire to alleviate their suffering."[25] Parent-child relationships are often sympathetic as well as empathetic, and they are sympathetic in the sense that parents do not wish to see their children suffer. But sympathy, if it is taken too far, can blur necessary lines of authority. It can cause a parent and child to identify too closely with one another, leading to the feeling that parent and adolescent are in this together. The parent may subsequently feel compelled to fight the child's battles, and thereby prevent the child from learning to fend for him or herself. The risk of sympathy is that it can minimize the potential for adolescents to manage their own lives and to pursue their own sense of self.

Relationships that involve "caring for" and that lead to an overly thick sympathetic response can compromise parent-child authority. Sennett describes the sympathetic response as an attempt to create a "purified" community where fathers can become "pals to their sons, and mothers sisters to their daughters." Sennett further notes that a consequence is that all signs of authority can be lost, resulting in a "feeling of failure and dishonor if the parents are excluded from the circle of youth, as though they were tarnished by being adult. A good family along these lines is a family where the people talk to each other as equals."[26] Sennett's critique warns that this sort of democratization of relationships can become oppressive. It also leads to ignoring the developing needs of children as they move into adolescence and then adulthood.

Surely children need the security of a caring adult; they cannot feel abandoned, abused, or neglected. As children age into adolescence, they naturally spend more intense periods of time with their own peers; they have romantic desires. Relationships with teachers, coaches, and other adults become emerging sources of empathetic identification. But a thin layer of empathy is required in these cases. Teachers cannot become too close to their students; they must grade objectively. This professional way of viewing a relationship is also the case for therapists, guidance counselors, and coaches. They are employed as professionals to evaluate, counsel, and render empathetic—not sympathetic—decisions.

Empathy and Juvenile Justice

Juvenile justice officials have long recognized the importance of empathy. In the early twentieth century, Denver judge Ben Lindsey advocated empathy for the delinquents brought into his juvenile court. He displayed empathy by trying to understand adolescence and the group context of delinquency. Lindsey was reported to have scolded police officers when they attempted to make adolescents snitch on one another.[27] He understood the norms against snitching. He placed himself in the shoes of the impoverished delinquents whom he saw in his court. In turn, he hoped that they would similarly identify with him and his efforts to place them on a straight and narrow path.

An equally significant early twentieth century figure is Ernest W. Burgess. He, too, advocated empathy as the best way for officials to prevent delinquents from continuing their life of crime. He believed that treatment providers needed to empathetically identify with young offenders. In his afterword to Clifford Shaw's *The Jack-Roller*, he wrote:

The first step in the course of treatment is the approach to the boy, not by sympathy, but by empathy. Through his life-history his counselor is enabled to see his life as the boy conceived it rather than as an adult might imagine it. Empathy means entering into the experience of another person by the human and democratic method of sharing experiences. In this and other ways rapport is established.[28]

Note the distinction between empathy and sympathy. Developing empathetic relationships with adolescents is part of what it means to be a youth service professional. But this attempt to understand is limited. Empathy is not easily achieved in the bureaucratic setting of officials. Decision-making must often be rendered by officials in a routine, non-empathetic manner. Officials hardly have the time to sit and try to understand all the life circumstances of their delinquents; often the life history and the intimate reasons for serious delinquency are considered irrelevant when meeting societal demands to see the adolescent punished.[29]

Empathetic Identification

Graduating from high school, moving on to college, and getting a job are milestones in the lives of not only adolescents, but also their parents. There is a shared celebration at each stage of the adolescent's meeting commonly agreed upon expectations. But these shared expectations are subject to revision, depending on the capacities of the child to graduate from high school, leave for college, and eventually land a job. Healthy adolescent development through empathetic identification recognizes adolescent capacities to meet certain milestones. It requires parents and their children to identify with one another.

As noted, this kind of empathetic identification is not easily achieved. There is theory, and then there is action. The offender is often framed as another—not one of us, a person whose plight we cannot easily identify with. The violent juvenile offender is another person's child—not possibly our own. Our own would be more deserving of juvenile justice, because we would know the personal traumas that might have led to the offense. The other would be more deserving of criminal justice, because we cannot identify with that adolescent's misfortunes; his or her traumas cannot be understood. But this is not how systems of justice were supposed to develop under the theory of modern-day criminal law. As Marcus Dubber states, "The Enlightenment was the age of empathy and abstract identity. The common man no longer was to be pitied for his unfortunate plight. Instead, enlightened gentlemen and reformers strove to empathize with the ordinary person— identify with them—precisely because he was identical to them in some fundamental sense."[30] To be relationally modern means to be able to empathetically identify with the other, not just those who are intimately connected to one's family, tribe, or corner group.

Trust

Willie Bosket and David O lacked adults whom they could trust. They could not trust their parents, teachers, neighbors, friends, or officials. There was no one they could turn to assist them in confronting their problems. In the case of Willie Bosket, the juvenile justice system had repeatedly failed to provide the secure treatment that he obviously needed from the age of nine. Officials were ill-prepared for his violent outbursts. They practiced the fine art of avoidance when Willie would throw chairs. His rejection by one treatment provider after another was indicative of the fact that they have given up on Willie, not just in adolescence but also in his childhood.

Similarly, David O could not reveal his deeply disturbing thoughts to another adult. Why should he? He learned to trust no one; he could not trust his rejecting mother or his physically violent father. He could not trust the teachers and administrators who would repeatedly threaten to expel him. And the trust he expected from those who professed to be religious was violated when he was too young to remember. No one knew of his abuse by Minister John, who would invite young David O to stay overnight at his home. David O wrote:

> He would rub my back and touch me in ways that confused me. The sexual abuse didn't affect my spirituality, because I had no spirituality or beliefs. I felt uncomfortable, and more confused by the minister's

behavior. Everyone thought and said he was a wonderful person. A good man, a man of the cloth. Everyone seemed to love him. I did not realize I was being groomed and manipulated.

Both David O and Willie Bosket are the victims of child sexual abuse who lost more than their innocence; they lost that critical sense of trust that is needed to buy into the beliefs, values, and norms of adult society. Their troubled childhoods produced troubled adolescence, which required more than a quick trip to a youth diversion center to address. No wonder they lacked the security, reliability, and stability of relationships that could have enabled them to have a normal adolescence.

The contemporary social science literature on adolescence recognizes the importance of at least one trusted adult in the life of an adolescent. As Scott and Steinberg state, healthy adolescent development depends on the "presence of at least one adult—typically, but not necessarily, a parent who is involved in the adolescent's life and invested in the young person's success."[31] This adult is presumably not only there to invest in the adolescent's success but also there to assist in confronting a range of possible troubles. Perhaps one adult is not enough. A well-organized community relies on many, including parents, neighbors, teachers, coaches, and youth service professionals. They may not offer the consistency or the thick layers of personal attachment that can come from a parent. But they are facets of a relationally modern world, providing the trust that can enable attachments to emerge in the ongoing pursuit of relationships.[32]

Ideal Parents

Modern-day views of how best to parent are reproduced in parenting websites and how-to-parent books and magazines. The objective of any ten-point parenting program is to produce relatively trouble-free, successful children. Successful parenting is believed to create successful children, although writers who are careful in their language suggest that this is not always the case. I have already alluded to bad parenting in the case of David O and Willie Bosket. Drawing on a relational theory of modernity, it is now time to describe the good or ideal parent.

First, parents and their adolescent children should feel secure. They should be able to trust each other. Children should feel secure not only in their parents' love, but also in their parents' having created for them a safe environment where they can thrive in their pursuits. A safe city provides a general sense of security as evidenced by its low rate of crime. Adolescents and their parents hardly worry about street robberies and assaults as they move about from one activity to the next. Secondly, parents should be responsive to the unique needs of their children. They should not assume that they will always obey the legal rules. Adolescents must be allowed to understand the meaning of rules, and they must be given the opportunity to reflect thoughtfully on the need for enforced rules. They should be given the opportunity to think about their mistakes. There must be mutual recognition of not only the rules, but parental reasons for enforcing rules, and the adolescent's responsibility for any violation of them.

Criminologists have studied styles of parenting described by Diane Baumrind[33] and related them to the incidence of delinquency.[34] The winning style is an *authoritative* as opposed to a repressively dictatorial *authoritarian* or a laissez-faire *permissive* parenting style. The research literature consistently supports the view that children raised in authoritative parenting households are less often troubled and similarly less delinquent; they are less likely to have a range of social and psychological problems.[35]

Steinberg's definition of authoritative parents summarizes several of their characteristics:

> Authoritative parents are warm but firm. They set standards for the child's conduct but form expectations that are consistent with the child's developing needs and capabilities. They place a high value on the development of autonomy and self-direction but assume the ultimate responsibility for their child's behavior. Authoritative parents deal with their child in a rational, issue-oriented manner, frequently engaging in discussion and explanation with their children over matters of discipline.[36]

In acting "warm," authoritative parents are empathetic. In contrast, authoritarian parents who are obsessed with rules clearly lack this warmth. Authoritative parents may also be considered negotiating parents for their willingness to discuss the rules. The important point here is that this parenting style promotes self-reflection and critical thinking. Steinberg writes further that "Family discussions in which decisions, rules, and expectations are explained—an approach to discipline called induction—help the child understand social systems and social relationships. This understanding plays an important part in the development of reasoning abilities, role taking, moral judgment, and empathy."[37] So the ideal parent is not only an empathetic parent but one who is able to recognize that rules are not easily understandable; children cannot learn them on their own.

Parents generally know that the world is a complicated place, and they wish to give their children the tools they need to find their way. The ideal parent is authoritative because this parenting style is most effective in enabling adolescents to graduate and to manage on their own. Based on an extensive review of parental attitudes toward child-rearing, Duane Alwin has documented several elements of modernity that I have outlined.He reports that in earlier generations, parents indicated that they valued obedience more than autonomy.[38] Contemporary parental attitudes have shifted away from this obedience, authoritarian model of discipline to one that emphasizes the need for adolescents to learn to think on their own. He found that

> There is a fairly clear pattern of increasing preferences for an emphasis that stresses the autonomy of children and a decline in the valuation of obedience. Over the periods and settings studied parental orientations to children had changed from a concentration on fitting children into society to one of providing for children in a way that would enhance their development.[39]

And where is this desire for autonomy most likely to be located? According to Alwin, "middle and upper classes tend to express a greater preference for autonomy or self-direction in children, while the working classes give a relatively greater emphasis to obedience and conformity to authority and tradition."[40] There are several reasons for why this is the case. Those who labor in positions as employees are subject to the supervision of their bosses and may reproduce authoritarian relationships when they return home. David Popenoe makes the point that middle- and upper-class family members "are more autonomous" today and more bound by values of "self-fulfillment and egalitarianism."[41] This is not an unfamiliar theme in the criminological and sociological literature.[42] Affluent parents tend to be more egalitarian parents, more willing to negotiate order and, in the process, become relationally modern.

Still, difficult children can lead parents to be less than patient and understanding. The reasons for a child acting out may be related to a learning or mental disability. A delinquent act like burning down the house can create a rift that is not easily overcome, and indeed may lead to a more authoritarian style of parenting. Still the ideal parent is not an isolated parent but a relationally-modern one. The Relo parents rely on more than just their parenting skills. They depend on the resources of a safe city, such as good schools and good before- and after-school programs.

Conclusion

Success in the modern-day sense of the word is the ability to achieve a sense of self in society's many places. Many youth are able to achieve that sense of self through their secure sense of place in familial, educational, and recreational settings. There, and elsewhere, they learn to grasp the complex demands of a modern-day society and gain the ability to be rational and autonomous. But as I have argued, they cannot easily reach that point without the assistance of others.

Trust and empathetic identification are essential. They enable adolescents and adults to recognize one another—each other's concerns and troubles. If they are unable to recognize and be recognized in more than one social setting, they are at risk of serious delinquency. Relational modernity is not just about the constraints imposed by parents. Rather it recognizes the fact that adolescents are in pursuit of on-going identities; their character has yet to be fully formed. The safe city enables the relational through recommended techniques of parenting. An enabling adolescent self is encouraged through critical thinking—and, if lucky, through late-night debates about the philosophical positions of Hobbes and Mill.

Not everyone in an affluent suburb is affluent. This is one of Amherst, New York's low-income, subsidized-housing subdivisions. It is located close to a shopping mall.

4

Beyond a Street-Corner View of Delinquency

The public street corners of car dependent suburbs like Amherst are the least desirable places for adolescents to hang out. They prefer the more private areas of shopping malls, fast food courts, diners, parking lots, and the wooded areas of their suburban subdivisions. They also like the privacy of their suburban basement recreational rooms. Suburban partying often takes place in the privacy of a house, especially on weekends when parents are away.

Hanging out on a public street corner is not only less common in suburbia, but also less relevant to the lives of today's youth. In an earlier, industrialized period of modernity, more of a city's youth lived in densely populated neighborhoods. Suburbanization had not yet arrived. Corner stores still existed, and many in the middle class resided in close proximity to one another in apartments and row houses. Plus there was less dependency on the automobile. In car-dependent suburbs like Amherst, a considerable amount of time is spent moving about on one suburban roadway after another.

The way youth choose to hang out relates to both time and place. More of today's youth are spending a considerable amount of time on their social media accounts. Technology has enabled adolescents to create large groups of distant friends. Through their Facebook pages, instant messaging, and blogging on their favorite Internet sites, they can quickly stay in touch with one another. This kind of social engagement is possible because of their ability to afford a computer laptop, tablet, or smart phone. Of course, there is still the occasional need to personally stay in touch through face-to-face settings. Although the physical in direct personal relationships has not completely disappeared, it seems to matter less in the affluent places of a post-industrial, technologically sophisticated society.

Theories of delinquency tend to rely on facts about adolescents from an earlier era. They tend to focus on the delinquencies of impoverished inner-city males, often under the assumption that serious delinquency is boys' gang delinquency. This group context for delinquency is still important. There still is a street-corner culture, especially among impoverished youth in inner-city neighborhoods. The youth of *Money Magazine*'s most dangerous cities are at a high risk of violence and imprisonment. The safe city remains safe because it lacks the violent delinquent gangs and the internecine warfare that have engulfed the lives of too many inner-city youth. Ancient battles over neighborhood boundaries and familial and personal honor still matter in the most impoverished neighborhoods of the inner city. Few of the young perpetrators and victims of this culture of violence reside in affluent suburbs.

So criminological theories have emerged to explain why higher rates of serious criminality exist among youth in impoverished neighborhoods. One criminological vision of the kinds of places conducive to high rates of crime focuses on the street corner as a metaphor for youth crime. There is no single view represented in a street-corner literature that is vast and a product of numerous authors. Although any summary of that literature would risk glossing over each author's unique theoretical point of view, collectively, they do make several common observations. First, adolescents are more in a world of their own; they are living in an age-segregated society where they must spend long hours in school with other youth who are similarly situated by age. They are more likely to hang out with one another, rather than working side by side with adults as in earlier pre-modern times. Second, adolescents are more likely than adults to be influenced by their peers; they often wish to appear cool when hanging out with their peers. The third point that makes the street-corner literature relevant to a study of delinquency is its focus on the adolescent gang or group as facilitating serious and frequent offending. The most serious kind of offending is usually associated with a street-corner group defined as a delinquent gang.

All the above points can be debated. Like the street-corner metaphor itself, the street-corner literature generalizes the kinds of problems that adolescents can face in adjusting to the values and norms of an adult society. Yet the adolescent gang, like adolescence itself, is in a state of transition. Not all street-corner youth are spending their time hanging out with friends; at various times, some of them may be home or in the library studying. Some may be especially good at thinking for themselves when the offending becomes really serious. Several of the Jocks in the Glen Ridge story of rape not only refused to participate, but left as soon as the assault began, although none made any attempt to stop the rape or report it to the police. Also, some youth seem better able to navigate the troubled waters of adolescence than others and to resist the negative influences of peers. Conversely, there is another segment of deeply troubled youth who pursue serious acts of crime on their own, such as David O. The street-corner view of delinquency can be further challenged by the fact that the vast majority of adolescents who participate in group acts of delinquency subsequently desist.

So my objective in this chapter is first to present a snippet of street-corner visions, and then to offer an alternative relational vision of delinquency and control. The theory presented in earlier chapters has its relational and societal components. First, there is the structure of society itself. This is the modernity part. It assumes modern-day societies are complex, segmented in ways that did not exist in earlier times. In earlier times, the city could be more neatly divided into identifiable concentric zones.[1] The delinquencies of suburban youth cannot be so well organized. Another societal component is the sort of complex competencies that are expected of youth in an increasingly technologically developed society. There are not as many assembly-line factory jobs; rather, there is a greater likelihood of finding work to program the robots that are now operating assembly lines. In order to obtain these high-tech competencies, adolescents must adapt to the demands of a complex society, which in turn means that they must begin to think for themselves in one complex organizational setting after another. Most importantly, they need to buy into the rationality of their schools early on, perhaps with their first elementary school science and language class. In learning the complexities of science and language, they also learn their place in school, among peers, and eventually in possible occupational pursuits.

The second component to a theory of delinquency and modernity is relational. How adolescents adapt to the complexities, autonomies, and rationalities of a modern-day world depends on their relationships. Of critical importance are their parents. But parents know they cannot do it all on their own. Home schooling may delay for a little while reliance on teachers and other youth service providers. Children depend not only on their parents, but also on extended family members and other adults. Parents want a good neighborhood with good schools so that their children can be taught by good teachers and be exposed to good neighbors. There is also the hope that their children will hang out with the good children of their good neighbors, and avoid the large pitfalls of delinquency. But the good in relationships is more than just being good in a nice suburban neighborhood in a safe city. Recall that the youth related in stories of Columbine, Glen Ridge, and Hanover High did not suffer from a lack of good neighbors or teachers. They suffered a deeper set of troubles, and because their troubles were not recognized by adults in their world, they in turn could not recognize the support that they needed to confront their difficulties. They lacked adults whom they could trust enough and who could trust them. They lacked adults who could identify with them, and with whom they could identify as well. If their adult and adolescent worlds could recognize their troubling behaviors, they might have avoided their serious acts of crime.

The relational elements of modernity are not mutually exclusive or exhaustive. The capacities to trust and empathetically identify assumes adolescent relationships are not on a one- way street. Adolescent attachments are a response to the expressed feelings of those who care about them. They may identify with their parents, as their parents may identify with them. Willie Bosket had trouble identifying not only with the law-abiding adults who attempted to assist him, but also those adults who in their personal as well as positional roles of authority had trouble empathizing with him. He could not trust them, and they could not trust him.

Several assumptions are implicit in a relational theory of modernity and delinquency. First, there is the assumption that adolescence is a transitional period of time. Adolescence is a relatively short but critical period in the life course of individuals. There is the expectation that adulthood will soon arrive. But how soon depends on an adolescent's particular trajectory toward adulthood, one that modernity no longer sees as dependent on the traditions of the past. There is segmentation in their developing trajectories: Some youth may take a while longer to move out; they might choose to delay college, marriage, and having kids of their own. Some may be emotionally or intellectually delayed. Others may have suffered the trauma of physical or sexual abuse. They may have had to cope with the early death of a parent. They may need more than the usual amount of time to navigate their familial, educational, and peer-group settings. The manner for allowing them to do so is relational. It demands that there be adults in their lives to provide the personal as well as positional elements of trust and empathetic identification—the sort that enabled Terribly Young to successfully complete his diversionary program. Terribly Young not only needed to dutifully follow the advice of his probation officer, therapist, and parents; he needed to trust their advice and identify with their stated commitment to his success. His renewed faith in adults did not end with his successful completion of probation. Rather, it continued as he matured into a law-abiding adult, able to graduate from college and pursue a viable occupation.

Street-Corners of Delinquents as a Metaphor

I now briefly revisit the street-corner literature with a theory of relational modernity in mind. As noted, the street-corner literature is vast, and so I limit my review to several classics that contain the words "street" and/or "corner" in their title. I already mentioned several classics in the sociological and criminological literature, such as Gerald Suttle's *The Social Order of the Slum*. So I reserve the main parts of my review to William Foote Whyte's *Street-Corner Society* (1948) and Elliot Liebow's *Tally's Corner* (1967), as well as Elijah Anderson's most recent book, *Code of the Streets* (1999). While published during distinct periods of the twentieth century, all remain influential in the criminological as well as sociological literature, and each is still required reading in many sociology and criminology graduate programs. Although their impoverished subjects varied in time and city, all three books attempt to explain why their street-corner subjects are different from the rest of the more law-abiding population.

I begin with Whyte's *Street-Corner Society*, which produced the first significant division between delinquent and non-delinquent through the metaphoric use of the terms "corner boys" and "college boys." It became a model for many generations of ethnographic studies, particularly those that focused on social network analysis.[2] Whyte's 1948 classic is valued for presenting a vision of social order within what was previously assumed to be a purely disorganized slum.[3] Whyte's observations took place during war-time industrialization, when a large proportion of the Italian immigrant boys and sons of immigrants whom he studied could find work and achieve a significant part of the modern-day American dream of moving out of their inner-city slum and into the outer suburbs.

Several generations later, Elliot Liebow's *Tally's Corner* presented a slightly different metaphoric use of the term "street corner."[4] He focused solely on the lives of impoverished men, who hung out at a local corner store. Liebow returned to the Chicago School theme of social disorganization to examine the dysfunctional inner-city lives of African American men during the 1960s. This was a time of rising expectations for basic civil rights and of high hopes from anti-poverty programs. Liebow showed how the men he observed were deeply troubled and unable to manage their lives. He described street-corner men as failed men, who saw themselves as "losers" in the larger world.

Like Liebow and Whyte, Elijah Anderson uses the words "street" or "corner" in the titles of his books.[5] Unlike Liebow, Anderson was able to look at African American inner-city neighborhoods from the perspective of a black ethnographer. Perhaps his ability to identify more closely with his African-American subjects allowed him to see distinctions among his impoverished inner-city subjects that Whyte and Liebow could not see. His insightful observations occurred in the most recent period of deindustrialization and highlighted its devastating impact on inner cities of America.

Whyte's Street-Corner Society

William Foote Whyte spent the years 1937 to 1940 observing a largely immigrant Italian inner-city slum of Boston, which he called "Cornerville." He described Cornerville as a place where "children overrun the narrow and neglected streets, . . . the juvenile delinquency rate is high, . . . crime is prevalent among adults, and . . . a large proportion of the population was on home relief."[6] Whyte lived in the neighborhood during the time he conducted his field research; he even learned Italian so he could speak to residents.

Whyte's street-corner subjects are Cornerville's delinquents. The street corners of Cornerville attracted a certain kind of youth to whom Whyte refers as a *corner boy*. The *corner boy* thinks and acts in opposition to a *college boy*. Both, however, are not only equally impoverished, but also equally intelligent. Yet the college boys are smart enough to avoid hanging out with the neighborhood street corner boys. Whyte further states that college boys prefer to stay home, presumably studying. They also think beyond their local neighborhood and are too willing to abandon it for the greener pastures of a good middle-class neighborhood.

So the classification of youth begins early, not only in the manner that Whyte identifies corner and college boys, but also in the way that groups self-identify. Is it Whyte's classification or that of the corner boys that distinguishes them from the college boys? Besides just hanging out, the corner boys are the more socially loyal. They depend more on each other, and are less autonomous than the college boys. College boys are presented as living more for themselves. Whyte states that

> The difference between them [corner and college boys] is that the college boy either does not tie himself to a group of close friends or else is willing to sacrifice his friendship with those who do not advance as fast as he does. The corner boy is tied to his group by a network of reciprocal obligations from which he is either unwilling or unable to break away.[7]

The unwillingness of corner boys to think beyond their local street-corner friendships can be devastating. It prevents them from pursuing their own "best interests."[8] The best interests that Whyte sees as critical include attending college and pursuing a good middle-class life, which requires the boys to leave their locally impoverished neighborhoods.

Besides their dependency on their local neighborhood relationships, corner boys lack the capacities to manage in complex organizational settings. They are unable to democratically negotiate rules of order. Instead, they prefer the simplicity of authoritarian relationships. Whyte refers to the corner boys he observed as "Doc's gang." Doc brought them together, and the story that he tells is about their allegiance to Doc and his allegiance to them. In contrast, college-bound boys recognize the importance of authoritative relationships. They learn the rationality of adult-supervised clubs where they can participate in an organization's codified rules of order. How the college boys reached that point was determined early on in their lives by school teachers who pre-selected which youth would later become members of the local Italian Community Club:

> In contrast to the corner gang, the nucleus of the Italian Community Club was formed by the teacher who ranked her pupils according to her evaluation of their scholastic performance. At an early age Community Club members were encouraged to look upon themselves as superior individuals. Membership in this group depended not so much on group action as upon the individual's intellectual accomplishments and upon his ability to please outside authorities. In college the emphasis was again on individual intellectual performance.[9]

Clearly, college boys were on the law-abiding side of the street, given their ability "to please outside authorities." They were assisted by their teachers' belief in their ability to be smart enough to be part of the Italian Community Club. So self-identification does not rely solely on the self. Teachers were identifying "at an early age" those who should be in the college-bound category of adolescents. In effect, they received all sorts of benefits based on their capacities to be relationally adept, rather than on their intellectual performance. How early they showed their ability to please others, Whyte is unable to state. But the important point is that gravitating to local street-corners or to adult-supervised community clubs was not solely a matter of adolescent choice. Most importantly, teachers and I presume other adults made distinctions that gave some youth more confidence than others to proceed with other societal demands, like acting rationally in one complex organizational setting after another.

But perhaps Whyte is confusing the sociable kind of intelligence that corner boys have with a more academic kind of intelligence. Corner boys might have more undiagnosed learning disabilities, familial traumas, depression, and a long list of other difficulties that could limit their ability to perform well in school and to please their teachers. In

Whyte's account, trouble in the corner boys' personal lives is not really considered a factor as to why they performed poorly in school. In any case, corner boys were left to fend for themselves—without the adults to steer them clear of a street-corner trajectory.

Corner boys are at risk because they have trouble buying into the democratically organized rules of a modern-day society. They prefer the laid-back, informal approach of an earlier pre-modern era. Their activities are not so much planned, as informally decided based on the exclusive preference of whoever happens to be in command. Whyte quotes Doc, the leader of the corner boys, as saying, "it is better not to have a Constitution. . . . It's best to get everyone to agree first, and then you don't have to vote."[10] To buy into formal bylaws would require corner boys to negate their preference for informal, direct personal relationships for more formal, positional relationships.

Why would they do so? Why would they prefer authoritarian rules over authoritative ones? First, corner boys are from an early age unable to adapt to a complex world. There are no organizational bylaws, codified rules, or clearly stated divisions of authority, as is the case in the larger middle-class world of adult society. They are living in a time that has long past, one that I have considered pre-modern. They lack the civilizing impact of an enlightened world where lines of authority are positionally recognized. Essentially, they are out of sync with the larger modern-day world.

Whyte gives several examples of how corner boys are not buying into modernity's demands. He describes the diverging careers of Chick (who is a college boy) and of Doc (who is a corner boy leader) by repeatedly noting that "intelligence and ability does [sic] not explain [their] different careers."[11] Instead, a middle-class ethos of work and save appears to be a main factor. Chick, like other college boys, worked and saved so that someday he could leave his impoverished Cornerville neighborhood. Chick was future-oriented, while Doc was not. As Doc himself indicated to Whyte, he had a present-oriented, live-for-the-moment view of life:

> Bill, I owe money now, but if I was paid all the money owed me, I would have a gang of money. I never saved. I never had a bank account. . . . If the boys are going to a show and this man can't go because he is batted

out, I say to myself, "why should he be deprived of that luxury?" And I give them the money. . . . And I never talk about it.[12]

Not only is a "work and save" attitude rejected by Doc and other corner boys; so too are the economic realities of modern society. Corner boys refuse to open a bank account, because their personal ties prevent them from saving and lending money based on the positional authority of banking officials. As the corner boys' leader, Doc is lending money with none of the safeguards that would characterize a lending institution. On the surface, this freewheeling approach to money with fellow corner boys seems admirable, but inevitably it produces the sort of interpersonal conflict that a formal organizational setting would avoid. Thick personal ties may be reason enough for why family members may give each other money without any formal agreements. But that kind of informal approach is not enough to finance long-term goals like taking out a college loan or a mortgage to buy a house.

Street-corner youth may indeed be closer, perhaps because of their opposition to formal organizational settings. But theirs is a disabling kind of closeness. It is too provincial; that is, it prevents street-corner youth from entering the larger world. Corner boys learn to trust their fellow street-corner youth, but not their teachers or employers who are embedded in a larger set of more complex organizational structures. They prefer personal relationships not positional ones.

Whyte quotes one street-corner youth as stating that he "judged a man's capacities according to the way he acted in his personal relations."[13] Relying just on informal relationships leaves street-corner youth closer to the old-country villages that their parents or grandparents left behind. While the college boy is prepared to move on, corner boys are not.

Yet there is more going on than just the loyalty that corner boys feel toward one another. They are described as more attached to their street-corner than to their homes:

The residence of the corner boy may also change within the district, but nearly always he retains his allegiance to his original corner. . . . Home plays a very small role in the group activities of the corner boy. Except when he eats, sleeps, or is sick, he is rarely at home, and his friends always go to his corner first when they want to find him.[14]

It is not place per se that they are attached to, but those who occupy a particular place in the corner boys' lives. Whyte does not tell the extent to which the corner boys' homes might be filled with abusive, traumatized parents. The reasons for corner boys being more attracted to the street than their home may have to do with relationships with their parents and extended family members. It is hard to tell the extent to which corner boys are rejected by their parents and other adults.

Whyte recognizes the corner boys' difficulties in identifying with the larger social world of adults. Teachers, social workers, and officials are too far removed from their own impoverished immigrant culture. Whyte quotes Doc, who states that

> "You don't know how it feels to grow up in a district like this. You go to the first grade—Miss O'Rourke. Second grade—Miss Casey. Third grade—Miss Chalmers. Fourth grade—Miss Mooney. And so on. At the fire station it is the same. None of them are Italians. The police lieutenant is an Italian, and there are a couple of Italian sergeants, but they have never made an Italian captain in Cornerville. In the settlement houses, none of the people with authority are Italians. Now you must know that the old-timers here have a great respect for school teachers and anybody like that. When the Italian boy sees that none of his own people have the good jobs, why should he think he is as good as the Irish or the Yankees? It makes him feel inferior."[15]

So if Miss O'Rourke were Miss Lorenzo instead, would it have made a difference in Doc's life? Would he have become a college boy instead of a corner boy? Perhaps, if Doc could have empathetically identified with Miss Lorenzo, and she with Doc. But in an inner-city public school with a class size much too large and her own kids to go home to, Miss Lorenzo after a long day at work might have been just as quick as Miss O'Rourke to classify Doc as a corner boy. Doc's wish for a Miss Lorenzo was a wish for someone to have been there for him early on in his life. He wished for more teachers, social workers, police officers not only with whom he could identify but also who could identify with him and his struggles.

Instead, the corner boys were left identifying with corrupt adults, the less law-abiding in their neighborhood. They saw and identified with policemen, judges, and politicians on the take, profiting from the illegal rackets in their community. They observed officials looking the other way for that occasional bribe, and they could better identify with those monetary pursuits than with those of teachers and social workers with their low salaries. Ultimately, the story of street-corner life cannot be just about the youth themselves and their network of friends. It is really about how from an early age street-corner youth learned not to trust and empathetically identify with the more law-abiding adults in their impoverished inner-city neighborhoods.

Liebow's Street-Corner Men

Not all ethnographies of impoverished inner-city neighborhoods present an easily identifiable division between street-corner and non-street-corner individuals. Nor are all lower-class inner-city neighborhoods equally impoverished. While some are more organized than others, others are less so, and the residents of these less organized neighborhoods tend to develop less organized lives. That means they are less motivated to be socially engaged in the enabling activities of the larger community. They are unlikely to participate in a community club and to have extended family members and friends on whom they can rely. They have graduated from being street-corner boys to becoming street-corner men. They failed to move beyond their initial street corner, as Doc and many other street-corner boys eventually did. They became deep-end, highly disturbed street-corner men, the subject of Liebow *Tally's Corner*.

In contrast to the society described in *Tally's Corner*, Whyte's street-corner society is too organized. The corner boys are too socially connected to one another. If they move into the category of street-corner men, it is because they figured out how to make money through organized crime. They largely avoid the devastating impact of terrible drug and alcohol addictions.[16] Racketeering, playing the numbers, and petty theft are more typical. Whyte's ethnography sold because it questioned the vision of a singularly disorganized impoverished inner-city life, as portrayed by early twentieth-century Chicago School sociologists. Social disorganization implied more than just the opposite of social organization; it meant that a large segment of impoverished residents of inner-city neighborhoods were too disabled to produce meaningful work, good housing, and decent schools for their kids.

But for many of inner-city residents, this kind of social disorganization cannot go for long. Once they can afford to move, they do, and their lives and that of their children change for the better. They suffer less from high delinquency rates, as Chicago School sociologists observed repeatedly in one city after another. The zone from which they transitioned was generally a dilapidated neighborhood that had the highest rates of officially recorded crime. It was envisioned only as a temporary place to live by the most impoverished first-generation immigrants. Once they found better jobs and could afford better housing, they moved to less impoverished neighborhoods where there were fewer street-corner men.

But what about those who could not move? They are the impoverished inner-city African American men whom Liebow observed in *Tally's Corner,* which was the name of a "carry-out shop" where local residents pursued "a wide range of activities, legal, illegal and extralegal."[17] The name in turn serves as a metaphor for a street-corner life with values that are contrary to those of the safer outer neighborhoods of the city.

Liebow identifies several characteristics of street corner men. First, the circumstances of street-corner men define their capacities to act. They are intellectually and emotionally disabled and cannot compete for the few jobs there are in their neighborhood. Moreover, street-corner men are unable to perform well enough in school and in places of occasional labor. They work only sporadically because they have trouble getting and keeping a job. Their failures are cumulative. They have failed in their places of school, work, and family. The reasons for this triple failure are interrelated. The problem of "getting a job, keeping a job, and doing well at it" cannot be separated from their inability to maintain and sustain relationships.[18] Reasonable work becomes a "low priority" because there is no one to empathetically state to these street-corner men: "You can do it; I believe in you; everyone has their special skills." They cannot be trusted, because they have learned not to trust the larger world of past teachers, employers, and officials.

For instance, Liebow describes how his subjects from an early age learned that they are "dumb," incapable of performing basic occupational tasks. They feel too incompetent to compete for jobs that Liebow sees they are capable of performing. He quotes one of his subjects as describing how he learned nothing at his high school, despite graduating with a degree:

> "I graduated from high school [in Baltimore] but I don't know anything. I'm dumb. Most of the time I don't even say I graduated, 'cause then somebody asks me a question and I can't answer it, and they think I was lying about graduating. . . . They graduated me but I didn't know anything. I had lousy grades but I guess they wanted to get rid of me."[19]

In effect, the externally imposed label of "dumb" becomes a self-definition of being "dumb," which, in turn, structures the thoughts and actions of street-corner men. Delving further into this cycle of self-fulfilling prophecy, Liebow observes how a street-corner man's "low self-esteem generates a fear of being tested and prevents him from accepting a job with responsibilities or, once on a job, from staying with it if responsibilities are thrust on him, even if the wages are commensurately higher."[20]

Liebow, like Whyte, suggests that street-corner men are more intelligent than their school performance or IQ tests indicate. But Liebow's street-corner men are even more troubled. They lack the self-confidence to even take a test; their difficulties and possible learning disabilities are not recognized. By internalizing their repeated record of school and occupational failure, they are unable to move beyond occasional minimum-wage work. Additionally, they lack a tightly knit group of supportive friends. Other street-corner men are in similar states of continuous frustration. The reasons for their low self-esteem are deep; Liebow is unable to provide the personal details, such as the physical or sexual abuse they might have experienced.

Further evidence of their deep-seated troubles is contained in Liebow's description of his subjects' personal relationships. They lack long-standing friends, in contrast to Whyte's corner boys. They suffer repeatedly from the instability of multiple romantic relationships, leading to jealousies, and at times serious acts of violence. Their personal instability is related to their own upbringing; their parental care was sporadic and often left to a single parent, if the other was in prison or addicted to drugs, or to a foster parent. Either way, they did not receive the consistency of emotional support deemed critical to an individual's well-being.

The street-corner men's pursuit of close relationships illustrates the kind of trouble that they are in. Their search for personal long-lasting relationships is unrealistic.[21] Liebow illustrates the point when he relates how occasional acquaintances become elevated to the status of "going brothers." The desire to turn a casual acquaintance into a long-lasting friend reflects a deep-seated desire for the familial love that the street-corner men never had—the sort of love that close family members generally have for one another. The relationships of street-corner men create a fantasy that is impossible to maintain. In "going brothers," street-corner men may create temporary symbolic attachments, but deep-seated frustrations arise when the expected friendship fails to materialize into long-lasting love. Disappointments turn to anger and the inevitable humiliation that leads to serious acts of violence.

So street-corner men are desperate men. As youths, they did not develop that modern-day sense of self that could enable them to manage life's difficulties in adulthood. Hence, their problems adjusting to societal demands did not end with their adolescence. They are overwhelmed as adults, and look to the anesthetizing effects of drugs and alcohol to cope with their failures. They need assistance to cope with life and the devastating effects of their addictions. But that assistance is not forthcoming, personally or positionally. Street-corner men are living in a space of their own, disconnected from the larger modern-day world. As Liebow describes, the street-corner man lives on the edge day to day:

> He does not, as a rule, have a surplus of resources, either economic or psychological. Gratification of hunger and the desire for simple creature comforts cannot be long deferred. Neither can support for one's flagging

self-esteem. Living on the edge of both economic and psychological sub-systems, the street-corner man is obliged to expend all his resources on maintaining himself from moment to moment.[22]

An image of street-corner men "living on the edge" is not that of a group of street-corner boys living "in a sea of want." Life for the former is even more devastating; it has become extremely chaotic, disorganized, and at times violent. Liebow's street-corner men are black men who have a harder time integrating into the larger society. They have become modernity's adult chronic offenders who populate maximum security prisons. Their disadvantages accumulate far beyond the impoverished circumstances of their birth. Their potential as human beings is repeatedly denied, creating a total absence of self-esteem and self-control and an inability to pursue self-actualization. They have moved from the status of street-corner boys to that of broken street-corner men.

Anderson's Street-Corner Places

Liebow's focus on black impoverished inner-city neighborhoods may have overemphasized their disorganized features, and lumped street-corner men into one singular category. Elijah Anderson, in a series of books, introduces distinctions within the inner-city neighborhoods, which he observed in research that spanned several generations. Each of Anderson's books contains the word "street" or "corner" in its title.[23] The distinctions he identifies among the impoverished recall Whyte's comparative organizational focus, and similarly, Anderson eventually returns to contrasting street-corner and non-street-corner individuals.

Anderson is sensitive to the adults in the impoverished inner-city neighborhoods. He relates the "folk" categories that residents of an impoverished inner-city neighborhood apply to themselves. Such iden-tifying terms as *old heads, winos, hoodlums,* and *down people* reflect divisions that reproduce divisions in the larger society. Anderson's *Code of the Streets* narrows that division even further, whereby inner-city residents are either street or decent folks.[24] Families matter in that street families raise street kids, while decent families raise decent kids. But street families stay impoverished and isolated; they are unable to adapt to the larger society; their code of the street is too restrictive, preventing them from developing the norms and values that would enable them to adapt to a larger set of societal rules.

Among the structural conditions that Anderson considers is late-twentieth-century deindustrialization, which has had a devastating impact on the African American inner city. Drawing on the writings of William Wilson, he notes that in the de-industrialized world of the 1980s, the "old heads" were no longer around to serve as an example to younger generations of youth. The factory and its jobs were gone. Inner-city residents were becoming more impoverished and more likely to become involved in crime.[25] Their low-level crimes were leading to longer sentences, increasing the likelihood that "old heads" would not be around to provide inner-city youth with the guidance they needed to avoid becoming street kids. Drawing on his earlier ethnographic observations, Anderson notes that inner-city black youth are too much in a world that lacks the guidance of law-abiding adults. As a consequence, they have become embroiled in a street-corner life.

Yet not everyone in the impoverished inner city is a street-corner youth. There are the decent kids from decent families who spend time in their local libraries or basketball courts. They differ from street-corner youth in that they abide by middle-class values. Decent kids are not allowed to just hang out, because they are strictly supervised by their parents. Their parents have jobs, attend church, and are able to properly raise their children. Decent families and their kids learn to adapt while street kids and their families do not. The street kids lose out because their parents and other adults are not there for them, because often they themselves are too troubled, drug addicted, or incarcerated to care.

The ability to adapt enables decent kids to become decent adults. Adapting means being able to move between sets of friends, to recognize the local drug dealer as well as the minister, to consider society's many settings and the adults in their positional roles. In other words, decent families and their kids are relationally modern. They can traverse the larger world by learning how to navigate a multitude of places. Anderson calls these decent adolescents "code switchers." They have learned to place a premium value on managing and negotiating a diverse set of social rules.[26] Decent kids are able to adapt to more than one definition of a situation, despite being raised in the same impoverished neighborhood. They are modern in the sense that they can traverse more than one social setting. They have learned to accept middle-class values as the most appropriate ones, while still managing to navigate the culture of their inner-city streets. According to Anderson,

> Decent people, especially young people, often put a premium on the ability to code switch. They share many of the middle class values of the wider white society but know that the open display of such values carries little weight on the street: it doesn't provide the emblems that say, "I can take care of myself." Hence such people develop a repertoire of behaviors that do provide that security. Those strongly associated with the street, who have less exposure to the wider society, may have difficulty code switching; imbued with the code of the street, they either don't know the rules for decent behavior or may see little value in displaying such knowledge.[27]

Anderson is clear that the street is a limiting place, a corner where its members lack the capacities to code switch. Street youth are unable to adapt to the larger codes of society. They are restricted to a code that is conducive to delinquency and crime. To share "middle-class values" means leaving their village-like street. They need assistance to do so. Street-corner youth are not just a product of poor parenting; they need some adult in the larger society with whom they can identify. To teach them how to navigate their impoverished neighborhood requires adults who buy into middle-class codes. The "old heads" served that purpose in the past, warning neighborhood youth not to repeat their own mistakes. The reasons street kids cannot identify their own difficulties and limitations and their teachers, coaches, and officials cannot identify with their struggles are never explicitly discussed. The cumulative disadvantages of being an African American in an impoverished inner city are in the foreground of Anderson's analysis. But some youth do make it, and how they are able to confront modernity's demands seems to rest solely on the decency of their families.

Anderson's street kids are not alone. They need a considerable amount of guidance and support to navigate the restricted code of the streets. In his ethnography of Spanish Harlem crack dealers, Philippe Bourgois relates the difficulties that they had in trying to find legitimate work. They had considerable trouble leaving behind their street-corner identities.[28] They failed to adapt to a world of legitimate modern-day work. For instance, several of his subjects had difficulties in dealing with women in supervisory positions. "Primo," for one, "was both unwilling and unable to compromise his street identity and imitate the professional modes of interaction that might have earned him the approval and respect of his boss,"[29] according to Bourgois. He further states that "The machismo of street culture exacerbates the sense of insult experienced by men because the majority of office supervisors at the entry level are women."[30] There is no mention of human resource workers, the supervisory women themselves, and therapists who might provide the sensitivity, understanding, and empathy that might have allowed Bourgois's drug dealing men to adjust their gender vision of who should be a supervisor.

Yet Primo and his fellow street-corner men do eventually adapt. Bourgois revisited his research participants ten years later in 2001, and found that the young men he studied obtained regular full-time employment. To some degree, they learned to adapt. How they matured into a state where they could find employment most likely involved a degree of self-reflection that they were just not capable of in an earlier period of their lives. But there may have been opportunities, social workers, and correctional counselors and programs that made a difference. For a segment of the seriously troubled, more is required than mere parental support.

Loic Wacquant's critical review of several street-corner ethnographies, including that of Anderson's, makes the point that the lives of the seriously troubled cannot be reduced to a singular dichotomy of value orientations. More is going on in their lives as implied by his statement that street-corner subjects are disabled by their "broken habitus."[31] "Habitus" may be interpreted as the practical, enabling mind-set of a particular group of individuals. For those with a broken habitus, the capacity to navigate their social settings is highly restricted. In this sense, those who are unable to leave the ways of the street are equally unable to adapt to the modern-day world. Their problems of adjustment are not just limited to adolescence; problems persist, and they need substantial help in overcoming their difficulties.

To conclude: corner boys, corner men, crack dealers, and street kids suffer from their inability to recognize and be recognized in a relationally modern world. They are on a one-way street that lacks the middle-class opportunities that could have allowed them to move into the larger set of preferred corners of society. Those who have been relegated to the category of society's street-corner men often have given up. Many of them are in prison, having been subject to the harsh, exclusionary punishments of the criminal justice system. They have been banished, further isolated from many of society's better corners.[32] David O is not alone in having been given an adult sentence in criminal court for a crime that he committed at the age of fifteen. Thousands more at even younger ages have been brought into criminal court instead of juvenile court for less serious offenses. Their terribly troubled adolescence has been denied.

Beyond a Street-Corner Vision of Delinquency and Crime

It is now that moment to present an alternative metaphoric vision of delinquency, one that is slightly different from the urban ethnographies that I just reviewed. The metaphor should reflect the car-dependent quality of suburban living and the absence of corner stores. It should also represent its lower population density—that suburban youth need not escape from their crowded apartments to hang out on their local street-corners. It should suggest that they can get into their car or onto their bike and head over to their friend's suburban basement recreational room. They have choices of suburban parklands and malls as well. Not only do they have access to the things that are supposed to make for a good middle-class life, but they also have adults who are willing to expend large amounts of money for good schools, terrific recreational programs, and a generally safe place to live. An alternative metaphor should include the enabling possibilities of a safe city and its host of adults.

The alternative image that I propose is, then, that of a multitude of interconnecting suburban roadways. Each of them contains a few bumps or potholes, which can create all sorts of troubles. Some of these potholes are clearly marked. They announce clearly the risks of drugs and alcohol, and the consequences of violating the stated rules. On some of these suburban roadways, adolescents can feel really lost; they have difficulty reading the signs. There are fewer adults to help them

understand how best to behave. At times they need to look for a roadway that is more isolated from adult words of condemnation. They wish
to ride along with similarly alienated youth. In these darker and more
distant streets, there is the risk that adolescents will have considerable
trouble finding their place in the adult world. There is the risk that they
will become a lost spoke on a wheel of loose affiliations.[33]

In retrospect, it is easy to simply say that the Columbine shooters were on the wrong kind of adolescent roadway and that there was
more going on in their lives than what could be readily observable. But
how they moved to a pathway where adults were not in the position to
assist them in confronting their troubles cannot easily be addressed. It
requires looking deeply at the reasons for their troubled pathway, and
why the juvenile justice system was ineffective in providing them with
the intense level of treatment they obviously needed. All that the relational in a relationally modern theory of control can suggest is that the
Columbine youth, David O, and other middle-class youth who commit
serious crimes require more than a good suburban school district and a
city's diversionary programs. They require a structured, intensely therapeutic setting where they can receive the understanding that would
better assist them in dealing with the real and imagined traumas of
their past.

The Glen Ridge rapists were also on a suburban roadway of serious
trouble. They had a history of harassing and abusing girls and those
who were not like them. If adults had been less blinded by their status as athletes or as sons of prominent citizens, their group act of rape
might have been averted. Their particular roadway was filled with society's many patriarchal signs of power—signs that state implicitly that
the more vulnerable in society count for less. They might have been
placed on a different path if they could have felt what those less fortunate feel; the negative consequences of mistreating girls should have
been addressed earlier in their lives. But this required more adults in
their lives to address the way they valued those who were different
from them.

Hanover High School's honor students who were caught burglarizing their school were on another kind of roadway. The roadway leading
bright adolescents to their Ivy League colleges cannot easily be distinguished from their need to cheat. They happen to have gotten caught

this time, but there were undoubtedly times when cheating worked. The accused youth wanted to reproduce the success of their parents. Their intention was good. They wanted to achieve in an achievement-oriented society, which meant figuring out how best to reach the stated goal—knowing full well the risks. Their pathway to success could have included a good moral compass—one that should have been reinforced by adults in each and every one of their social settings.

And then there is the lonely roadway of the adolescent who is isolated from friends, family, and who has lost all sense of trust. This is the roadway that David O traveled on. He was virtually alone with the most terrifying of unconscious desires. He had no peers, no parents, no teachers, and no minister whom he could trust. He was badly beaten by his father, abandoned by his mother, and sexually abused by the leader of his church. His is not only the story of youth who have killed, but also the stories of youth who have killed themselves. Their stories repeat themselves: they had serious troubles and those around them had serious trouble assisting them, leaving them to fall into the abyss of self- and other-directed acts of violence.

Relational Accounts of Delinquency

A suburban roadway metaphor should incorporate Norbert Elias' definition of a civilized society, in which self-control becomes critical to navigating society's many traffic jams. The controlled self is a psychologically controlled one; it resides in an individual's mind and is independent of anyone being there to supervise him or her. Suburban roadways are not just physical places of supervision. They depend on people operating their lives on their own. There is the expectation for autonomy—the need for individual decision-making to make a modern-day society work.

There is an emotional side to driving on your own, as Jack Katz relates in the stories he tells of middle-class delinquencies in *Seductions of Crime*.[34] Although his book focuses mainly on violent crimes, Katz devotes an entire chapter to the delinquency of middle-class youth. They are on a suburban roadway that he relates to the emotional and sensational aspects of crime, and its attractions. Their reported acts of delinquency fall into the less serious category of offending; otherwise they would be in prison instead of college. For them, delinquency has a "sneaky thrill." This comes through in one youth's narrative quoted by Katz:

> "I grew up in a neighborhood where at 13 everyone went to Israel, at 16 everyone got a car and after high school graduation we were all sent off to Europe for the summer. . . . I was 14 and my neighbor was 16. He had just gotten a red Firebird for his birthday and we went driving around. We just happened to drive past the local pizza place and we saw the delivery boy getting into his car. . . . We could see the pizza boxes in his back seat. When the pizza boy pulled into a high rise apartment complex, we were right behind him. All of a sudden, my neighbor said, 'You know, it would be so easy to take a pizza!' . . . I looked at him, he looked at me, and without saying a word I was out of the door . . . got a pizza and ran back. . . . (As I remember, neither of us was hungry, but the pizza was the best we'd ever eaten.)"[35]

The quoted youth had traveled far. A trip to the Middle East to visit a country in a constant state of war was not risky enough. The suburban roadway of a good middle-class life was too well paved. More was required—hence, the thrill of theft, which came with the full knowledge that the delivery boy, pizza shop, customer, or some other entity would suffer the loss. The boys' lives may be too secure, involve too much of the same, have no limitations that would require them to work as pizza delivery boys. A spark of excitement enlivens the mundane—a spark that depends on a lack of empathetic reasoning about what it means to steal someone's pizza. Perhaps Katz's subjects are also aware of the fact that they have affluent parents in their lives who could prevent them from suffering the serious consequences of their act of theft or property destruction. Like Terribly Young's parents, they have the money and the wherewithal to get the best possible legal representation.

Not all middle-class parents provide their sixteen-year-olds with money, travel, and the luxury of having their own car. There are levels of affluence that distinguish the middle class from their upper-middle-class neighbors. These distinctions reflect not only the money that families have but also the power that they are able to generate, often less consciously through parental pursuits. In other words, the "sneaky thrill" of getting away with it is not a thrill that every adolescent can afford to enjoy.

There is a subtle quality to power and how power along with control reproduces itself from one generation to the next. John Hagan's power-control theory is meant to explain class as well as gender differences in rates of delinquency.[36] But I see the class distinctions that Hagan relates as being closely linked to a relational theory of delinquency, which shows how relationships are reproduced, so that the authority that the middle class feels and gains from their positions of affluence makes delinquency feasible. Affluent adolescents can experiment with illicit drugs and commit petty acts of theft like stealing pizzas, knowing full well that they will not be severely punished. Like their parents who are often in a position of power through their own occupational pursuits, they have learned to manage the risks of delinquency and that of modernity.

Hagan shows how the positional power of parents as measured by their authority at work relates to self-reported delinquency rates. He reports that adolescents who have parents in the employer or supervisory class reported higher rates of delinquency than those in the employee or unemployed class. This is a controversial point that has been disputed, because it suggests that affluent kids are more delinquent than less affluent ones. But Hagan's comparison is not between the affluent and the impoverished. It is between gradations in middle-class life—differences between those who have authority in their full-time places of work and those who also have full-time work but lack that authority.

In Hagan's vision of power and control, relational dimensions are distinguished from the more physical ones in such contexts as parental supervision. Hagan finds that there is less control of boys, and more freedom granted to them. The Jocks in Glen Ridge, where "boys will be boys," were not closely supervised. They could assert their power, as glorified athletes. Honor students who cheat are also asserting their autonomy when they do all that they can to obtain that winning grade. Bill Gates was also given the autonomy that his parents and therapist deemed essential, and of course there was a different kind of trajectory. Boys would seem to come out ahead not only in the world of paid work, but also in their delinquency rates. There are exceptions when both boys and girls are raised in egalitarian households. For Hagan, gender equality translates into a rise in delinquency rates among girls.

But there is a relational element that Hagan and associates highlight in their explanation of why girl delinquency rates are generally lower than those of boys. They draw on Nancy Chodorow's psychoanalytically oriented writings and discussions of how relationships are not just personal but also positional.[37] The positional controls are abstract, representing the thin as opposed to the thick in relationships. The positional is a function of a complex society where the places of labor are no longer close by. Girls are subject to more personal controls because of the presence of their mothers, presumably in more traditional households, whereas the relationship of boys to their fathers is more positional, according to Hagan and associates, who call attention to

> the father's immediate absence, because he is so often away at work, and the mother's immediate presence, because she is so often tied to the home, in gender role identification processes. A consequence is that the son must identify positionally with an absent male role model, while the daughter can identify personally with an omnipresent female role model.[38]

Although this may be too dated a view of gender differences as they relate to delinquency rates, the point is that constraints depend on an adolescent's ability to identify with the adults in his or her life.

Why Positional Relationships Matter

In the industrial and post-industrial eras of modernity, positional relationships are on the rise. Max Weber first noticed this to be the case as soon as the farm, village or home no longer became the place of work.[39] As parents began to spend long hours away from the intimacy of the household, problems with identification inevitably arose. Those problems persist in the post-industrial digital age, as relationships are increasingly positional, even between parent and child.[40] To be modern means acknowledging the fact that individual identities are in a state of flux and that they have to be discovered through a process that can no longer be neatly structured, at least in a stage of life that is defined as transitional.

In his widely cited book on *Delinquent Boys*,[41] Albert Cohen acknowledges Talcott Parson's theory of Western aggression, wherein the primary sources of support for twentieth century wars are linked to widespread status anxieties.[42] Cohen speculates that in middle-class homes, boys are less able to identify with the labors of their fathers because they are too far removed from the home, and so their image of what it means to work as a man is correspondingly vague. Where a segment of middle-class boys has trouble identifying with their fathers, those boys could act in ways that would heighten their risk of delinquency. Thus, according to Cohen, "Male delinquency in families which are culturally middle-class is primarily an attempt to cope with a basic anxiety in the area of sex-role identification; it has the primary function of giving reassurance of one's essential masculinity."[43] Yet there is more going on here than gendered parental identity problems. Middle-class delinquents are not just suffering in their search for a suitable identity; they are also reacting to problems in moving mentally beyond their father's identity. Indeed, they may have significant trouble identifying with their fathers, but then there are all these teachers, coaches, and neighbors with whom they could identify.

Earlier, I mentioned Travis Hirschi's vision of social control as one that emphasizes adolescents' relational attachments. Those attachments are not based solely on the extent to which parents supervise and restrict their adolescents' activities. They are based on feelings of closeness, as in the child identifying with one or more parent. Hirschi states that "the child is less likely to commit delinquent acts not because his parents actually restrict his activities, but because he shares his activities with them; not because his parents actually know where he is, but because he perceives them as aware of his location."[44] Perceptions matter. But they are the perceptions of adolescents not just of their parents. The adolescent's attachment to parents must be reciprocated. So too are the less personal and more positional attachments adolescents develop as they move about from one social setting after another.

But how do adolescents reach that point when they become so disengaged from their parents, teachers, and other adults? What is the source of their lack of attachment? The answer recognizes that life can be a struggle for a segment of adolescents; difficulties can stem from a learning disability or parents who are unable to provide them with the recognition that they need. At times their frustrations can be sufficiently repressed. But then disappointment can take on a reality of its own, as in the "going brothers" of Liebow's street-corner men. This subjective element of the strains of life requires adolescents and the adults with whom they have contact to recognize their mutual struggles as they navigate one suburban roadway after another.

Yet the bumps in suburban roadways can be just as hazardous for suburban as for inner-city youth. One bad turn can lead to another. James Short and Fred Strodtbeck recognize the risks of lower-class gang delinquency. The adolescents in the neighborhoods of Chicago they studied face the risks that go along with their impoverished inner-city neighborhood. They are too much on their own—left to figure out how best to manage their lives. They lack adults to warn them about the risks of unprotected sexual activity, gun possession, and membership in a gang. If they can avoid parenthood and violence at a young age, they are lucky. But some youth are not. They have stood their ground in a fight with no intention of committing a lethal act of violence. But then the gun went off; its threatened use became its actual use. Short and Strodtbeck describe such situations in which one bad turn can lead to devastating consequences as "aleatory." In such aleatory circumstances, one non-intentional action places the individual at risk of another.[45]

The risks for suburban youth are considerable as well. They too can be isolated and unaware of the risks of their own suburban pathways. Delinquent groups may fail to see the long-term consequences of being on their own. Although hanging out in a basement recreational room is in itself not of significant concern, when hanging out leads to intense isolation, adolescents are at risk of serious trouble.

Short and Strodtbeck provide considerable amounts of data to support their aleatory view of delinquency and control. Particularly revealing is their finding that inner-city gang members are more likely to rate adult power lower than non-gang members. Using an 8-point scale, they found that black and white gang members rated adult power at around 4.5. In contrast, middle-class non-gang members rated adult power at 7.4. The authors further state that gang members had few adults to whom they could talk about their concerns, particularly problems at school.[46] The adults are not present in the gang member's society. They have little access to them. And those who do have access are too troubled to care.

For those inner-city delinquents who manage to make it into adulthood, their prospects are generally good. In their follow-up study of a cohort of officially identified lower-class delinquents, Robert Sampson and John Laub relate the reasons for their eventual desistance from crime.[47] Although they note the importance of childhood attachments, they also acknowledge that emotional bonds can emerge in adulthood through occupational and familial pursuits. They emphasize that a good loving marriage is a source of relational support that contributes significantly to an offender's desistance from crime. Equally important is a social network of support that develops through other life-altering events, like military service and a good job. But the choice to pursue a good as opposed to a bad relationship emerges in interaction with a whole host of professionals in the business of giving advice. The social workers, prison counselors, or therapists whom court-identified delinquents typically encounter may have had an impact on their choice to enter the military and to achieve satisfying work and a good marriage. They may have made the difference in the on-going ways that adolescents think about themselves and how they wish to create their own stories.

The typology of a street-corner view of delinquents negates the on-going quality of adolescence. It negates the transitional and the fact that on all levels—biologically, psychologically, and socially—life will be transformed. Past difficulties may become transformed into sources of strength, or they may lead to more serious troubles. My suburban roadway metaphor draws on contemporary social theory to suggest that modern-day identities are on-going.[48] Suburbia not only contains a complex network of subdivisions, but also a maze of roadways. It can be a lonely place. Its lower population density creates more room for taking off on one's own and pursuing one's own roadway. Along the way, adolescents encounter more or less visible signs of how best to proceed. Each sign contributes to the adolescent's own unique set of on-going narratives. These narratives are the stories that adolescents tell about themselves, as they are driven and begin to drive from one place of activity to the next. They are the definitions of the situation that both shape and mediate their lives. According to Giddens, "Each of us not only 'has,' but *lives* a biography reflexively organized in terms of flows of social and psychological information about possible ways of life."[49]

Now it is time to leave the stories of other youth and to focus specifically on how the youth of Amherst tell their own stories of delinquency and modernity as expressed through personal interviews and surveys with them, their parents, and a range of youth service providers.

Amherst Central High School is located in an older neighborhood close to the city of Buffalo, New York. It was built at a time when cities were more centralized than they are today.

5

The Trouble with Youth in America's Safest City

The youth of a safe city are able to share their difficulties, discontents, and serious troubles. In comparison to the youth of impoverished inner cities, they are more able to be relationally modern because of the adults in their lives. As a consequence, their troubles are not the same. Yet the youth of Amherst do have their share of concerns, worries, and conflicts, and at times, their difficulties can also culminate into the sort of troubles that lead them into frequent offending.

This chapter is about the troubles of Amherst youth. It avoids trivializing their troubles by identifying their stated sources of discontent, which, in turn, explain why they are more or less attached to their parents, teachers, coaches, and friends. It draws on the reasons they present for their delinquency, and why a whole host of adults is critically important. A range of youth service professionals along with parents often enable them to confront their difficulties. The presented reasons for delinquency are based on a sampling of Amherst's young adults. Their words are linked to earlier surveys, which were conducted when they were adolescents. I also link their words to surveyed responses by their parents—surveys that were conducted about the same time as that of their adolescent children. The stories that the sampled Amherst young adults tell provide a partial view of how their parents, teachers, counselors, and friends viewed their delinquency. They relate reasons for offending and for ultimately desisting. The seriousness of offending is based not just on its legal ramifications, but on the situations that adolescents describe as significant. Survey data in combination with their personal interview data allow me to check the validity of their claims and the consistency of their identified troubles. An analysis of the data enables me to distinguish my subjects' acts of theft, property damage, and violence from illicit drug/alcohol consumption, cheating in school, and thoughts and acts of running away or suicide. These distinctions mirror legal categories that impact the status of adolescents in and out of the juvenile justice system.

In addition to their type and frequency of offending, I highlight how they view others in their lives. I assume that adolescents are not completely isolated with other adolescents; there are adults in their lives who have more or less influenced the particular pathways that they have eventually decided to pursue. In the course of moving from one grade to the next, they must be able to recognize the rationality of their familial, educational, and recreational pursuits as well as the irrationalities of some of their peer group associations. In this sense, adolescents are navigating a multitude of social settings along their own particular suburban roadway to tell an on-going story that ranges from mild to serious discontents.

But the complex and the transitional aspects of adolescence and modernity should not be neglected. It is not easy to specify exactly the source of adolescent discontents, even in the intimate setting of a family. Parents may be aware of their child's history of difficulties, but unable to respond in a way that prevents a bad situation from becoming even worse. In other words, the adolescents and their parents may be unable to explain why they find each other so annoying. Parents may be too befuddled by their adolescents' many piercings, tattoos, loud music, and too tightly or loosely fitting clothes. The reasons the music is too loud and disturbing may reflect more than just a cultural trend; deep-seated discontents may have accumulated, thereby making a not-so-good situation even worse.

To tell the stories of Amherst youth, I draw on levels of difficulties that culminate into a form of trouble. The term "trouble" can have various meanings. First, trouble can indicate the impact of violating a commonly accepted rule; the greater the violation, the more serious the trouble. But there is a subjective side to this use of the word "trouble," which can supersede the actual objective harm. For instance, some parents may respond to a curfew violation more harshly than others. They may have less tolerance for any rule-violating behavior. Other parents may be more selective in their response, ignoring certain offenses like an occasional act of pot-smoking or the consumption of alcohol at a house party. Thus, the extent to which an act is viewed as particularly troubling is not merely determined by a set of legal rules. There are parents, teachers, peers and a whole host of others (including social scientists) who are in the business of defining delinquent acts as more or less troubling.

Another way that trouble is perceived is through the practical knowledge that parents, teachers and others have about the consequences of an adolescent's rule-violating behavior. Parents may say to their youth, "You're in trouble," and adolescents might talk of "being in trouble." These statements are based on what has occurred in the past. Further definitions emerge when an adolescent draws on expressions of remorse through phrases like "I'm sorry" or "I wasn't thinking." The sincerity of these words is a judgment call. Undoubtedly, that judgment call is influenced by the knowledge that parents and others have of the adolescent—of his or her unique history and capacity to think ahead.

The practical knowledge that parents, teachers, and other youth service professionals possess of adolescents creates a sliding scale of trouble whereby some adolescents are viewed as more troubled than others. The reasons that they are more troubled may be based on their inability to successfully function in school and in society's many other competitive settings. They may also be troubled by a history of abuse and victimization, as discussed in the stories of Willie Bosket and David O. Their offending and subsequent expressions of remorse may be understood based on the fact that they have been so troubled. For example: "Johnny has been bullying me for some time and when I found the chance I hit him real hard." This kind of trouble is framed in the past tense, and is part of the victim-turned-offender narrative.

To highlight their possible adolescent troubles, I weave data obtained from the subjects' high-school surveys into my analysis of their personal interviews. I further link surveys of their parents to provide a larger picture of their familial relationships. The vast majority of those personally interviewed produced basically good stories of how they were able to transition into adulthood. No one reported having been adjudicated as delinquent in juvenile court or criminal in criminal court. This is because few Amherst youth experience the full legal consequences of their acts of delinquency. Of course, this is not the case for all affluent suburban youth, as my previous reference to the case of David O and others has revealed.

Sampling Young Adults Surveyed as Adolescents

Subjects were sampled from a larger population of 615 youth who were randomly surveyed six years earlier. At the time of their personal interviews, they were between nineteen and twenty-five years of age. When they took their high-school survey, they were between the ages of fourteen and nineteen. Their high-school and parental surveys were conducted in 1990, and their personal, young-adult interviews in 1996. Additional personal interviews with parents and officials cited in this chapter were conducted between 2001 and 2012.[1]

The parts of the surveys I link most to their personal interviews asked parents and their youth the extent to which they got along with each other. One set of questions asked if the youth had fun with their parents and how they decided the rules (such as how late to stay out at night). Another set of questions asked youth about the extent to which they trusted, empathized, and identified with their parents. Their parents were similarly asked the extent to which they felt relationally close to their adolescents. An additional scaled item is the willingness of parents to provide for an attorney if their children were in legal trouble. These parental and youth sets of scales are referred to as the relational part of scaled items. On a never-to-always scale of possible responses, youth who scored the highest on this relational scale indicated that they "always" 1) shared their thoughts and feelings with their parents; 2) spent time talking to them; 3) would like to be the sort of persons they are; 4) trusted them; 5) and knew that they would always provide for an attorney if they got in trouble. The tabulated responses were standardized so that the top of the scale would be 10 points. The same transformations were made for the instrumental questions that asked about parental monitoring. The combined relational and instrumental scales produced a 20-point maximum of parental attachment.[2] Youth who scored at the top of the scale would be at or close to 20.

The personally interviewed represented 4 percent of the total youth population surveyed in 1990. As is the case with other research studies that survey and interview subjects over an extended period of time, many of those surveyed in 1990 had moved and were no longer living at the last address we initially obtained from their school boards.

Another potential methodological problem is that the personally interviewed may be more self-selective than random. It does not include the
incarcerated, chronic, and violent group of offenders. It misses youth
who are away in therapeutic schools or military academies. The personally interviewed may have been more influenced than those who
were unwilling to participate by the financial incentive that was offered.
Those in the non-response category may have been out of town or too
busy working at their full-time jobs to respond to the mailed interview
request. Another possibility is that eligible subjects did not wish to participate in a study that could link their high-school surveys to their personal interviews as adults. Last but not least, some of those who were
not interviewed may have committed serious offenses and were imprisoned during the period of the personal interviews.

Still, a comparison of those who were personally interviewed and
those who were not revealed few demographic differences. There is
no significant difference in social class measures based on parental
occupational status or assessed housing values; occupational status
was obtained from the parents' surveys and assessed house value from
public records. A higher percentage of females are among the personally interviewed as well as the adolescent surveyed population. Yet
the interviewed population includes a good proportion of youth who
reported plenty of acts of delinquency. The interviewed population has
a significantly higher rate of self-reported delinquency than the non-
interviewed group.

Classifying Troubled Youth

High-offending Amherst youth may not be considered serious delinquents relative to the higher rates of arrest and incarceration among
impoverished inner-city youth. My measure of high-offending youth
is relative to the surveyed population. I distinguish high- from low-
offending Amherst youth by the frequency of their adolescent self-
reported delinquency. My measure of frequency is based on surveyed
responses to questions about theft, assault, and property damage, which
are common acts of delinquency and belong in a category of their
own, distinguishable from drug/alcohol use, cheating in school, and
status offenses like running away. I use the frequency of self-reported

common acts of delinquency for the past year as well as for earlier surveyed years to divide high- and low-offending adolescents. The next
chapter discusses the middle-category of offending adolescents.

Besides the issue of relative seriousness of offending among middle-
class youth, there are the usual problems of classifying youth based on
survey data. First, the adolescent's age at the time of the survey matters. For adolescents surveyed in their freshman year, there would be
fewer incidents to report than those who were surveyed in their senior
year. Another problem with a frequency measure of trouble is that low-
offending youth could have committed serious offenses. For instance,
David O would be considered a low-offending youth because his only
offense was his act of murder. Moreover, adolescents who committed
few acts of delinquency but offended by consuming lots of alcohol and
pot would fall into the category of low-offending youth.

The justification for focusing on common acts of delinquency includes its seriousness. I assume more consistency in the reaction to
theft, assault, and property damage, as well as to hard-core drugs and
large quantities of marijuana with the intent to sell, and less consistency in response to alcohol and pot use, cheating in school, and other
non-index types of offending. I also define the seriousness of offending
based on its frequency.

My reference to adolescent troubles is based on those that they are
willing to share in the personal interview situation. Undoubtedly, I
report only a sampling of troubles—the ones they are most willing to
discuss. But they are also often significant enough to be recalled directly
and indirectly in their high-school survey. The personal interviews
combined with their surveyed responses taken at an earlier period of
time provide a more reliable picture of Amherst adolescents, more so
than would be possible based on only one source of data.

I begin by summarizing the population of young adults who were
personally interviewed. After listing the subjects, I detail their sources
of trouble and their delinquencies. I first list the least and most delinquent based on their self-reported acts of theft, property damage, and
assault. I refer to these offenses as acts of delinquency; they can lead
an adolescent into juvenile or criminal court. The distinction between
high-and low-offending adolescents is based on the categorization
of the sixth highest and lowest offending youth. In between these

extremes, there is a middle group of fourteen subjects whose sources of trouble are discussed in the next chapter.

The Personally Interviewed

Here are the personally interviewed and a summary of their troubles, delinquency, and status as young adults.

ALAN *resented his parent's decision to move to Amherst.* At the time of his survey, he was sixteen years of age. He self-reported eighty-one acts of property damage and no drug use or alcohol consumption. At the time of his interview, Alan was in graduate school, studying to become a pharmacist.

BILL *attributed his bad temper to his father's violent outbursts.* His survey revealed fourteen separate acts of delinquency. He got drunk, smoked pot, cheated, stole and damaged property. Bill successfully graduated from a large state university. He planned on a career in business just like his dad.

CHRISTINE *developed an eating disorder. She was also troubled by her mother's dislike of her boyfriend.* She felt tremendous pressure to succeed. Later, she graduated from an Ivy League university and was planning to attend medical school.

DEE *did not get along with her younger sister. The two fought constantly.* She frequently attended house parties where she often became drunk. At time of her interview, Dee was about to graduate from the University of Buffalo.

DENISE *suffered from Attention Deficit Disorder.* Denise reported attending nine house parties where she often became drunk. She also said she cheated in school five times. At the time of her interview, she was attending community college and working as a waitress.

GARY *could not participate in school sports because he lacked transportation.* He reported cheating in school three times and stealing or damaging property five times. But he did not report acts of alcohol or substance use; he never attended house parties. At the time of the interview, he was enrolled at a local state college and was unsure as to the kind of career he wished to pursue.

JACKIE *fought often in her neighborhood.* Her father seemed to care more about her ability to fight well than to perform well in school. She lived in one of the lowest income subdivisions of Amherst. She cheated in school twice. She dropped out of college and at the time of her interview, worked part-time as a secretary. She married and planned to return to school.

JEFF *had a difficult home life. His parents divorced when he was sixteen.* He said his mother was too strict; subsequently, he moved in with his father. He reported cheating in school twice and attending lots of house parties where he often became drunk and smoked pot. He was picked up by the police once, but never officially arrested. He was admitted to five of his six top choices of universities. But after his first year, he dropped out.

JOAN *thought she could have performed better in school if her parents cared more about her school performance.* She was raised in a less affluent section of Amherst. Her mother was the school cook. She skipped school often but reported virtually no acts of delinquency. Joan went to the local community college, and at the time of her interview she had transferred to the University of Buffalo, majoring in human services.

KAREN *was troubled by her classmates' lack of religiosity.* She reported several acts of theft while attending her religious high school, but no acts of substance abuse. She graduated from a Christian Bible college and was planning on performing missionary work in New Guinea.

KARL *did not like Amherst. He said it was too rich. He had a difficult time fitting into its "white-collar" subdivisions.* His parents decided to move when he was in sixth grade from the less-affluent, blue-collar town of North Tonawanda. He wished his parents had never moved. He reported numerous acts of delinquency. He stole, damaged property, committed acts of assault, and abused alcohol and drugs. He attended community college after high school, worked in a local auto factory and at the time of the interview was pursuing a degree at Buffalo State College.

KERRIN *is African American and felt isolated. She wished Amherst schools had more non-white students.* Her parents moved from the inner city so that she and her siblings could attend good public schools. She reported lots of house parties (more than most) where she frequently got drunk. At the time of her personal follow-up interview, she had received a B.S. degree in fashion, was unmarried, and pregnant. She said she no longer drinks and is in pursuit of a career in fashion design.

KIM's *father was accused of sexually abusing her sister.* Kim partied often, reported lots of substance abuse, cheated in school ten times, and was at the top of the scale in reporting thoughts and acts of running away and suicide. She reported virtually no acts of delinquency. When we interviewed her, she had just graduated from the University of Buffalo and was a stage manager at the local theater.

LEE *was troubled by familial pressures to succeed in school.* He emigrated with his parents from Hong Kong, and knew that school was extremely important. He reported no acts of delinquency, but numerous acts of copying and distributing copyrighted materials (videos and music). Also, he said he thought about running away/suicide. At the time of our interview, he was attending graduate school in engineering.

LUKE *was bullied in elementary school. He felt rejected by his parents.* He revealed personal difficulties with school officials as well. His self-reported high rate of delinquency placed him in the top 1 percent of surveyed youth. He was a frequent user of illicit drugs. He is the only subject to report having dropped out of high school. Soon after dropping out, he started experimenting with serious drugs and developed a heroin addiction. At the time of his personal interview, he said he no longer was a drug user, thanks to rehab, and was attending the local state college.

MARIE *recalled that her father rarely praised her and often criticized her.* She reported several acts of delinquency, attending house parties, and cheating, but no substance abuse. She transferred from a local private college to the University of Buffalo, where she majored in psychology. When we interviewed her, she said she did not wish to live in Amherst and was pursuing a variety of out-of-state jobs.

MARY *also disliked her neighborhood. She said it was too transient.* She wished she could have lived in a place that had more of a sense of community where she might have known more of her neighbors. She reported few acts of delinquency, but attended lots of house parties where she often got drunk. She graduated from an out-of-state private college where she majored in economics. She planned to move to Florida and explore her career options there.

NANCY *disliked the kids in her neighborhood because they were too status conscious.* She switched from the local high school to one further away for that reason. She attended lots of house parties, and reported twelve acts of pot smoking and ten acts of getting drunk in the previous year. At the time of her follow-up interview, she was a senior at the local state college and planned to become a social worker.

PATTY's *teacher touched her in a sexually inappropriate way.* She reported attending lots of house parties, and getting drunk several times. She also reported cheating in school twice. At the time of her interview, she was attending an out-of-town SUNY college where she was majoring in communications.

PHIL's *parents divorced when he was only two, and subsequently he moved frequently.* He spent his childhood living with his mother, but decided to live with his father and step-mother in Amherst during high school. Although he had trouble fitting in, he reported few acts of delinquency. He reported cheating in school five times. He went to a Catholic college in western New York, and decided to pursue a career in business.

RENA's *father repeatedly hit her.* Although he was a psychiatrist, his parenting style was apparently authoritarian. She understood the culture of India where her father was raised. Despite the traditional way in which she was raised, she reported cheating three times in high school and committed six acts of delinquency, three of them involving shoplifting. She was on her way to attending medical school.

ROCHELLE *suffered from anorexia during her high-school years.* She moved from Rochester during her first year of high school and had trouble making friends. Her parents were insensitive to her depression. She reported no drug or alcohol use but did report cheating twice in school, and six acts of theft. At the time of the follow-up interview, she was attending dental school.

SANDRA *performed poorly in school. She felt Amherst was too competitive.* While she reported few acts of delinquency and no alcohol consumption or drug use, she drank frequently in college. She graduated from a state college where she majored in business. At the time of her interview, she worked at a personnel agency.

SUSAN *was troubled by her classmates; she thought they were too concerned with status.* Susan reported seven acts of delinquency (four of which were shoplifting,) but no instances of drug or alcohol use. She graduated from college and at the time of the follow-up interview planned a career as a midwife.

TERRY *resented her parents' move to Amherst and found the town terribly boring.* She reported many delinquent acts, as well as frequent drinking and partying. She was also caught shoplifting and nearly arrested. At the time of her interview, she was attending dental school at the University of Buffalo.

TOM *disappointed his father by dropping out of football and pursuing his own career path.* He reported numerous acts of property damage and theft. He indicated that he cheated ten times in high school. He graduated from the University of Buffalo with a major in theater. At the time of his interview, he was employed as an actor in a local theater company.

The Stories of High- and Low-Offending Amherst Youth

Christine and Luke: The Least and Most Delinquent

Christine and Luke exemplified diverging suburban pathways.[3] They attended the same Amherst high school and were in the same grade when they responded to the 1990 Amherst youth survey. They lived relatively close to one another, only one census tract away. They might have passed one another in their school hallways or in the Boulevard Shopping Mall without knowing each other. They clearly had different sets of friends. And they clearly followed different kinds of suburban pathways from the time they were in elementary school. Christine was able to pursue the high honors track, while Luke could hardly tolerate his high-school years. While Luke was arriving at school too stoned or drunk to concentrate, Christine was paying attention in her Advanced Placement classes. By graduation, she attained a near perfect grade point average. Luke was not allowed to graduate with his class. Christine studied for her classes and attended the University of Buffalo's accelerated high-school math program for gifted students. The hours Luke spent taking and dealing drugs may have been about the same amount of time that Christine was busy with her extra-curricular activities. She practiced her piano and sang in her school *a cappella* group. The stories of Luke and Christine illustrate more than just diverging suburban roadways toward adulthood; they reveal how segments of adolescents are able to be relationally modern.

CHRISTINE

Christine's personal interview as a young adult largely confirmed her surveyed responses as a high-school student. Her high-school survey responses indicated that she identified with, trusted, and empathized with each of her parents. She also answered a series of questions that showed that her parents were well informed of her activities—that is, who she was hanging out with and where she was going.[4] Christine indicated that she always 1) shared her thoughts and feelings with her parents; 2) spent time talking to them; 3) would like to be the sort of person they are; 4) trusted them; 5) and knew that they would always provide for an attorney if she was in trouble. Christine scored at the top of the parental scale, 18 out of 20. Her parental relational score is significantly higher than the average of 13 for the entire youth population.

In her personal interview years later, Christine confirmed that her parents were highly supportive and that she felt very close to them. Both her parents were practicing psychologists. They spent time talking to Christine. Her mother worked as a psychologist in the city of Buffalo schools, and told Christine of the troubled youth whom she counseled. That seemed to have impressed Christine, she said.

At the time of her survey in her junior year, she reported no delinquent acts, no troubling emotional behavior, and no sexual relations. Her personal interview six years after she had taken her high-school survey confirmed her exceptionally low rate of delinquency. Still, there are indications of trouble in her life, which could not have been determined from her high-school survey. Her troubles emerged in her senior year, when expectations for her success became rather unbearable. She recalled losing a considerable amount of weight. Although she never received the diagnosis of anorexia, it was a very difficult time of her life. She said:

> I was sick a lot when I was in school; in high school I missed like all these days of school, and then they implemented the attendance policy, so I was afraid I was going to fail all my classes 'cause I just wasn't going to be there, and so the guidance counselors would like talk to me, they thought I was anorexic, they thought I was depressed or whatever, and like it just wasn't

true you know I was just sick, you know there was really no reason, and they would like talk to all these people about it, they tried to talk to me about it and I just never got the sense that they knew what was going on, they always thought they knew what was going on.

It is hard to believe that Christine was really at risk of ever failing all her courses. But the comment reflects the seriousness with which she viewed her emotional difficulties. She had the capacity to realize the stress she felt. Although she does not believe the guidance counselors correctly diagnosed her difficulties, she was still able to relate to their concern. In the process, both she and they were being relationally modern in recognizing and being recognized for potential sources of adolescent troubles.

Christine listed other possible sources of excessive stress. One was her mother's disapproval of her choice of boyfriends, which became a source of tension.

I started dating when I was a senior; [he] was sort of one of those rebel types whatever, my mom didn't like that, she thought I was too serious about him . . . he smoked, he drove a little red car, like now he's getting a tattoo, stuff like that. . . . My mom was just really upset, she couldn't really stop me from going out with him, she couldn't ask me not to see him, well she could ask me but I'd just say no, but she was always upset and I knew she was upset, and I always felt guilty that I, I liked him so much and she didn't really like him.

The feeling of guilt that Christine expressed suggests that high levels of attachment can be a potential source of significant trouble. That does not seem to be the case with Christine. Despite the familial difficulties that Christine related, they were not enough to prevent her from staying on the high honor track. Whatever the reasons for her inability to eat well, they were not serious enough to prevent her from finishing her senior year and from being accepted to an Ivy League university. Christine continued to take the Advanced Placement college-credit classes that her high school offered. She was on her way to medical school at the time of her interview.

LUKE

Luke had a terribly difficult childhood, adolescence, and young adult-hood. Each turn of events that he related placed him closer to the edge of becoming a chronic adult criminal. He reported the most frequent and serious offenses among those personally interviewed. While Chris-tine's pathway toward adulthood is clearly honorable, Luke's would be commonly viewed as dishonorable. He failed repeatedly to meet soci-ety's expectations of him, especially as first encountered in school.

Luke said his difficulties in school began early in elementary school. He recalled hating school at the time—not because of the academic work, but because of being repeatedly bullied. According to Luke, "*I got beat up a lot in elementary school, 'cause I was like ten pounds soak-ing wet.*"

He also revealed that he had a difficult relationship with his parents. This is not surprising, given the fact that they were school teachers; they would not be pleased with his poor school performance, especially later in his middle and high school years. It was then that he began to listen to punk music and hang out in the city with others who shared his taste in the punk music scene, though his parents repeatedly complained.

Luke mentioned that his relationship with his parents reached a low point when "*they threw out all my records.*" He started his illicit use of drugs early in seventh grade, when he was first introduced to smoking pot. He found a crowd of friends who he said were less judgmental than his parents, teachers, and clean-cut adolescents like Christine. With these less judgmental youth, he was able to enjoy marijuana and then subsequently other drugs. Luke followed an all-too-familiar path into the frequent and serious use of alcohol and drugs. His relationship with his parents and family members became even more strained. His two younger siblings sided with their parents, and he felt further isolated.

Luke's personal interview as a young adult confirmed his surveyed responses. Based on his responses to his high school survey, Luke's rela-tional and instrumental parental control measures were relatively low. Luke's parental relational score was only 8 compared to a mean of 13 and Christine's of 18. Luke's parents confirmed that he was a difficult child. They said they only managed to "*sometimes have fun.*" In contrast, Christine parents indicated that they "*always*" had fun together. Luke's and his parents' surveyed responses disagreed regarding the extent of democracy about rule-making decisions; he saw less democracy in the household than his parents. In contrast, Christine and her parents were in sync about how they viewed familial rule-making decisions.

Luke felt rejected by his family and by his classmates from the time he was in elementary school. He could not recall ever performing well in school. The school was not a place of honor for Luke as it was for Christine. His familial and school settings were too emotionally complex. He found a simpler world through drugs, eventually turning to harder drugs and dealing as well. He sold dope in his high school, and began to regularly arrive at school stoned.

School officials repeatedly warned Luke. They insisted that he enroll in the school's drug awareness program. He did so but said it had *"absolutely"* no impact on his subsequent drug use. He was rarely at home, and those few times that he did do his homework, the results were not good. He was flunking out of high school and was warned that he must arrive at school sober. In his senior year, school officials started to watch Luke more closely. He felt even less at ease in school and subsequently dropped out and pursued education in an alternative setting.

Luke eventually received his high school equivalency diploma. He then attended a small private college. His parents remained supportive; they certainly hoped that his drug use in high school would no longer be an issue in college. Yet that first year away from home was difficult for Luke, and he reverted to drugs and alcohol. He found a new crowd of drug-using friends. Perhaps it was the fact that he was no longer at home that led him into more serious trouble when he started to take that extra step into harder drugs. He did so in his first year of college and subsequently had to drop out mid-semester when he became addicted to heroin.

It was during one late night of partying that Luke hit a bump on his suburban roadway that changed the course of his life. He had driven home drunk and swerved into a ditch. He was injured but not seriously hurt, and fortunately there were no other passengers in the car. The police arrived and arrested him for driving while intoxicated. Luke's parents hired a private attorney who was able to work out a deal with the prosecutor. It involved Luke agreeing to an intense drug rehabilitation program. If Luke succeeded in his drug rehab and avoided another arrest, his case would eventually be dismissed.

So in the brief story of Luke there is an all-too-familiar pathway from childhood difficulties to serious adolescent and young adult troubles. But Luke was also fortunate; he had the sort of parents who were willing to stand by him in a courtroom and to pay for a private attorney. As a young adult, Luke began to appreciate his parents more than ever. Although it was not always that way, he referred to them as "*awesome*" and happily married.

At the time of his personal interview, Luke was attending the local state college. He was optimistic and apparently drug free. The suburban roadway to adulthood for Luke was a particularly difficult one. He ranked as reporting the highest rate of delinquency. He had experienced quite a few bumps in the road, and could have been officially classified as delinquent. But thanks to his parents and a system of juvenile justice and criminal justice that believed in giving Luke another chance, he managed to get back on track. Indeed, he was fortunate to have officials who were not quick to adjudicate him as delinquent or criminal. Those officials were undoubtedly influenced by parents, who despite throwing out his punk music, cared enough about him to see him through some difficult times. They did not abandon him even as a young adult. They were willing to pay for the private attorney that he required in order to avoid conviction and possible imprisonment.

Jackie and Karl: The Second Least and Most Delinquent

Jackie and Karl would have preferred a less competitive Amherst. Jackie's personal interview told a slightly different story than the one that might be gathered from her high-school survey. Her low surveyed rate of delinquency did not include the fights that she reported in her personal interview. Jackie dropped out of college after her first year. Now at the age of twenty-three, she was considering how best to return. Karl's rate of delinquency was second to that of Luke's and would place him in the consistently high-offending category of delinquent youth.

JACKIE

When Jackie took the Amherst survey, she was seventeen years of age. She reported only one incident of assault, and no drug or alcohol use. She also responded that she was highly attached to her parents, scoring above the average—a 16 out of 20. Jackie and her parents indicated that they often had fun together. Her parents also agreed with her on the extent to which they democratically decided on the rules. At the time of her survey, Jackie seemed attached to school. She was on her way to college. Her grade point average was in the B range, and she reported that she liked school. Based on a scale of seven questions, her school attachment score was 26 compared to 30 for Christine. This score of 26 was substantially higher than the mean of 20 for the entire youth population, and 22 for the survey population. All would seem to be well in Jackie's life until she arrived in college.

According to Jackie's personal interview, given when she was twenty-three, she could not manage her freedom away from home. As a young adult, she was unable to resist the influence of her friends. She was away from home; she would not have dared to smoke pot or to drink alcohol if she were still living at home. In her first year at a local state college, she joined a sorority where drugs were prevalent and where her fellow members introduced her to the pleasures of marijuana and alcohol. She not only enjoyed smoking pot regularly, but also began to drink often. She was too drunk and often too high to maintain the grade point average required to stay in college. After her first year, she dropped out.

Jackie lacked the self-discipline to live away from home. Her suburban roadway to adulthood was too sheltered. When she lived at home, she managed reasonably well. Her high-school performance was good; she was closely supervised by her parents. She was hardly tempted by drugs or alcohol, as was the case with other kids whom she knew. Her parents were clear that her punishment would be severe if she disobeyed their rules. She said in response to a what-if question about delinquency: "*I probably would get one major butt-ass kicking, probably wouldn't be allowed out of the house for a month or two.*" But once her parents were no longer physically there to watch over her, Jackie had considerable trouble managing the next stage of her young adult life, which started in college.

I was living at the sorority house, I was away from my mom, and I could come and go as I pleased, do whatever I wanted, I didn't have to worry about trying to sneak in drunk, that kind of thing. . . . I had never drank or done any kind of drugs in high school and this was pretty much a new experience and I kinda went full force, and uh, my whole year was dedicated to that pretty much.

Despite Jackie's strict upbringing and her parents' close supervision, she could not quite manage college and her social life. Her young adult trajectory into drugs and alcohol suggested that her level of self-control was dependent on her social setting.[5] Jackie's substance abuse and subsequent dropping out of college could not have been anticipated based on her high school surveyed acts of delinquency. Although she reported only one incident on her survey, her personal interview revealed quite a few neighborhood fights.

Jackie talked about the many fights that would occur among her neighborhood kids. She said, "*It would usually just start out as one fight that someone else jumps into so another person jumps into it and it just ends up being a big mob fight.*" Apparently, her father believed that violence should be fought with violence. He was a police officer and insisted that Jackie take karate lessons so that she could physically defend herself. She wished her father had been less interested in teaching her how to fight and more interested in how she could obtain good grades.

Although Jackie performed reasonably well in her high school, she felt her life was too influenced by her peers. She could have achieved better grades if she was less peer-oriented:

> I guess you pretty much live up to what your peers are doing and so if my friends were all getting this grade, I would always end up getting that grade just cause I wouldn't try any harder . . . when they put me in a class where everyone was getting higher grade and expecting more of themselves, that's what I did.

Jackie was not prepared to confront the complexities of modern-day living, which required her to act as an autonomous, well-functioning adult. She was highly influenced by her peers, and in college apparently did not know when enough was enough. She may have also been influenced by disparities between the wealth of Amherst's larger population and her family and neighborhood income. Her neighborhood had the second lowest income and the fewest residents with a college degree. It also had a relatively high concentration of minorities—14 percent compared to 3 percent for the entire town of Amherst. The assessed value of her home was below that of all the other interviewed subjects.

Once Jackie left college, she no longer consumed alcohol or illicit drugs. She married a recovering alcoholic, who had just started his own home-improvement construction business. At the time of her interview, she was optimistic about her future and life with her new husband. She was also planning to return to college to finish her degree.

KARL

In contrast to Jackie, Karl reported numerous acts of delinquency in his high-school survey, which he then confirmed during his personal interview. He started to drink at an early age; his survey indicated that he often got drunk. Karl had all the risk factors associated with high rates of delinquency and crime. Like Luke, he did not get along with his parents. His surveyed responses indicated little in the way of any parental attachment or control. His total parental control score was 8, similar to Luke's and five points below the average of 13.

Karl also expressed considerable discontent. He hated Amherst and the subdivision where he lived. He preferred the more working-class neighborhood where he had previously resided and visited often. His parents favored the move because they wanted Karl and their other children to attend Amherst's well-funded schools. But Amherst's schools and high priced homes hardly impressed Karl. He identified more with his father's working-class roots than with Amherst's professionals. His father worked initially as an auto worker, and subsequently was promoted to supervisor and several years later into a high management position. When Karl moved, he was in middle school and his father had just become director of personnel. They purchased a newly built home in one of the better subdivisions. Karl's house was assessed at three times the price of Jackie's. This is how Karl described his move:

> I moved into the area in sixth grade and then sixth, seventh and eighth grade I felt that I was very out-casted. I didn't understand everything that was going on and it was a whole, alien sort of world where people act differently and do different things and you have to sort of adapt to that.

So Karl felt that the Amherst schools were too academic. He was not interested in school for reasons that he described briefly. "*I was more interested in being cool than with learning, which I really feel is kind of opposite of how I really am, but I think that was a part of how I had to grow up.*" Although Karl recognized the importance of school, he said his interest in academics decreased even more once he entered Amherst's public high-school. He would have preferred to stay in his Catholic school, but his parents were unwilling to pay the extra tuition given the excellence of the public schools and the high school tax.

Karl started at the regents level (the academically college-bound degree) and then moved down to a general degree. According to Karl, "*Being just the barely passing student that I was, I basically convinced my guidance counselor that would be the best thing for me and in reality I was just looking for the easy way out again and I still got just passing grades.*" His parents were not pleased when Karl told them that he would not pursue an academic degree.

> *Yeah, [my parents] had always been concerned. I've always been at that level. I've always had a lot of potential and a lot of aptitude. I just never used it until recently and they were discouraged of course but as I recall now it doesn't seem like much of a big deal now but I'm sure it was at the time. They were concerned.*

Karl developed an outcast identity. He rejected the sort of professional identity that his father worked hard for; it was not the kind of identity that Karl preferred. He no longer wanted to compete for good grades. He preferred the "*slacker,*" "*non-competitive crowd*" for reasons that may have reflected the trouble he had learning the required subjects. His preferred identity became a more deviant one. He was drawn into "*the drug using kind of slacker atmosphere where there wasn't so much competition.*" His friends were more like Luke. Their friendships crystalized by driving to school together and smoking pot together. "*We started carpooling in the mornings . . . and then we started smoking at the same time, and that was sort of a friendship bonding thing I think.*"

Karl graduated from high school with a general degree and then worked in various jobs in the Buffalo area, including the auto factory where his father was in a management position. At the time of his personal interview, he was attending a local state college part-time.

The take-away message from Karl's interview is that he had trouble meeting the educational demands of a society that honors those who perform well in school. He may have had a learning disability that prevented him from staying on track with an academic degree, but he insisted that he was capable. His point was that the reasons for his becoming a high-offending youth had more to do with resentments about cited parental decisions, such as where his family would live and the kind of public high school he would have to attend. Karl felt his parents did not empathize and identify with his concerns, and he certainly did not identify with their desires for him.

The narratives of Karl, Luke, and Jackie are stories of youth who become involved in drugs and alcohol. Their zones of comfort cannot be found within an affluent suburb's excellent schools or in the strict controls of parents. All may be well at first, as in the case of Jackie, but at some point they learned to make their own decisions. They had trouble dealing with the complexities of their school settings. For Jackie it was in college where societal demands became overwhelming, as she discovered once she left home and was no longer subject to the kind of personal and social controls that went along with living at home. Karl and Luke felt lost earlier, in their high-school years, while Jackie lost that critical element of self-control once she moved from home.

Yet all was not lost. In each of the cases reviewed so far, there was a slight detour in the adolescents' suburban pathways toward adulthood. The road may have become rather slow-going, but it nonetheless avoided serious, frequent adult criminality.

Lee and Alan: The Third Least and Most Delinquent

Lee and Alan are Asian Americans. It is coincidental that they should happen to be third least and most delinquent youth. Their delinquencies might be considered trivial and of little consequence, especially considering how well they were able to perform in school, and then subsequently obtain admission into professional graduate programs. They were on their way to achieving good jobs and the status that goes along with becoming a high wage-earning American.

LEE

Lee was born in Hong Kong and felt a lot of pressure to succeed in school. He reported no acts of delinquency, including no acts of substance abuse. He never attended house parties nor did he commit any delinquent acts; he even said he never cheated in school. However, he did indicate that he had his share of troubling thoughts, including once thinking about leaving home and twice thinking about taking his life. His surveyed emotional troubles are within the average range. Lee spent a lot of his time playing computer games. He also reported a high rate of copying copyrighted materials. He was in the top 3 percent of youth who committed this common violation.

Lee felt pressured to succeed. He and his family had high expectations. They believed having a good education was the key to having a good job. He explained: "*Well, they always say that you know if you don't study hard or something like that then you cannot go to college, and you're not gonna get a good education, and then you're not going to get a good job.*" Lee identified closely with his father and older brother:

> *I think my dad and my brother have influenced me. You know my dad, back then, he didn't have a good education, and then you know, he just moved himself up through engineering. I think that takes a lot hard work, a lot of um, will, a lot of determination, and, so I think he's my role model, and my brother, I think, he's smart.*

Lee became interested in engineering at an early age. He said, "*In my family I think everybody likes math.*" Lee also liked that his mother was a stay-at-home mom. "*She had more time to spend with me and my brother which is good, so we can get more attention, which I think is a good thing.*" He reported that the rules were non-negotiable, and the parenting style he lived under was authoritarian.

When Lee was not studying, he played video games, often with friends who were equally studious: "*Most of my friends uh, are almost like me, you know uh, um, I mean they're interactive people and they're quite smart you know and I can learn so much from them, it's good.*" Lee scored high on all relational indicators. He was able to manage well on his own and was not as peer dependent on other youth, as was the case with Jackie.

Lee was accepted to all the universities where he applied. He decided to stay home and attend the University of Buffalo. At the time of his interview, he was about to complete a graduate degree in engineering and then planned to obtain a Master's in Business Administration. He hoped to work someday for a defense contractor.

ALAN

At the time of his survey, Alan was sixteen. His self-reports place him on the high end of the delinquency scale of property damage and theft offenses. Like Lee, he felt intense pressure to perform well in school. He reported no delinquent friends and a higher than average level of parental supervision, but a lower level of parental attachment. He and his parents indicated they had fun only some of the time. His parents indicated there was little democracy about the rules, while Alan indicated there was none.

Alan felt isolated. He moved from Buffalo to Amherst at the beginning of his high-school years. Although he reported plenty of thefts and acts of property damage over his lifetime (eighty-one), he never drank or used substances. He said he lacked friends. Alan had strong feelings about those who would use drugs: "*I thought they were shooting themselves in the foot. I mean it's a waste.*" He also explained that he never thought of having a house party: "*I mean most of the people that I would invite anyways wouldn't fill up a full room.*"

He attributed the reasons for his delinquencies to his move from Buffalo to Amherst. He resented the move and often returned to visit his city friends. He also felt he was raised in too strict a household; his father worked as a minister. Alan seemed sociable and adept at school. He prided himself on his ability to navigate more than one social group. He maintained relationships with his city friends, although he indicated he had few close friends.

Alan would fit the category of youth to whom Elijah Anderson has referred as "code switchers."[6] These are youth who can navigate between several groups. In Alan's case, he was able to be friends with honor and non-honor students. According to Alan, "*I was a bridge between the regents and the honors program, because I didn't take all honors classes or all AP classes like my friends did, and I didn't take all regents classes, so I was a bridge. So I was in with both sides but I was also isolated from both sides.*"

At the time of his personal interview, Alan was attending the University of Buffalo's school of pharmacy. He was fortunate never to have been arrested. The take-away message from Lee and Alan's stories is how culture matters in enabling youth to perform well in school, but not without their share of adolescent troubles. Based on their self-reported delinquency, which was confirmed in the personal interviews, Alan was more troubled than Lee. If the legal system was more efficient, Alan would have been arrested and charged as delinquent. He might have been on a different trajectory despite his ability to perform well in school. Alan's preference for a less academically oriented crowd placed him on the edge. He could have been drawn into more serious delinquencies which could have diverted him from the career objectives that seemed to be not only in his interest but that of his family's as well. Lee's objective offending might be considered trivial, but reports of thoughts and attempts at running away or suicide should not be taken lightly. They are indicative of relational problems that should be considered serious. They both were able to succeed thanks to a culture of strong familial support that allowed them to adapt to modernity's demands, particularly in one educational setting after another.

Joan and Bill: The Fourth Least and Most Delinquent

Joan cared little about school and reported few acts of delinquency. Bill cared enough about school to survive high school and gain entrance into a decent university. He reported numerous acts of delinquency. Joan was a junior when she took the Amherst survey. She described herself as someone who *"kept to herself"* in high school, but she was active in student government and in the community as a volunteer at a nursing home. At the time of the follow-up interview, Joan was still living in Amherst, attending a local college, and working part-time at an insurance company. She planned a career in health care administration.

JOAN

Joan was raised in a modest section of Amherst; the assessed value of her home was well below average. Her father worked for the town, and her mother was the school cook. Joan reported a higher than average rate of parental control, scoring 9 out of a possible 10 for the supervisory, instrumental measures of control. Her relational score, however, was about average, at 6. Joan perceived her parents as quite knowledgeable about her whereabouts. Her parents' responses to their survey indicated otherwise. They thought that they had given Joan a considerable amount of freedom. Her parents further indicated that they had more fun with Joan than she with them. Both she and her parents scored high on our democracy index, which tapped into dimensions of shared rule-making.

Joan's low rate of delinquency is in spite of her parents laid back approach toward her school grades. Although most of the interviewed subjects reported considerable parental pressure, Joan told of too little. She believed her parents should have been less laid back in preparing her for school. She wished they demanded more of her: "*I could have done better; I didn't try hard enough in high school. . . . I don't think I realized in time in high school if I would have tried harder I probably could have gotten into a better college.*" She further attributed her mediocre school performance to her parents' own lack of higher educational degrees. Consequently, education was not stressed. "*Well, my father went to a two-year school; my mother didn't go to college.*" She further noted, "*My parents never showed an interest; well I don't want you to think they didn't show interest but they never tried to push me to do anything.*" She elaborated, "*I never got yelled at or anything . . . my parents never really were strict about that, I mean as long as I did okay they were happy.*"

After high school, Joan attended the local community college where she majored in the social sciences. She performed well enough to transfer to the University of Buffalo, where she majored in health and human services with a concentration in gerontology. She describes her program: "*Oh I love it, I started taking classes for a minor in human resource management, so far everything's going really well.*"

She started volunteering in a nursing home while in high school, and continues to do so every Saturday.

BILL

In contrast to Joan's parents, Bill's yelled at him a lot. He felt highly pressured to perform exceptionally well. He lived in one of the most expensive subdivisions; his house had the highest assessed value of those we interviewed. Although at the time of his survey he was only fourteen, his surveyed responses placed him in the top 2 percent of property offenders and the top 6 percent in school cheating. He reported the following offenses: beating up someone on purpose; stealing things worth more than $5 and less than $50; taking a car for a ride without the owner's permission; taking things from a car; vandalizing school property; and stealing with a group of friends. He was also picked up by the police. These acts were confirmed in his personal interview, which detailed additional acts of taking things from his father's pharmaceutical company. He reported getting drunk and smoking marijuana regularly.

Bill's relatively high rate of delinquency would seem predictable based on his reported rate of parental attachment. Bill's instrumental and relational scores were both 6 out of 10 in contrast to Christine's whose scores were 9 out of 10. His combined score of 12 for the parental attachment measures was slightly below the average for the entire sample of youth. Part of the reason for his low parental attachment score is that his father had a temper that was difficult to control. He would scream not only at him but also at his mother and the rest of the family. *"He would be yelling at her all the time, and, you know, just a lot of tension, you know, he's yelling, you know, um, you know he hit me a few times, a bunch of times, that was a big deal."* This was especially the case when his father heard about Bill's misconduct at school: *"[I got] hit when I got in trouble in school. I got the belt, which is not a fun thing when you're sixteen years old . . . pull your pants down and get whipped by your old man, you know."* He feared his parents, particularly his father, and said that he rarely had fun with them.[7]

Instead, he had fun with his friends and lots of it. He often attended house parties. A typical party consisted of *"a lot of booze, a lot of marijuana, um, some fights I'd say, that wasn't a big thing, lots of booze."* He drank wherever he could, in parks and behind the high school where kids would congregate. His drug use, alcohol use, and acts of delinquency continued throughout high school. He started dealing in drugs. He explained the reason he was never arrested: *"I guess I just didn't get caught you know, by the police, just kept it out of the house pretty much."*

Bill attributed his delinquency to his father's bad temperament, and his trouble with persons in positions of authority.

I just didn't like authority I guess, I mean I didn't really like school, I didn't enjoy school, I didn't enjoy Amherst, high school was a difficult place to go. . . . I guess it's hard to be a high-school teacher and be, be the same way to everybody, but I didn't like school, I didn't like authority figures.

Despite his temperament, problems with authority figures, and his continued drug use, Bill managed to perform well enough to gain entrance to a well-ranked out-of-state university. In his freshman year, he continued to use drugs and party whenever he could.

There was lots of partying, you know the alcohol is there, the drugs are there, you know the sex and rock and roll is there . . . there isn't just one place to be, you can go to bars, you can stay at the fraternity house, you can go to somebody's house . . . there's a thousand parties, there's dorms, there's, a lot more, I'd say options I guess, cause there isn't, like in high school, just one place to be, where everybody's at, there's just tons and tons of parties.

Eventually Bill started to care more about his school work and his future than about getting high. He insisted that he never lost that balance, and he may be one of those individuals who could manage both the demands of school and the pleasures of drinking and drugs. He said many of his friends did not do as well. This is how he distinguished himself from the rest of his drinking and drug using and dealing friends:

I cared more I guess. I wanted to be something. I wanted to be rich and successful and they don't care; their goal is living day by day. You know I always have that future plan of being successful; you know, doing four years of college on top of high school. It's what society dictates. If you don't do it, you don't pay the bills and you get farther behind, and I just always knew that.

So Bill was relationally attuned to the demands of society. He had the intellectual capacities that allowed him to reflect not only on his past but also on his future and how he could best find his preferred sense of place.

As far as his offending, it helped for Bill to be away from home. College became a turning point.

I mellowed out, really worked on my temper and was more calm, you know, relaxed, didn't have a job at school, away from the house, you know no worries, all my bills were paid for, you know relaxed, I already got into a good school so I had really no worries except in just passing which wasn't a big thing.

He looked back at his life and felt that even his father's beatings were not all that bad for him. "*I guess now that I look back on it and I don't understand; grateful's not the right word, but it was a positive thing because it sure kept me, somewhat straightened up.*"

At the time of the interview, he was finishing his junior year of college, majoring in business. He hoped to return to Amherst and work as a financial planner. "*I'd like to do financial planning, investments, turn money into money, make money for people . . . that's my goal I'd say.*"

Two different take-away messages can be derived from these two very different subjects. First, in the case of Joan, it is hard to tell if her parents' laid-back attitude might have directed her on to a more prestigious pathway. She did not get into any prestigious college at first, but she did well enough in her community college to gain acceptance to the University of Buffalo. Plus, she committed few delinquent acts. Bill, by contrast, was on a very rocky and risky pathway toward adulthood. He did not have a close relationship with his parents. He got into drugs and started stealing at an early age, and remained on this pathway of delinquencies throughout high school. His freshmen year in college was a period of transition, but he was still smoking weed and regularly getting drunk. Although he was in a party subculture, he could manage well enough to graduate from high school and then set his sights on a clear professional path.

Both Joan and Bill were relationally modern in the sense they could find their place in society, despite looking back and stating that they would have liked to have been on better suburban pathways toward adulthood.

Kim and Tom: The Fifth Least and Most Delinquent

Kim and Tom have a lot in common. Their rate of surveyed delinquencies tells only a small part of their stories. It is coincidental that they should both end up at the fifth least and most delinquent in the surveys. Prominent among their cited reasons for delinquency was their troubling familial relationships. The means by which they were able to manage those relationships are not unique to their stories. They show that trouble in a familial setting can be confronted through another social setting and the support of a whole host of non-family members.

KIM

According to her high school survey, Kim had numerous attempts and thoughts of running away. She also thought of suicide on several occasions. She ranked in the top 5 percent among females in the frequency of going to house parties where there was alcohol. According to her self-report for the last year, she ranked in the top 9 percent. She also ranked in the top 7 percent in the frequency of getting drunk and 15 percent in the last year. These rankings are of the entire sample, not just those interviewed.

Kim was terribly troubled by an accusation that her father sexually abused her sister. She said the accusation was based on a story her sister had written for one of her classes. Her high school formally investigated the allegations. According to Kim:

> I don't know exactly what happened, when I was a freshman and my sister was a senior, she had written a paper or something, or something happened and like they thought um, that our father was molesting us . . . and so we got sent downtown and they were gonna remove us and all this weird stuff, but uh, then nothing ended up happening from it . . . eventually, but you know we had to go through interviews and stuff and say that it wasn't true and you know, all that kind a stuff . . . and it was really awful and weird so . . . I mean my dad, I know my dad is like creepy.

Kim had an especially difficult time when her sister left for school and she was alone in her home, during her sophomore year: "*I can remember like when finally my sister that's next oldest from me went away to college which was like damn, you know I was like alone with my parents.*" Her personal interview confirmed her survey responses: Her parental attachment scaled measure was only 10 out of 20, 40 percent lower than that of Christine's. She also indicated that she and her parents never had fun together; her parents disagreed with that assessment, indicating that they sometimes had fun together. She responded that there was no negotiating the rules, while her parents indicated that the rules were sometimes negotiable.

Her personal interview six years after her survey suggests that Kim as a young adult was deeply troubled by familial dynamics that remained unresolved. She viewed her parents as the source of her problems; they failed to provide her the emotional support that she needed to confront her troubles. She was able to prevent her offending from becoming even more frequent and serious through her school extra-curricular activities. She found the emotional support that she was missing at home in her school. She was able to cope with her troubled home situation through friends and a teacher who seemed to really care. He ran the drama club. She said: "*Actually the teacher who was in charge of the drama club was really amazing especially looking back.*" She and her friends were devoted members of the drama club: "*I guess it gave us a kind of purpose.*"

Kim was not alone in the support that she found in her drama club teacher. She elaborated: "*Everyone had like alcoholic parents or abusive parents, or something, you know if that drama club hadn't been there, we would I don't know, we'd probably be dead, you know 'cause there was nowhere to go and nothing to do.*" She believed that he made a difference in the direction of her life. "*I think he saved a lot of people from committing suicide too . . . we all felt that way.*" Kim was able to avoid serious delinquency and a life of drugs and alcohol. She was able to confront her fear of her father. At the time of her interview, Kim had graduated from the University of Buffalo with a major in theater and was employed by a local theater company as a stage manager.

TOM

Tom reported twelve acts of delinquency, including several acts of theft, property damage, and assault. He also indicated that he had numerous thoughts of suicide/running away. Tom reported cheating in school more often than most of our subjects. He scored high on parental supervision (10 out of a possible 10), and low on parental attachment (6 out of 10). If these two scores happen to have been combined, as is often the case with studies that examine the effects of parent-child relationships on delinquency, we would mistakenly assume that Tom's relationship was about average. There are other indications that all was not well, given his responses to questions about perceived democracy and the extent to which he and his parents had fun together. Tom said that they rarely had fun together, while his parents indicated that they often had fun together. Similarly, Tom saw little in a negotiated order in regards to parental rules, contrary to his parents who indicated that the rules were always discussed. In his personal interview, Tom revealed that all was not well. He also said that his parents did not get along with one another. He said they stayed together for the kids, and they slept in their own separate bedrooms.

So family life was stressful for Tom; no one seemed to get along. His parents also expected more from him than he was willing to deliver. His father was a school principal at a local school. Although Tom did not attend the school, he felt constantly watched by the school administrators his father knew. He said his parents were highly competitive, insisting that each of their four children achieve high grades, play competitive sports, and pursue high-paying occupations.

Tom disappointed his parents on several counts. First, he no longer wanted to play high school football, despite his father's insistence that he continue. Tom explained that his father was "*a sports freak*" who competed in football and baseball and wrestled in high school and then in college. Tom had to contend with his father's disappointment. He felt he was not good enough: "*It was embarrassing. I tried to gain respect by playing football, and um, 'cause that was the only way to get respect.*" He described his father's disappointment when he told him that he had quit the team. "*When I quit, oh god, he just, I, I handed him the pads, and he looked at me and shook his head and walked away.*"

Tom preferred theater to sports. He, like Kim, found comfort in the theater club. He enjoyed school musicals. "*I wanted to be an actor; that's what I wanted to be but my parents said no, because there's no steady work, there are no jobs. I was a good student and they said don't waste all of your time and energy on being an actor.*" Both his parents tried to dissuade him from a career in the arts. They thought he had the ability to be a doctor. His mom would say to him, "*You'd be a great podiatrist.*" He said that his parents evaluated people by how much money they were able to earn. He recalled his mother saying that "*she never wanted anyone to be anything that, that did not make lots of money."* He further stated, *"It's important to them because they don't want their kids not to have anything when they get old."*

Tom and his parents seemed to have built up some resentment. They were not on the same page as to whether he could attend an out-of-state college. His parents said they could not afford the out-of-state tuition. Tom believed otherwise. Yet he agreed to attend the University of Buffalo and strived to be even more independent of his parents. At the time of Tom's interview, he was working in local theater and proud of the fact that he was paying his own bills. He hoped to move to New York City, where he viewed his opportunities as significantly better for making it as a professional actor.

The take-away message from Tom and Kim is that, despite their delinquencies, they were able to address their troubles through extracurricular activities. A good teacher made a difference in Kim's life. The high and narrow expectations of Tom's parents could be avoided by his pursuing alternative law-abiding activities. Both Kim and Tom took advantage of opportunities that enabled them to move reasonably well into adulthood.

Karen and Nancy: The Sixth Least and Most Delinquent

Based on her personal interview, Karen should technically rank close to Christine in the least delinquent category. She is quite different from Nancy; quite religious, devoted to her family, and disengaged from the vast majority of adolescents. Nancy was more into her friends, and highly influenced by them. In the personal interview, Nancy revealed that she was more delinquent than her survey as an adolescent revealed, while Karen indicated no delinquencies, contrary to her earlier survey.

KAREN

According to Karen's survey, taken in ninth grade, she never got drunk, smoked pot, or used any illicit substances. However, her high-school survey revealed three acts of delinquency, two involving property and the other fighting. She was one of a few adolescents to indicate in her survey that she never cheated in school. She was slightly above average

in emotional difficulties, with a total score of 8. But there is a discon-
nect between her survey and her personal interview, which leads me
to move her up the least delinquent scale ahead of Phil, who will be
included in my discussion of the fourteen remaining personally interviewed youth. Based on her responses to questions about parental
supervision and attachment, she scored 17 out of a possible 20. Karen
and her parents agreed on how they decided the rules, the extent of
parental control, and that they often had fun together.

Karen described herself as living a highly sheltered life. She said that
besides her interaction with people at school, "*I had interaction with
the kids from the youth group that I was in at church but that is pretty
much it.*" With regards to delinquency, "*I guess I was always the goody
two shoes. Just because I wanted to please, I wanted to please my parents and yet I wanted to be my own person too.*" She described how she
learned to respect authority at home and how that respect carried over
into school. She described how being a "good" Christian was important
to her: "*It influences every area of my life.*" According to her high-school
survey, she never watched television. She also indicated spending a lot
of time on her homework and receiving excellent grades.

Karen said both she and her parents are very religious; she attended
Christian religious schools throughout her life. Her father worked as a
carpenter and her mother as a nurse. They lived in a modest neighborhood in a section of Amherst that was located at the furthest point away
from the city of Buffalo. Despite Karen's apparently sheltered life, her
high-school survey revealed her several reported acts of delinquency.

Karen seemed to be troubled by her peers and their status-oriented
values. She believed that her classmates were not taking their religious
teachings seriously.

> *Well, it's a Christian school. Not everybody there is a Christian. Not every-
> body there believes in what Jesus Christ did on the cross for their sins. Some
> of them are sent there because they were bad in other schools and their par-
> ents want to send them to a kind of reform school. Some of them are there
> because their parents have money and their parents don't really know what
> to do with it. Some of them are there just to make it look good because
> their dads are pastors or whatever and they're supposed to go to a Chris-
> tian school and become Christians and stuff.*

Karen's feelings about her classmates extended to her neighbors, who, she said, were also too oriented toward status and money. She said their beliefs were superficial. Karen's religious feelings seemed to inform her points of view. She and her parents were equally religious, and according to her survey and personal interview responses, she identified strongly with them and they in turn identified with her religious pursuits. Although they were on the same page in their own religious community, there is a pre-modern aspect to Karen's life that leads me to speculate she is unable to meet one of modernity's most important demands: This is the ability to move beyond the intensity of a small community into a spectrum of relationships.

Karen noted how expert opinion conflicted with her biblical fundamentalist interpretations. For instance, she disagreed with today's experts on child rearing who state that parents should never resort to physical punishment. Karen said she was raised with a good dose of old-fashioned corporal punishment. She explained:

> Spanking's good. No matter what they say, ha-ha. . . . I'm glad [my dad] spanked me because I know that even though I didn't understand it then I understand that they loved me and I see kids who aren't spanked and whose parents say "you shouldn't do that, don't do that." And their kids totally controlled their parents. But I knew who was in charge and my dad did it out of love. . . . My dad spanked me with his hand because he felt that he knew how hard he was hurting me and he knew when to stop and I don't think he ever overdid it. But it let me know that when he said to do something, that it meant to do it and not because my dad was power hungry or because he never told me to do anything that was unreasonable, but it taught me to respect authority and to obey. . . . I respect authority, and I trusted my parents that they knew what was best for me because they've always done what was best before and they could see things that I couldn't see.

I quote the "ha-ha" to indicate that it might be a nervous laugh, an expression of anxiety about her beliefs when contrasted to the "they" in "what they say." Thus, in the social science literature, the ideal parent avoids resorting to physical punishment, as Laurence Steinberg has stated in his book on The Ten Basic Principles of Good Parenting.

Karen's view conflicts with principle 8: "Never use physical punishment."[8] Clearly, Karen and her father prefer religious dictums like "sparing the rod will spoil the child." Moreover, Karen's attitude toward physical punishment differs from how Bill or David O spoke of their beatings. The physical is tempered in Karen's case by a religiosity that has set limits, at least in their familial world.

Karen's identity is entwined with a tight coupling between religiosity in her familial and religious school settings. She felt enabled by her Christian education and most recently by her subsequent graduation from a Christian Bible college. At the time of her personal interview, Karen was planning to pursue missionary work in New Guinea.

NANCY

While Karen managed to resist the influence of her peers, Nancy desperately tried to fit in. According to Nancy, she was much too devoted to her peer group. She viewed her peers as part of her problem. Although she is our sixth most delinquent on our delinquency scale, she is the most delinquent among all the girls interviewed. She scored at the higher end of delinquency based on data from the general surveyed population. She repeated in her personal interview much of the survey information she previously reported; this included acts of cheating in school, frequently getting drunk and smoking pot.

Nancy emphasized that her friends became very important to her early in middle school. Her delinquency is largely related to her drug use. In middle school she first tried pot. It was at that point that she became more interested in her friends than in her school performance. According to Nancy, "*When I was younger I used to always do well, and then as I started getting older I just kind of, found that you know it's more fun hanging out with my friends and stuff, so my grades dropped a lot.*"

Nancy related that she was often punished for coming home drunk, and doing so past her agreed-upon curfew. She related how earlier in high school, her parents would ground her and prevent her from going out at night and seeing her boyfriend who lived in Buffalo. "*Normally I would be confined to the house, I couldn't go out even on the weekends.*" Nancy also indicated how she would negotiate the rules. She would "*keep nagging and begging them, and begging them, and you know try to get them to the point where they'll just like, you know give me a little leeway; sometimes it would work and sometimes it wouldn't."*

Nancy was not, however, a life course delinquent. She was able to desist from her acts of delinquency and drug use. In college Nancy made the decision to focus on her school work, and subsequently gave up smoking marijuana: "*I just realized that I didn't really like being high. I didn't like the way it affected me.*" That decision, however, was already in her mind at the end of her junior year. It was then that she reconnected with her school and her parents.

First, she became more engaged with school clubs. Nancy described how during her junior and senior year, she started to take school more seriously. After school, she described participating in a business club:

> *I participated in DECA [Distributive Educational Clubs of America]. . . . It's just basically like a, business club, and I participated in that my junior year, and then I went to state competitions, you know . . . you're put in a business situation like say, restaurant management, and it's like role play.*

Nancy said she became involved by taking business courses in school and had a few friends who were also involved. Her father's business also interested her, and they spent more time together talking to one another, mostly about her involvement in the club. She mentioned her father's reaction: "*I know he was happy that I joined the club, but he didn't really stress anything upon me; he let me make my own choices, my own decisions.*" Her father encouraged Nancy to make her own decisions, and she, in turn, subsequently identified with her parents occupational pursuits.

Unlike many Amherst youth who are expected to leave the Buffalo area to attend "*good*" colleges, Nancy wanted to stay local. She attended the local community college and then the local state college to complete her four-year degree. At the time of her interview, she was finishing her senior year and planning a career in social work. She said, "*I'm more of a people person.*"

The take-away message from the different stories of Karen and Nancy is that of the religious and the secular. The modern-day secular world emphasizes autonomy—the freedom to pursue life with your own chosen friends even if it means occasional acts of delinquency, as exemplified in the story of Nancy. Fortunately, Nancy was able to desist and to pursue activities that her parents encouraged. Karen's story is a religious one, and may be considered rather pre-modern. She was sheltered from the larger adolescent population. She lacked the freedom of place and thought to pursue a variety of relation-ships, including romantic ones. She did not express envy for what she might have missed by not attending one of Amherst's five large public high-schools. She felt loved, albeit not in the modern-day sense that Nancy experienced.

Summarizing the Least and Most Delinquent Youth

The young adults I quoted are a sample of the larger Amherst youth population. Their cited sources of trouble were most often resolved as they transitioned into adulthood. They were both constrained and en-abled by their parents, teachers, therapists, and youth-service profes-sionals. Each of those interviewed told a story of more or less conflict-ing relationships. At various times, troubles were attributed to their frustration with familial, educational, and peer-group demands. But the lasting impact of their cited troubles seemed minimal. Some were more troubled than others. But even the more troubled spoke of how they were able to eventually transcend their frequent delinquencies as they transitioned into young adulthood.

As is the case with *Money Magazine*'s list of safest cities, trouble and definitions of success may be viewed as relative. For a segment of par-ents and their adolescents, success is defined by the adolescent's ability to achieve an adult identity that produces considerable status. For Tom's parents a high-paying job was all that mattered. Christine's graduation from an Ivy League university and her eventual graduation from medi-cal school gave her the sort of status that Tom's parents wished for their son. But if Tom did not follow the path his parents wanted him to, his pursuit of theater, like with Kim's, enabled him to make law-abiding choices. Both could cope with their frustrations through pursuits that they found satisfying. They might be viewed as successful for the mere fact that they avoided more forms of trouble. They were enabled in the same way that Christine was by a good public school and teachers who seemed to really care. They could resist deep-end troubles because they never managed to fall into the category of the seriously discontented.

The difficulties adolescents face in their attempt to grasp all that is required of them in a modern-day society cannot easily be summarized. But the first point is that some youth have more of a cumulative set of troubles, making it more difficult for them to adjust to life's demands. Like Luke, they may have been bullied at a young age. They may have a learning disability and for related reasons dislike school. Luke was able to reflect on his difficulties and eventually find an alternative route. He was lost, disconnected from the rationality of showing up on time, sober, and ready to perform. He could not manage the demands of his high school and then that of his first year of college. He was not alone; the same holds for other youth, such as Jackie, who reported few acts of delinquency in adolescence, but once she arrived at college, she became embedded in a group of hard partying youth, and she subsequently dropped out.

And then there are youth like Karl and Bill. They, too, were unable to stay on a straight and narrow suburban path to adulthood. For their own reasons, they disliked where they lived and how their parents acted toward them. Karl preferred a less competitive route. An academic degree was not for him. He had trouble identifying with middle-class and upper-class Amherst. Bill wanted to reproduce his parents' good life, but was troubled by their relationship and by his father's beatings. He could manage school, delinquency, and drugs. He could graduate while Luke could not. Not only could Bill manage to attend a good out-of-state university, but he could say when enough was enough. He was able to get back on track.

As young adults, Bill and several other Amherst young adults interviewed could appreciate their parents. Even the tumultuous relationship that Luke had with his parents as an adolescent became a good relationship as an adult. They were there for him, and he appreciated their support. The good stories that I told in the second chapter of Terribly Young, Barack Obama, and Bill Gates are not that different from the stories of the most and least delinquent. Relationships in their modern-day form are important; they provide the relational support that prevent youth from becoming frequent and chronic serious offenders.

But so far, I have related only the stories of the least and most delinquent youth. There is an in-between category of adolescents that has yet to be mentioned. I discuss this middle category of adolescents whose offending is about average in the next chapter.

This signage from an Amherst, New York, roadway symbolizes several possible pathways.

6

Suburbia's Discontents

The middle category of offenders is more of the average than Christine or Luke. Any statements generalizing about this group of youth based on a high school survey or personal interview risk neglecting some of the biographical details that go along with a more focused look at each subject. For instance, Jackie did not become a frequent user of drugs and alcohol until her first year of college, while Bill quit soon after his first year. At the risk of neglecting several personal details, this chapter presents the narratives of the remaining youth who describe their personal and social discontents. I organize their stated discontents based on their feelings toward Amherst, parents, school, and peers. The larger social setting is Amherst itself, as a good or not-so-good place to reside. The next source of discontent is more personal in that it involves how interviewees perceive their familial relationships. School is also a major source of discontent, even among those who perform well. Last but not least, peer-group relationships are described, and those relationships can indeed be difficult.

The middle group of adolescents consists of the remaining fourteen subjects whose rates of delinquency are closer to Nancy's and Karen's than to Luke's and Christine's. Recall that their surveyed rates of delinquency (which place them in this middle category) are based on self-reports taken in one particular grade during their high-school years. Subsequently, as young adults reporting in the personal interview, they could reflect on troubles that they may have had throughout their adolescence. These acts of self-reflection provide a glimmer of how Amherst youth think about their reasons for offending. The narratives of the remaining group of personally interviewed youth suggest that their sources of discontent revolve around more than one particular social setting.

But before proceeding, I need to further qualify my use of the word "discontent." The interviewed youth in this chapter and the previous one were not seriously discontented to the point that they committed serious acts of crime. Few Amherst youth fall into this category. The Glen Ridge Jocks who raped and the Hanover high-school students who burglarized their school are rare. Few middle-class youth like David O are incarcerated for life. The vast majority of Amherst adolescents are able to manage their discontents so that they do not lead to frequent and serious acts of delinquency. The closest to that category of delinquent is Luke or Karl. Rather, the discontents of this middle category of adolescents are managed in ways that enable them to transition into adulthood. Still, I view their discontents, no matter how trivial they may seem, as being significantly related to their acts of offending. The stated discontents I view as falling into categories that typify the reasons for their trouble. Typifications are the core of any complex organizational setting.[1] Officials, teachers, and other youth service officials categorize the adolescents they regularly encounter. They must classify based on a limited set of characteristics. In the course of making routine decisions, they tend to consider only a limited set of facts, such as grade point average or score on a scholastic aptitude test. This does not mean that low-scoring adolescents lack other attributes worthy of praise and mention in letters of recommendation. But the bottom line for many in modernity's many complex organizational settings is that a select set of metrics is predictive of success or failure, however these may be defined.

At the same time, adolescents are also in the business of making judgments, including judgments about the places where they are made to live and the schools they have to attend. Adolescents complain not only about the adults who have structured their social world, but also about their peers whom at various times they consider to be more or less their friends. The previous chapter has already defined trouble in terms of a limited set of discontents. Recall Karl and Alan's dislike of Amherst; Luke's hating school and being bullied by his elementary school peers; Kim's confronting the possibility that her father might have sexually abused her sister. All these dislikes, conflicts, and fears can be summarized in words of discontent that distinguish the general from the specific.

Discontents and Drift

Distinguished delinquency theorists have long recognized the trouble that adolescents have in trying to fit into their group of peers and the larger adult society. David Matza has argued that one is not totally in opposition to the other. The term "subterranean convergence" implies that there is a meeting ground of value orientations that enables the sort of offending that subverts a range of legal norms. Adolescents drift between the world of adults and that of their peers. They take the values of one place of activity to another. Matza expresses the situational and transitional quality of adolescent values when he states that

> Drift stands midway between freedom and control. . . . The delinquent transiently exists in a limbo between convention and crime, responding in turn to the demands of each, flirting now with one, now the other, but postponing commitment, evading decision.[2]

The transitional is facilitated by the fact that adolescents are not yet firmly set in their identities: They are in an on-going search, exploring various rules of order along more than one possible suburban pathway, even as they are not yet independent, self-supporting individuals. Matza's definition of drift indicates that few adolescents are hardcore offenders or committed gang members. Drifters are not members of a delinquent subculture; their social world is too loose. Rather, they are in constructed social worlds in which it is OK to shoplift or to smoke pot at certain times and in certain places. The ambiguity that surrounds occasional acts of delinquency is related to the fact that the subject population drift into and out of delinquency. They can drift into delinquency because of a suburban roadway that has emphasized their right for individual, autonomous pursuits. They can also drift out of delinquency because of the enabling force of relationships that supersede the effect of any singular set of discontents.

Obviously, the concept of "drift" would not apply to Willie Bosket, because of his history of repeated violence. Similarly, David O would not fit into the category of drifters, because of the severity of his offense. David O's deadly act of violence was a product of deep-seated, emotional troubles. He lacked the enabling features of a modern society that could have prevented his act of murder. There was no one to offer him the counseling and understanding that would have led him to realize he was on a path toward serious trouble. There was nothing typical about his discontent, nor for that matter about the other seriously discontented individuals discussed in earlier chapters.

Sources of Discontent

Amherst

Terry described Amherst as a boring place to live. She resented her move from Texas to Amherst at the beginning of her high-school years. She described Amherst as *"peaceful, quiet, very low crime with boring, wealthy upper-middle-class suburbanites."* She went on to state that

> *Amherst is completely boring. I read the police blotter in the Amherst Bee [town newspaper] and it's funny. The crimes are houses that were egged and bones found on Sweet Home Road, which were later determined to be from a barbecue. Beer stolen from a Maple Road grocery store, and all sorts of little crappy things like fireworks going off.*

How could Terry complain about a city with a low rate of serious crime? There was more to Terry's statement, though. She was concerned with how trivial acts could become serious offenses. As her own self-report data reveals, her acts of delinquency were acts of defiance, attempts to make her life less routinized. She went beyond a street-corner view of delinquency by implying that the adults of Amherst made too big a deal about minor acts of offending.

Several youth spoke about how living in Amherst produced an unrealistic view of the world. Kim stated that *"growing up I didn't realize that every place was not like Amherst."* She described how driving down the streets now made her realize *"how weird this place is. . . . I guess just all the money or just not realizing like it's not like that everywhere . . . it was difficult to grow up in a community that was white collar and rich."* Kim also expressed her share of resentment when she stated that *"my family didn't really have money, and I guess everyone I grew up with made fun of me for my clothes and everything. . . . My parents got them at Kmart, or my brother's hand-me-downs, or whatever."*

Marie, like Kim, was surprised to learn later in life that not everyone was as affluent as her neighbors in Amherst. She said, "*It took me to get to college to know that not everybody had two or three or four cars at their house. You know, you see a lot of different people that are on scholarships or financial aid and stuff.*" Marie described the importance her parents placed on their country club membership. She further described them as being anxious during the few times they traveled into the city of Buffalo: "*It was lock your car doors as soon as we got into the city . . . very condescending I would say.*"

Rochelle's view of Amherst is similar to Terry's and Marie's. She moved at the beginning of her high-school years and felt she could never fit in. As was the case with Terry, she recalled her previous neighborhood as a better place to live. She described her Amherst neighborhood as

> snobby . . . *There's not a sense of community. It's an affluent neighborhood so our neighborhood wasn't friendly. I don't really know my neighbors . . . I would rather have lived somewhere closer to the city where it was more accessible to things in the city. A bigger variety of things to do and you don't have to drive so I was not so dependent on my parents to get from place to place.*

Some subjects expressed their mixed feelings about Amherst. For instance, Gary, who lived in a less affluent section of Amherst, initially described his subdivision as better than most. He referred to his neighborhood as "*modest,*" and that one "*can't really categorize Amherst . . . it depends on the area . . . you have rich areas of Amherst; they're high up, you know, nose in the air type of people.*" Still, Gary said there was little sense of community: "*None of the neighbors talk, like we don't have relationships with anybody that lives across the street or next door or, anything like that, you basically just keep to yourself in your own yard.*"

He further stated that his neighbors

> aren't *nosy, you know, and they're not always getting into our family's business. But it would be nice to be at least on a first name basis with them. . . . 'Cause we don't even know what our next door neighbors' names are, you know, really, and, and I don't think anybody in the neighborhood, really confers that much with anybody else.*

Sandra saw community in her immediate neighborhood, but not in other areas of Amherst. She saw her particular Amherst neighborhood as a good place to be raised. She said, "*all the neighbors knew one another and socialized with each other regularly.*" She noticed that more families were friendly with each other in her neighborhood than in other neighborhoods. She explained why she thought her block was different than other blocks: "*We do have a block party every year so everyone knows each other and I know talking to my friends, they're all like 'block party, what's that?'*" She went on to relate, "*it used to be just a beer party for everyone and since we had so many kids they turned it into more of a real block party with kids' games and we would have entertainment, like square dancing for everyone and we'd be out to like 12:00 or 1:00 in the morning. We'd have pizza later and casino every year.*" Sandra expressed that sense of community when she stated that "*we know every single person on the street and how long they've been there, their kids, what they do, just everything about them.*"

Yet Sandra, like Gary, had her share of discontents, particularly about Amherst as a car-dependent place. Both Sandra and Gary said that it was difficult to get to meet friends and to pursue all sorts of activities outside of their immediate neighborhood. According to Sandra, "*it was sometimes difficult to leave the block to get to friends and places. . . . I didn't want to take like a long bike ride and there isn't a sidewalk; I remember people used to honk or something and scare you. It was kind of hard from where I was coming from.*" Similarly, Gary stated that he no longer could participate in sport teams because

I had problems with travel so I couldn't. When my parents were working it was hard for them to get me to practices and stuff like that. It seemed they were always working when practices would start and obviously you couldn't start them later because then it would get dark . . . I couldn't drive or take a bus or anything like that . . . There was no bus that came and got you. You had to get there by car.

Others related that they had found ways to adjust to their car-dependent status. For instance, Alan told us that all his friends lived in different areas of Amherst and many of them lived miles away, "*so I met everybody pretty much through school, or I would ride my bike.*" For those youth who lived in more densely populated sections closer to the city, transportation was less of an issue.

The list of discontents about Amherst included its nearly all-white population. Kerrin was one of the few African Americans in Amherst. She understood the reasons for her parents' decision to move from Buffalo to Amherst based on its "*better public schools.*" But she felt isolated and wished that Amherst was more diversified. Kerrin echoed the opinion of others when she described Amherst as too homogenous, lacking the diversity of the city. She said, "*I think more should be done to include the growing number of minorities living in this area.*" She also stated that "*more could be done to recognize black students and to provide programs geared toward this population. . . . A lot of black students are very displeased.*"

Parents

Parents were a large source of discontent. They were generally seen as too strict and too controlling. The gender of interviewees mattered. Girls said their parents were more protective of them; they complained their parents were too strict, too protective, and demanded that they conform to curfews that were not required of their brothers. In contrast, boys noted how their parents tended to be rather permissive, not always knowing what was going on with them. This gender difference reflects differential levels of control based on beliefs that girls require more protection than boys. As was the case with Christine, girls had to contend with parental concerns about their choice of boyfriends. Several subjects also felt their parents did not trust them and unfairly demanded that they be subject to more supervision than was necessary.

Terry was especially resentful of her parents for having moved to Amherst. She expressed her anger through her music.

> I had this favorite Metallica album I played, that just made my bad mood worse, ha-ha. Basically, leave me alone, kinda lyrics, and I'd just play it really loud and that sort of stuff. 'Cause that really pissed my father off; loud music really pissed him off, so ah, you know, that makes it all the more better; loud heavy metal music really just got to them, really bad, you know they're like Neil Sedaka kind of parents.

Terry's parents expressed their disapproval not only in her choice of music, but also in her choice of boyfriends. They particularly objected to her dating an older guy. "*My mom didn't appreciate that when I was in ninth grade, I was going out with this, like, senior who had like excessive amounts of money.*" She further related that her boyfriend bought her a $1,500 stereo system, which led her parents to question his source of funds and what he was expecting from her in return. Despite their complaints, Terry continued to date her older boyfriend throughout her high-school years.

Terry's discontent with parental demands culminated in her senior year. She said they had promised that if she performed consistently well in high school and made honor roll, she could attend any college that would accept her. Terry made honor roll and was accepted by her favorite Ivy League school. She said her parents subsequently changed their mind, and told her she could not attend an out-of-state college because of the higher cost of tuition. So she ended up attending the University of Buffalo.

> *They didn't want to spend all that money on me. . . . Well UB's [University of Buffalo] a very good school, and you'll like it once you start school, and that sort of crap . . . But Ivy's a better school. And I got the big Ivy box with little stickers for my car and little Ivy banner and stuff like that. I was all set, and I was accepted and I even got the financial aid packet, and the packet for like orientation and all that stuff, like, I mean that's how late it was they told me that I was going instead to UB.*

She described how she felt toward her parents: "*I thought they were just big dicks. . . . I was not talking to them for like months, I mean that was the most pissed I've really ever been. I mean that really hurt my feelings. I sulked and complained to my friends mostly.*" She said that her friends responded: "*Yeah my parents lied to me too!*"

Sandy described the source of her discontent as the non-negotiable rules of the house. She was required to work in the family business, and had a strict curfew. If she happened to be home a bit late, she would be grounded. "*I always had dishes at night, and we were expected to do the housework and make sure my room's clean and be there and help out on Sundays and Saturdays. I had to help out with the gardening or whatever.*"

Pretty strict I would say." She felt her parents were stricter than her friends' parents. She explained: "*I had friends who had no curfew at all and friends that stayed out until 1:00 or so. . . . I felt bad, ya know, telling people I have to go home.*"

Yet Sandy followed the stated rules.

> *I never really stayed out past 12:00. I think for my prom I got an extension until 3:00 and that was a lot. That was a big thing. I had to argue for that. They didn't quite understand that most kids don't even have a curfew for proms, but I had one for 3:00 and I think I was out until 4:00. But I think I was home after 3:00 but the guy I was seeing at the time, we were just hanging out at my house until 4:00 and that was it so I was really home.*

Sandy also described how along with not permitting her to stay out late, her parents would place restrictions on where she could go. "*I remember one year I wanted to go to this concert and I knew they wouldn't let me. They're very, very strict and they probably didn't like the group or something like that.*" She indicated how at the time she "*hated*" all the rules.

> *I couldn't wait to go away to school but I did what I was supposed to. . . . I didn't really want to have to deal with being in trouble. I knew if I listened to them, and do what I'm supposed to do, then, I knew I was going off to school and I would be out of their hair basically, so . . . I guess I took it in stride and just dealt with it.*

Yet Sandy found ways to resist the stated rules. She explained how she would attend the forbidden concert: "*I told them I was doing something else and I covered my tracks making sure that no one would know.*" She recalled telling her parents one thing and then doing another. She said: "*Oh yeah . . . usually I would say I'm sleeping over and I would sleep over at a friend's house. I would just go there and then sleep over at the person's house.*"

Rena also complained about her overly strict parents. She felt they were too demanding of her following all the stated rules. She attributed their demands to the way they were raised in their country of origin and to the values that they brought to America. She explained her father's tendency to use physical forms of punishment:

He was transplanted from India in 1965 when he came here. And he just remembers India from 1965; he hasn't, you know, changed, and India has changed. It's become a lot more liberal, but he didn't change because he was transplanted, and so he is still as strict as his parents were with him because he doesn't have his peers to, like, show him how to be with his kids.

She further explained that strict rules were always enforced by her dad, who worked as psychiatrist:

My dad's very protective. You're not allowed to smoke, you're not allowed to drink, you're not allowed to talk to boys, you're not allowed to dance, you're not allowed to swear, you have to learn how to cook, and you have to learn how to clean.

She reported that if she broke a family rule, one parent would typically reprimand her verbally while the other parent would usually be on her side. When she was caught using her parents' bank card, her parents yelled at her and wanted to know what she did with the cash. She replied that she purchased books, but actually "*I got it for pot, ha-ha.*" She said that although both parents would not hesitate to reprimand her verbally, it was her father who physically punished her.

My father believes in physical discipline, like not like beating but like just a slap, like if you did something wrong you were slapped once and you had to go to your room . . . that's like an Indian thing and like you were sent to your room and you didn't come out until dinner and you ate dinner in complete silence and then you went back to bed. And when we were slapped our mom was always on our side. She would like hold us afterwards, you know, let us cry. My mom never hit us, like, if my mom reprimanded us she would yell and scream and then we'd go to our father and our father would be like "It's OK," and he would comfort us.

Rena said she was unfairly punished in contrast to her brother. Her brother would assist her in circumventing parental rules, particularly when boys called on the phone. She said: "*Like boys would call my brother to talk to my brother . . . they'd give him the message and then he'd tell me.*" In her later years of high school, she was allowed to go out only one night a week, Friday or Saturday. Although she reported that her parents usually knew where she was and whom she was with, she said that she would routinely go into the city without their knowledge. "*I would say that I was going out with my next door neighbor when I was going out with my city friends; you have to do what you have to do.*"

Marie, like Rena, occasionally committed acts of delinquency. She reported five acts of delinquency and had become drunk on several occasions. Her discontent focused on her father whom she saw as too demanding and much too critical. "*He was very harsh. He's very critical. He was the type of father that if I got a 99 on my report card he would say why didn't you get a hundred? You know he was very critical.*" Her father's high expectations produced the kind of discontent that led her to admit that as a young adult

> *I really don't talk to him. Honestly I don't have a real relationship with him. Never, my whole life! Well actually when I was really young I remem-ber when I was like nine and ten . . . he would kind of treat me like I was an adult and I don't know what happened. I kind of grew to resent him. I think for pressuring me, pushing me and nothing was good enough and I just felt like I couldn't please him so I did things myself. He's very high strung. He's got a bad temper and he's a workaholic. He'll come home and if you do something wrong it's like the end of the world. He's Italian. It's like an Italian man thing.*

Marie described that she had a better relationship with her mother whom she saw as "*overprotective.*" She felt that her family had stricter rules than others. She said: "*I kind of always remember that I was the one that had the curfew. I was like 'Everyone else . . .' and this and that and I would always have to check in.*" Marie also complained that her parents limited her self-expression. She felt that her parents were more concerned about what people would think than her own opinions:

> *I think that my parents very much prescribe to the status quo, you know, they are very into the golf and the societal, very into image in appearance and I think it takes away from self-expression extremely. They cringe at anything other than what they find is the norm, which is exactly what they*

live. You know, these clothes and this pair of shoes and how to do this in the
stock market.

Several youth said that their consumption of alcohol and other drugs was enabled by either too much or too little parental involvement. For example, Jeff's parents divorced when he was a sophomore, and he initially lived with his mother. He noted several incidents. For instance, he said he *"got in trouble for like a long time"* when his mom came home and found him and his friends smoking pot. He subsequently decided to live with his dad because he was permissive. When he had friends over, they would openly drink beer. Once, when he had a house party, he recalled his father merely telling them to "quiet it down." Jeff further stated that his father *"just seemed kind of clueless about the whole thing. There would be a lot of beer cans I think. He would say things sometimes but it wasn't too hard to get around it."* Jeff's discontent with his mother and father reflected the fact that they were not on the same page with regards to drug and alcohol use.

Jeff expressed discontent not only about his mother's efforts to punish his drug use but also about his dad's laid-back attitude about drugs and alcohol as well as other details in his life. *"He was more interested in his work and what was going on with his partners."* This was even the case when he and several of his friends were picked up by the police and driven home. He said, *"We were drinking beer at my house and decided to walk up to the Perkins [restaurant] at about 3 o'clock in the morning; we had beers in our hands and all of a sudden this cop shined a spot light on us and he drove us all home to our houses."* Despite having been picked up by the police with alcohol in hand, Jeff said he hardly faced any late-night or early-morning repercussions for his acts of delinquency.

Phil's parents divorced when he was two. Like Jeff, he shuttled back and forth between two households, and, like Jeff, during high school, he decided to live with his father and step-mother. He too referred to his father as *"relaxed as far as his rules. He wasn't always trying to control everything in my life, which was good I guess; he was fairly laid back as far as that goes. . . . I don't even think I had a curfew."* Phil, however, reported few acts of delinquency and basically saw himself as following the rules. He said, *"I had this weird sense to please him; just, maybe it was 'cause of my brothers. I remember what a pain in the ass they were.*

I wanted to be the good son." Phil's parental demands were limited to a few instances when he would be grounded for violating the house rules.

Kerrin similarly related that her parents were generally happy with her behavior because her *"brothers and sisters were more difficult to raise."* She said that her older sister was *"wild"* and that her parents had a hard time with her. *"They just couldn't control her . . . when we were little, like she would run away sometimes because they wouldn't let her do things you know, just like that . . . she basically got to do what she wanted to do."* She described learning the boundaries in her family by watching the demands placed on her oldest sister and brothers. She described how her sister along with her brothers would have house parties for the entire school when her parents were out of town; when they came home, they would find burnt cigarettes and furniture out of place. Because of her siblings, she felt her parents did not trust her to be alone at home.

School

Nearly all Amherst youth said school is important. They are inundated with that message. The survey data are remarkably consistent on that point; only 3 percent of our sample said that school was not important. Most students (54 percent) ranked the importance of school at the top of the scale (that is, extremely important); another 33 percent said it is very important. Parents and their adolescents stated that it is important for students to produce top grades so that they could compete for admission to the top schools and the most desirable professions. Many Amherst youth had little difficulty in meeting this definition of educational success. A segment, however, had its difficulties, and the reasons for their troubles followed a list of educational discontents. On top of the list was boredom. Just as youth stated Amherst was a boring place to live, so, too, they described their schools as boring. A second source of discontent was school competitiveness. Parental pressure to succeed in school is closely aligned with stated perceptions. Teachers, guidance counselors, and other school officials were cited as being insensitive to their educational discontents.

Terry, for example, was a high achieving student, yet she repeatedly stated how bored she was in school: *"I went to school, I brought other* books so I wouldn't have to pay attention in class because, I mean I hate to say this but they weren't really teaching me anything I wanted to hear most of the time, So you know I read a book and went from class to class." Terry was constantly late and would miss school. She never missed a whole day of classes she said, but became quite adept at forging notes so that she could be absent during extended periods of school time and

> go down to Elmwood [Buffalo] and go shopping or something like that . . .
> by senior year, they [school officials] hadn't seen a real note from my mom
> for years because, you know I didn't want to be caught so if she wrote me a
> note I threw it away . . . I forged whatever real note with special stationary
> with my mom's stationary, and it would say please excuse Terry because she
> had a doctor's appointment. I periodically varied it orthodontist appoint-
> ment, allergist appointment, that sort of stuff. By the end of senior year I
> was going to all sorts of interesting specialists . . . if anybody actually read
> those notes they would think that I had some serious medical problems.

Despite these acts of deceit and other acts of delinquency, Terry managed to continue to perform well in high school and then in college. At the time of her interview, she was enrolled in dental school. Her drift into delinquency was limited to just her adolescence.

Patty's educational discontent appeared to be more serious than Terry's. She performed poorly in school and skipped numerous classes. There were two incidents that limited her trust of teachers. The first incident occurred in sixth grade when

> I had a very touchy feely teacher, and I didn't like it one bit . . . he was a
> male, and I was not going to put up with it. . . . One day, he was standing
> over my desk and getting touchy feely with me. I told my parents about it
> and stuff like that, and I warned him, I said, "You stop touching me now,"
> and he's like "Oh what's the matter," and he kept it up. So I couldn't take it
> anymore, so I slapped him across the face, glasses went flying. He tried to
> get me kicked out of the school. I had this big war with him. Here I am a
> little twelve year old, and the principal believed him over me.

Then in high school, there was a second incident that caused her to distrust teachers and school administrators. She recalled:

I got suspended when my boyfriend beat me up in class. They suspended me for fighting, even though I just stood there and took the punches; I still got suspended. . . . I was with him from sixth grade to ninth grade. We had just broken up, and it happened there in the middle of class that he actually beat me up in the middle of one of my classes. . . . My teacher liked him more than he liked me, so I basically was in trouble again.

After these two incidents, Patty said, "*I could no longer trust teachers.*" She started skipping school and drinking at school. "*I just started becoming a troublemaker.*"

A lot of her troubling behavior occurred in school. She said, "*I would empty out my hair spray bottle and put some schnapps in there and me and my friends would stand at my locker before homeroom, talking about boys and our hair and stuff like that while we would be pounding schnapps, you know.*"

She described taking alcohol from her parents, and how it changed her social world.

It was my parents' and I stole it out of their bar, and it was probably about ten years old too . . . until that point I had never had a drop of alcohol. I did it because I couldn't get the respect from the adults so I was trying to get respect from new friends. . . . Next thing you know I'm invited to parties of all these upperclassmen . . . I'm hanging out with all the seniors and juniors, because I could drink more than them . . . it was kinda like, well if the adults aren't going to believe me, then maybe the students will.

Eventually, Patty was caught drinking at school.

I got caught . . . we were standing at my locker one day drinking schnapps and the nurse walked by and the nurse knew. . . . She was really the only one that actually felt sorry for me, you know. She understood, and we talked for a while. The nurse said she wouldn't tell anybody as long as I promised to go to counseling with the school psychologist. He said, "You can trust me; it is totally confidential," but then he turns and tells my parents that I have a serious drinking problem . . . he just read all his notes to my parents . . . plus the fact that he misunderstood half of it . . . it's like another adult I can't trust.

Patty's excessive drinking was limited to her high-school years. In college she started to minimize her drinking. She said,

> College made a difference. It taught me basically to voice my opinion. . . .
> In college I made friends with those who boosted my self-esteem. . . . They
> lifted me up on a pedestal; they didn't look up to me or anything like that,
> but they'd be like, "Yeah, you're the one and only Patty; you're so cool." They
> were very sure of themselves, and hanging out with them, I was more sure
> of myself, and it was like, we were always together.

At the time of the interview, Patty was about to graduate from the local state college she had been attending for the past four years.

Dee said she consistently scored in the B range, but her father would repeatedly tell her that she could do much better. He was quite vocal about the importance of school.

> When we got our report card I would kind of get yelled at, get the lecture.
> . . . He would say, "You can do better than that . . . you have to work . . . it
> will pay off in the long run . . . I know you can do better and you know you
> can do better. Everyone knows you can do better."

Dee attended many house parties where she would repeatedly get drunk.

Denise said that she had trouble paying attention in class; she suffered from Attention Deficit Disorder. According to Denise, "*I have a problem even now in school. I can't sit in the back of class because I watch kids out the window. I can't sit by the door because everything bores me. Everything is boring. Few things have kept my interest.*" Denise attended a small private school where she was in small classes and received the attention that she needed. Still, Denise reported attending nine house parties where she got drunk. She also said she cheated in school five times. At the time of her interview, she was attending the local community college and working as a waitress.

Peers

Nearly all our interviewed subjects indicated that Amherst was too cliquey. Several of the interviewed subjects stated that they were never that involved in these status-generating cliques. Just as their parents had a multitude of ways of describing their status, so adolescents saw peer-groups as means for generating status. This includes the status that emanates from looking cool based on peer-group styles. This is how Tom described peer groups in his school: "*There was the popular clique, the clique that everyone was afraid of, you know, the clique that people strived to be in and, there's the music clique, the nerds, geeks. It's funny because some of them even overlap.*" Yet the overlap could produce problems, according to Tom. "*If you had friends out of that clique then you'd be chastised by everyone, it was unfortunate, because I had, I had a popular friend, [but] I was not in one clique.*"

Patty, who lived in a modest section of Amherst and attended a high-school different from Tom, described her peers as

> *Cliquey, very cliquey. . . . You had your really popular group, your study bugs, your nerds or whatever you want to call them; then you had, you know, cheerleaders, stuff like that. . . . I was one of those people that just associated with everybody. I was, you know, not in one particular clique, but, it was very cliquey.*

Patty articulated the point that cliques were a way of creating status by producing a hierarchy of those who were considered the most and least desirable. She said,

> *They looked down on a lot of people . . . it had nothing to do with personality . . . they looked down on you because of your appearance; there was no overweight popular kids or no black popular kids, they were all white middle class beautiful people, like how it is on TV.*

Then there were the wannabes:

> *I couldn't stand being around them; they were trying to be in the popular groups, like they would just follow the popular groups like puppy dogs, and, you know carry their books or whatever, they were trying really, really hard, they were just so sorry.*

A few other subjects noted their own struggles to fit into a group of their peers. For instance, Patty stated that "*I would do anything to fit in.*

. . . You were very lucky if you got invited to those [house parties]. I mean there were parties with every group of people, obviously, but the ones I went mostly to were with older people." In the case of Patty and others, the need to "*fit in*" motivated the house party, the drinking and drugs. This is the group context point of delinquency.

Several subjects reported how they navigated their status-conscious peer groups. Nancy avoided the high school in her residential area because "*the majority of the kids come from families where they have a lot of money so they have an attitude to go along with it. . . . I just didn't want to have to deal with that so, I went to North instead.*" She elaborated: "*A lot of my friends went to North, and that school's not as bad with the cliques and stuff.*" She described her friends from North as "*true friends*" and said that "*they were more down to earth.*"

Dee also noted differences. "*The kids that went to East were richer than the ones that went to South and North. There were newer subdivisions that they lived in. Their parents were more of the lawyers and the doctors and the people that made a ton of money.*"

But discontents about peers were focused not just on cliques. A few youth noted that adolescent party-goers were to be avoided. For instance, Gary was critical of kids who attended house parties.

> *I couldn't figure out why people were so proud of the fact that they threw up or they were hung over the next day. Some people would come to school hung-over and I'm like, okay? I just knew which ones would succeed in the world and which ones wouldn't. You could just tell. I mean I don't want to stereotype, but I am, there are just certain people that would come hung-over or just like miss a week of school at a time, and I'm like, well, I don't want to do that.*

Gary was not alone. Other youth said they desisted after observing their friends' troubling use of drugs and alcohol. Patty became less interested in the party drinking culture that she was a part of after seeing its impact on her and her friends.

> *I saw that my friends were going nowhere. . . . I just got sick of it, I felt like I was getting too old too quick, you know. I didn't even like the taste of beer,*

but I was drinking it anyways, you know, and I just woke up one morning, and I said time to start over, and I basically did, you know. . . . I broke up with my boyfriend and I dropped my older friends and I started hanging with people my age, just from a different school.

Patty's drift out of delinquency was facilitated by her recognition that she could no longer continue to tolerate a partying identity. Others similarly pointed to how their identification with peers had shifted. They view their relationships with peers as dynamic and subject not only to the place of the school, but also to the place of their religious activities and family gatherings. Rochelle indicated her friends "*were a part of my youth group. . . . So pretty much during school, I didn't have a lot of friends in school but with people outside of my school.*" Similarly, Patty said,

I started hanging out with my cousins a lot more . . . junior and senior year, I kind of, drifted away from the Williamsville crowd to the Orchard Park clan. I still hung out with them once in a while but it was getting too difficult. . . . I started hanging out with people I grew up with when I was younger and then we came back together again for junior and senior year. I hung out with people from other schools and family members, and then, I started hanging out with, people I grew up with again.

Relational Modernity Revisited

The vast majority of those interviewed were able to transcend their personal difficulties and transition into adulthood without committing serious and frequent acts of delinquency and crime. They could deal with their troubles because they could rely on more than one place of activity in which to reflect upon their discontents. They were enabled by opportunities that adults and friends provided to confront their discontents—whether those discontents involved a lack of community, of parents being too strict, of teachers behaving abusively, or of other adolescents being too cliquey. They had ways of coping and managing their troubles so that they could avoid a pathway leading to serious acts of delinquency.

But sources of discontent can accumulate to the point where they can justify violating stated parental and legal rules. They facilitate the drift into delinquency, as do the rationalizations that Matza refers to as neutralizing the "moral bind of the law."[3] Yet there is not just one legal set of legal rules to be neutralized. Indeed, there can be instances in which the rules of the house conflict with the rules of the state. As was the case with Jeff and others whose parents were divorced, one parent could be more tolerant than the other, permitting what was not permissible by another. The rules of modern-day society are routinely disputed, often as parents come to the defense of their own adolescent child. Some parents may be facilitating subterranean convergence by identifying too closely with their adolescent's troubles. According to a youth service professional,

> We had one incident where the family counselor went there, and the parents were not happy that she was there. . . . The father was irate. He said, "I hold the arresting officer's mortgage." He had the nerve to pursue this. So what message does that give? The kid had clearly broken the law, had definitely, and he had that kind of attitude the whole time. Well, we knew where that attitude came from. And we see that more and more. When I talk to the school social workers they said they had a parent come in screaming that they dared to call his kid down to the office and question him without legal representation. Or they come in and say, "OK, the kid did some vandalism, what's the bottom line?" and they just get out their checkbook. . . . I think the kids are really being done a disservice because they're not having to be accountable. I say that to kids all the time, "Who paid your legal fees?" It used to be that almost always the kids had to pay the legal fees. Now maybe it's 60 percent pay the legal fees. They don't even know what the legal fee was.

Is this good parental behavior in defense of an adolescent child or is it parental indulgence? The message is less than clear, and its lack of clarity is due to modernity's dispersed sources of authority. This was the case in the incident that I described of honor students burglarizing their school. Their parents came to their defense, as parents are expected to, especially in a decentered world where my ability to recognize the good in my child is different from my ability to recognize that in a stranger's child. That recognition through the relational force of modernity has its intended and unintended consequences.

But the fact that some parents have the kind of power that allows their youth to circumvent the consequences of their illegal behavior is not new. What is new is that it has become more prevalent in modernity's post-industrial cities. For instance, Amherst police officials are finding more parental resistance to their occasional attempts to enforce the law. According to one senior thirty-year veteran,

> *It used to be that we would return a kid to his home, and parents would thank the officer. . . . Now there are more times when we bring a kid home because of pot, and the parent will say, "No big deal" and may mention that they drank alcohol or smoked pot as a kid as well.*

To be relationally modern means to recognize that adolescent difficulties are often parenting difficulties. These difficulties are apparent in the contrasting stories of Christine and Luke. Christine's parents could not have been as troubled as Luke's. Christine grasped from an early age all that society demanded from her. She could compute complex mathematical equations and practice piano on her own. She was able to accept the rules of her school, home, and other places of activity. Luke's pathway was filled with lots of troubling events; his was a less honorable roadway toward adulthood. Luke struggled, and his parents struggled as well. On his trajectory, he reached a point where he developed a hardcore addiction to heroin. But his parents were there for him, as were therapists at a residential drug rehabilitation facility. The good and not-so-good stories of youth are stories of parents, teachers, police officers, and a whole host of others who are more or less there to assist youth as they transition into adulthood. In some families and in some settings, the struggle may be more complex and more deeply disturbing; expectations for conformity may not be easily met. Dee's father may not have been following the right set of recommended parental techniques when he yelled at her, "*I know you can do better, and you know you can do better.*" It is difficult to know for certain, as Karen related in her justification of her father's spankings of her.

Fortunately for the subjects interviewed, they eventually found their young adult sense of place. Although Tom disappointed his father by not pursuing his father's passion for football and his mother's desire for him to pursue a high-paying career, he found plenty of support for his calling in theater. Although his delinquency as reported was initially at the high end, he was able to desist. So, too, did Bill and the many other youths who drifted into and then out of delinquency. But they could do so only through a certain degree of empathetic identification and trust that allowed them and the adults in their lives to be personally and socially engaged.

As I have tried to emphasize, the right way to parent is not easily determined given modernity's many expert opinions and the fact that there are fewer traditions from the past to guide the conduct of youth. To most safe-city parents, the rationality of discipline and punishment makes sense if it allows their youth to resolve their difficulties so that they do not get into serious trouble. Yet this is not the case for all middle-class youth, as I have highlighted in earlier chapters pertaining to the seriously discontented who have committed serious acts of crime. It is critically important that adults in their positional roles recognize the difficulties that a segment of adolescents face in order to help them avoid more serious troubles.

In a study of middle-class, drug-addicted youth, Elliot Curie astutely observes that the most troubled are those whose parents believed their adolescent should be able to solve their own problematic behavior.[4] He refers to these parents as blindly believing in a "social Darwinist" approach to child rearing, which entails

> a belief system, a cultural and psychological orientation toward the world —especially toward the bedrock issues of responsibility and mutuality, discipline and nurturance. Most of these parents were not just victims of this belief system but subscribers to it. It was, after all, a worldview shared by the most affluent among them, who did not suffer from significant economic stresses, who could afford help, and who had sufficient resources to buy a variety of services for their children. The rejection of the idea of mutual responsibility, a righteous distaste for offering help, the acceptance or encouragement of a view of life in which a competitive scramble for individual preeminence and comfort is central, the insistence that even the most vulnerable must learn to handle life's difficulties by themselves and that if they cannot it is no one's fault but their own.[5]

I imagine Luke's parents and the many other parents of seriously delinquent youth were torn between the more instrumental saying of "Either you do it my way or it's the highway" and the more relational response of "You're troubled because of us, school, and the kids who have bullied you." In the end, Luke's parents chose a more inclusionary response: they were there for him, as an adult, to prevent his conviction in criminal court and possible imprisonment. Luke was fortunate to have another chance and the opportunities that go along with living in a safe city, including officials who are slow to arrest and convict their delinquent youth. Luke was eventually enabled by the force of relationally modern parents.

More questions remain, though: How might relational modernity matter in a larger population, a more representative sample of Amherst youth? To address this, it is critical to return to the notion that the familial, educational, peer-group, and community settings adolescents face matter. In the next chapter, I turn to several years of survey data to conclude my analysis of delinquency and modernity in America's safest city.

This Amherst, New York, youth center is located near an athletic field, ice rink, and swimming pool.

7

Safe-City Offending

Official arrests represent only a fraction of adolescents who could be arrested and adjudicated delinquent. As I noted in introducing *Money Magazine*'s designation of Amherst, New York, as America's safest city, few acts of delinquency are reported to the police. Crimes recorded by the police are more accurate indicators of serious categories of violent and property crimes. By relying exclusively on the FBI's index of part-one offenses, *Money Magazine* has ignored the larger spectrum of non-index offenses. To suggest the extent to which that broader spectrum of offending is more or less common among Amherst adolescents requires me now to present the self-reported delinquency data that I briefly referred to in previous chapters.

To describe the extent of youth offending in Amherst, I draw on several surveys that were conducted with representative samples of youth and their parents. They are based on samples of respondents surveyed during several periods of time. In two of the surveys, a total of 1,353 youth were questioned about the incidence of delinquency. Many of their parents were also surveyed as well. I refer not only to the parental surveys to explore the reasons for their adolescent child's delinquency, but also to a sample of Amherst youth service professionals. By linking these various surveys together along with archival and official data, I hope to present a more complete picture of delinquency and the means for its control—one that draws on social science techniques that allow me to go beyond the stories of youth that I have so far told.

The data that I present allow me to describe not only the extent of offending in Amherst, but also how adolescents, their parents, and officials feel about its seriousness and programs aimed at controlling its occurrence. I have suggested that after-school programs and programs to divert youth from the formal legal system as well as other community organizations are the settings for the control of delinquency; these are the middle-class settings that make a city relatively safe.

My description of the reasons for delinquency draws on a theory of relational modernity, as outlined in the previous chapter. The personal interviews revealed how the offending acts of adolescents were related to more than one social setting. Several related questions that emerged from their interviews can be further addressed with a larger sampling of youth. For example, Luke related that he was bullied as a child. Is this just Luke or are rates of surveyed victimizations correlated with self-reported delinquency? Bill related his father's bad temper. Could Bill's delinquency be related not only to his father's temper, as he suggested, but also to his father's possible drug and alcohol use? I will not refer specifically to Bill but to the larger Amherst youth population when I relate how victimization or parental consumption of alcohol relates to youth offending.

To further address how relationships matter in the lives of adolescents, I move from percentages and average values to correlations and statistical effects. Multivariate statistical techniques allow me to analyze the possible effects of parents, schools, peers, and community on adolescent offending. The analysis is based on a cross-sectional snapshot of feelings that adolescents expressed through their responses to their surveys. Rather than lump all these settings into a single causal model, I prefer to analyze them separately—each for its possible relationally defined effects on adolescent offending.

So recall that Christine could be unhappy about how her relationship with her mother was going, but quite happy at other times with her school performance. In contrast, Luke's problems seem to have overwhelmed him; his early troubles at school and most likely his relationship with his parents created familial troubles that could not easily have been resolved.[1] Are the sources of discontent identified in the previous chapter similarly related to adolescent offending among a larger, more representative sample of youth? For those youth who are particularly troubled, my suburban roadway of relational modernity suggests that discontents are critical. Although they are interrelated discontents, I consider them separately for the purpose of understanding modernity's major places of activity. I begin with parents as a critical source of support as well as of discontent. My next major social setting is the school. Its demands for adolescent competency can be overwhelming for a small segment of youth, as in the case of Luke. The extent to which peers matter is also important and may contribute to relational sources of support, or the reverse. Recall how Nancy attributed her offending to the need to fit in with her peers. Last but not least, there is Amherst itself and its programmed activities. Those who are discontented by its available programmed activities should also be less likely to indicate participation in them. Recall that Terry said Amherst was a terribly boring place. Recall also that Bill lived in a considerably more expensive house and subdivision than Joan and reported a lot more delinquencies. Is the wealth of a subdivision neighborhood related to rates of delinquency in the larger population? Is the larger, surveyed population of youth doing equally well as young adults? To address these questions, I draw on measures of adult occupational and educational status from a survey of their parents taken ten to thirteen years after the Amherst youth surveys. I end the statistical portion of my analysis where I began by returning to official rates of delinquency, as gathered from the Amherst police department's youth division.

Amherst Youth Studies

Surveying Amherst Youth, Parents, and Officials

Surveys were conducted with parents and youth who had given their written consent, as required by the University of Buffalo's Institutional Review Board and by the Amherst Youth Board and school boards. The surveys received the support of Amherst officials for the initial purpose of creating a Needs Assessment Study, which included evaluating various town-wide programs, such as its diversion and recreational programs, which I later describe. The surveys and data presented in this chapter as well as the interviews discussed in the previous chapter could not have been generated without the full cooperation of town officials and the support of many Amherst residents. The research proceeded through several contracts between the Town of Amherst and the Research Center for Children and Youth at the University of Buffalo. The research center's co-director, Murray Levine, and I were the principal investigators, and our research agreement provided full access to school board lists, public and private school officials, and samples of youth and their parents. On a more personal level, the Amherst Youth Board director, Joseph Bachovchin, made the research possible by providing access to youth workers, program directors, and other officials. He also facilitated group meetings with youth and parents, and enabled us to obtain the permission of school superintendents and their school boards. Additional insight and support came from Detective Michael Torrillo, who worked as the chief of the Amherst Police Department's juvenile division. Detective Torrillo explained police policies and provided the aggregated adolescent arrest data. Statements about official sanctioning in this chapter and earlier ones are based on numerous lunch and coffee time conversations. Several weekend nights were spent accompanying Detective Torrillo and other officers as they responded to reports of adolescent delinquency.

The Sample

In 1987 and 1990, random samples of high-school youth were generated from school board lists. These lists consisted of every Amherst youth in public and private school. Letters were sent to parents requesting permission to survey their adolescent child. In addition, the randomly selected youth were asked for their permission and offered a financial incentive (a gift coupon) for participation. While the public school youth were surveyed during school hours in a designated study hall or during a lunch-time period, the private school students were surveyed after school in town-operated youth centers. If students were absent, they were contacted and given the opportunity to take the survey on three other occasions. In anticipation of a lower response rate among private school youth, they were oversampled.

Based on census and school district data, the survey samples appear fairly representative of the town's high-school population. The grade and age distributions in both surveyed periods are within 2 percentage points of the distributions in the high-school population. The percentage of boys and girls in the survey and total population are within 1 percent of each other. The total combined sample of 715 youth in 1987 represented 13 percent of the senior high-school population, a high percentage for surveys of this kind. Moreover, the sample population closely resembled both the racial and the marital characteristics of the town: 92 percent of the surveyed sample are white compared to 93 percent in the population, and 15 percent of the surveyed sample indicated their parents are single parents compared to 18 percent in the population. In 1990, we randomly selected a 20 percent sample of 930 public school youth from the 4,504 youth in Amherst senior high schools. Of the 930 letters to parents requesting their consent for the participation of their son or daughter in the survey, we received 629 consents. Out of the 629 youth who had their parents' permission, 524 actually took the survey. The remaining 105 youth with parental consent did not wish to take the survey or were absent on the several occasions when the survey was administered. The 524 youth who took the survey represent a final response rate of 56 percent for the public school sample.

We selected 449 youth out of 879 youth from the private school sample. Parental consent was received for 30 percent of this sample (136 youth). Out of this population, 114 youth came to the Amherst Youth Board offices, where they completed the surveys. The response rate for the private school sample is 25 percent, which is substantially lower than the public school sample. The total sample in 1990 is 638: 114 private school youth and 524 public school youth. The percentage of private school youth in the population is 16 percent; private school youth constituted 18 percent of our sample. Although the final survey population slightly over-represents private school youth, there is no reason to believe that this larger proportion of private school youth produced any bias in our analysis. The total combined sample of 638 youth represents 12 percent of the senior high-school population, a high percentage for surveys of this kind.

The parent sample was composed of either mothers or fathers of youth who took a telephone survey conducted by professionals at Goldhaber Research Associates of Amherst, New York. Out of 638 parents telephoned, 560 responded to the parental survey. Twenty-eight percent, or 178 parents, were not at home after three calls or refused to participate in the survey. The parent survey response rate was 72 percent, an unusually high response rate, which indicates the importance the vast majority of parents placed on youth concerns.

The youth surveyed as freshmen in 1987 were surveyed again in 1990 as seniors. Out of a freshmen population of 147 youth interviewed in 1987, we located 122 names on the school board lists in 1990. The proportion providing consent and completing the interviews was comparable to the general population, producing a completed sample of 72 youth who had agreed to take the surveys as freshmen in 1987 and then again as seniors in 1990.

We also were able to conduct several additional surveys. We surveyed public middle-school youth in 1993, as part of a needs assessment concerning the building of a fifth Amherst youth center. The report we produced was based on a sample of 238 public school youth. The 238 middle-school youth surveyed were asked about their experiences in one of four Amherst youth centers. This survey is referred to as well. Last but not least, in 2000 we conducted a follow-up with parents of youth who were interviewed in 1990. We were able to locate and interview 35 percent of our initial youth survey respondents' parents.

Based on these multiple sources of surveys and their sampling distributions, I have no reason to believe that there are serious biases that would impact my analysis beyond those that are reported in other published studies of youth. As is the case with this and other surveys, there are selection effects. Not all parents and youth provided the active consent that the university's Human Subjects Review Board required. The sample excludes troubled adolescents who were incarcerated and away in therapeutic schools, as well as those who were persistently absent from school.

Another question is whether delinquency rates could have changed significantly since the data were first collected. Based on a 2009 survey conducted of Amherst youth by the Search Institute,[2] there is good reason to believe that delinquency rates have not changed significantly. For instance, the Search Institute survey found that 24 percent of youth said they used marijuana in the last twelve months. This is the same percentage that we found in 1990. The percent in both these surveys varies by gender and age in the expected direction in that older boys report the most frequent use while younger girls the least frequent. The similar rates of self-reported offending between the more recent 2009 Search Institute survey and the earlier Amherst surveys are particularly impressive given differences in sampling and survey procedures.

The following sections tell a largely quantitative story of delinquency and modernity. I avoid the longer statistical story produced for the contracted Amherst reports. For the purpose of avoiding a sea of numbers,

I illustrate the extent of offending and reasons for its control by drawing on a select group of tables, graphs, and diagrammed figures that summarize a larger set of statistical analyses.

Dimensions of Delinquency, Drug Use, Cheating/Dealing, and Emotional Troubles

Several dimensions of offending are commonly defined. These include offenses involving categories of theft and violence. Another dimension of adolescent offending is illicit substance use, such as alcohol, marijuana, cocaine, and other non-prescription drugs. Illicit substance use is distinguished from other types of self-inflicted harm. Harm against self, as defined by answers to questions about having thought about or attempting to commit suicide or run away, is classified as an emotional trouble. Although emotionally troubling offenses might not be thought of as delinquent acts, they can lead an adolescent into the juvenile court through the legal category of status offender. A more nebulous delinquent categorization is cheating in school, which I describe as a category of its own.

Delinquency

How common is delinquency among Amherst youth? To answer this question, I draw on 1990 self-report data. Accordingly, the vast majority (71 percent) committed a delinquent act that could have landed them in juvenile court. Each act of theft, property damage, and violence could have led to the adolescent's adjudication as a delinquent.

Figure 7.1 displays the percentage responding to each of the surveyed offenses. The most common delinquent offense is theft of items worth less than $5; self-reports of theft decrease the higher the dollar value. The thefts represented consist largely of acts of shoplifting. The next most common offense is the destruction of property (banging up something): 29 percent of Amherst youth said they committed this offense. Vandalizing school property and stealing with a group of offenders are the next most common property offenses, 16 percent and 15 percent, respectively. Group and lone fighting are also rather common, with about one in four Amherst youth indicating that they either had been in a group fight or beaten someone up. The percentages are substantially lower for each offense when looking at reported delinquency in the last year. But even when the total likelihood of one or more of these eleven delinquent acts is limited to just the last year, the percentage involved in acts of delinquency drops from 71 percent to 64 percent.

The theft, property damage, and assault measures produced the delinquent offending dimension, which will be referred to in the subsequent multivariate analysis. Not included in the delinquent offending dimension are the percent picked up by the police, and if they were ever charged by the police. Only a small proportion of adolescents was ever arrested and charged for their offenses. But this percentage is actually smaller than it appears according to police records, as I will report later in this chapter. Many adolescents may have thought they were charged when they were not formally charged or arrested.

The second row in Figure 7.1 refers to the offense category of cheating in school. This common offense is also excluded from the delinquency total. Figure 7.1 shows that 74 percent of Amherst youth said that they had cheated in school. The percent who said they cheated was even higher in 1987, when 84 percent said that they had cheated in school. When we asked about cheating within the last year, 33 percent said they had done so. Age is not related to having ever cheated or having cheated just in the last year. Boys have a slightly higher rate of cheating: 76 percent of boys cheated compared to 71 percent of girls.

The surveyed distribution of offenses repeats well-known patterns in delinquency. In this sense, the data are representative of other self-report studies. Most of those who reported an act of delinquency would be considered one- or two-time offenders (37 percent). Another would fall into the recidivating category of three- to five-time offenders (27 percent). Frequent delinquency as defined by five or more offenses constitutes 36 percent of the offending youth.

Gender and age repeats well-known patterns. The delinquency rate for boys is 81 percent, compared to 63 percent for girls. Although the difference is relatively small for the entire delinquent population, substantial variation in the ratio of boys to girls emerges when broken down by type of offense. For instance, theft of more than $50 yields a ratio of 9 to 1 boys, while it is only about 2 times as large for boys

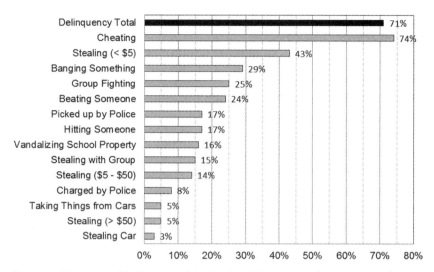

Figure 7.1. Percentage of Amherst youth indicating delinquency, police contact, and school cheating. *Note*: Delinquency Total includes all offense categories except for Cheating, Picked up by Police, and Charged by Police.

when theft is less than $50. The data confirm the well-known point that boys not only offend more, but that when they offend, it is considered more serious.

The relationship between age and delinquency also follows a familiar curve. It tends to peak at sixteen and then declines in the senior year. As in the case of Luke and Karl, a small segment of youth repeatedly commits their offenses throughout their high-school years. In the case of Luke, he reported a large number of delinquent acts in each of his school years. I was able to more accurately assess the age distribution based on a subsample of youth who were surveyed in 1987 as freshmen and then again as seniors in 1990. Most adolescents (66 percent) who reported an indexed delinquency in their freshman year reported an act of delinquency in their senior year. But those who did not report any delinquent acts in their freshman year were substantially less likely to report an offense in their senior year; there, the percent drops to 42 percent.

The eleven acts of delinquency exclude cheating, which I examine as a category of its own. The combined measure of delinquency offenses had a statistical reliability coefficient of .67; that is, adolescents who committed one of these delinquent acts often said they committed another.

Substance Use

We asked respondents to self-report if they had smoked or consumed a variety of illicit substances within the past year. Our alcohol question asked specifically if they had "*been drunk or high on alcohol.*" As indicated in Table 7.1, most Amherst youth (67 percent) said they had used illicit substances within the last year. The percentage saying they got drunk within the last year is 59 percent. Alcohol was the drug of choice, with tobacco and marijuana next. Only 1 percent said they had used steroids, 4 percent cocaine, and 5 percent amphetamines. There are significant differences in the use of tobacco and marijuana. Girls reported smoking more tobacco than boys (45 percent compared to 35 percent), and boys reported more pot than girls (27 percent compared to 21 percent). Older adolescents reported more frequent substance use than younger ones. However, alcohol use in the last year and attending house parties where alcohol was present is only slightly correlated with age; .08 for alcohol and .11 for house parties. The younger an adolescent was when he or she first tried an illicit substance, the more frequent his or her subsequent use. In total, six indicators of substance use are combined to create a substance abuse category with a statistical reliability coefficient of .64.

Table 7.1. Percentage of Amherst Youth Indicating Use of Illicit Substances (Last 12 Months)

Substance	Percentage
Alcohol	59%
Tobacco	41%
Marijuana	24%
Steroids	1%
Cocaine	4%
Amphetamine	5%
Total illicit dubstance use	67%

*Table 7.2. Percentage of Amherst Youth Indicating
Emotionally Troubling Thoughts and Attempts
(Lifetime)*

Type of Thought or Attempt	Percentage
Thought about taking life	43%
Attempted to take life	12%
Thought about leaving home	67%
Attempted to leave home	13%
Thoughts and attempts total	73%

Emotional Troubles

Early use of drugs correlated with emotional troubles; the correlation
is significant for drugs and emotional troubles, but not for alcohol consumption. Emotional troubles are defined as thoughts of and attempts
at leaving home or taking one's life. Gender is significant for suicidal
thoughts and attempts: 53 percent of girls compared to 31 percent of
boys thought about taking their own lives, and 15 percent of girls said
they had tried to take their life compared to 7 percent of boys. A less
extreme indication of emotional troubles reflects desires to leave home
and actually trying to leave home. The percent distribution of youth
indicating emotionally troubling thoughts and attempts is presented in
Table 7.2. Although most youth (67 percent) said they thought about
leaving home, only 13 percent actually tried to do so. In total, 73 percent
of Amherst youth indicated they had either thought about or attempted
to take their own life or to leave the place of their home. Emotional
troubles are highly correlated (.72 alpha) and are combined to create a
dimension that I refer to as emotional deviance.

Youth and Parental Perceptions of Offense Seriousness

Youth, parents, and officials were asked to rank on a 10-point scale the
seriousness of various offenses. We were interested less in an absolute
measure of seriousness than in a relative measure—how youth compared to parents and officials in their assessment of various offenses. We
asked youth, their parents, and a sample of eighty-four Amherst youth

Table 7.3. Parent, Youth, and Official Perceptions of Offense Seriousness in 1990 (out of 10)

	Skip a day of school	Use cocaine	Beat up someone	Get high on marijuana	Shoplifted $10	Get drunk	Break a streetlamp
Parents	6.9	9.9	9.1	9.6	9.4	9.1	8.6
Youth	5.3	9.3	6.1	7.7	7.4	5.8	5.4
Officials	5.9	9.8	8.6	8.9	8.7	8.6	7.8
Average	6.0	9.7	7.9	8.7	8.5	7.8	7.3

service professionals to rate the seriousness of offenses on a 10-point scale of most to least serious.

As might be expected, many parents and their adolescents disagree about the seriousness of various offenses. Some parents are more lax than others about the legal rules, especially when they, themselves, are or were involved in the consumption of alcohol or the smoking of marijuana. As previously noted, a segment of parents is upset that the police would even dare to charge their adolescent child for any offense. Still a substantial portion of parents viewed various acts of offending as highly serious.

Although Table 7.3 indicates parents and officials generally viewed surveyed offenses more severely than youth, they all agreed on the severity of cocaine use. For other offenses, however, youth service professionals were more in agreement with the surveyed youth population than with parents. While adolescents and their parents generally agreed about the seriousness of cocaine, there was less agreement about skipping a day of school. As would be expected, adolescents were more likely to see the listed offenses as generally less serious than their parents. This is also the case for getting drunk and using marijuana. Similarly, vandalism was viewed slightly more seriously than skipping school. Moreover, parental and adolescent perceptions of seriousness between 1987 and 1990 seemed highly consistent. For both populations, there is a slight increase in the perceived severity of getting drunk. This increase in severity may be attributed to the fact that Amherst Youth Board and school officials launched a campaign to make parents and youth aware of the risks of alcohol abuse after the 1987 survey.

The substantially higher ratings that parents gave to the seriousness of various offenses are illustrative of how they may see their potential consequences. I read the numbers as suggesting that parents are more aware of the trouble that can develop through an arrest and conviction for even a minor offense. Parents view the use of cocaine as substantially more severe than marijuana because they, along with officials, know the penalties for marijuana are mild or non-existent compared to cocaine. The same can be said for acts of larceny or skipping a day of school.

As expected, perceived offense seriousness among youth is correlated with offending. That is, the higher the frequency of reported delinquent acts, the lower the perceived seriousness of the offense. The inverse relationship between perceived severity and frequency of offending was at its highest for marijuana and the lowest for cocaine, $-.42$ compared to $-.12$. Getting drunk has a correlation of $-.38$. In total, the correlation between the frequency of delinquency and perceived seriousness was $-.32$. This supports the point that there is a continuum of harm associated with adolescent offending, and that there is ambivalence about some legal rules, especially when they involve the consumption of illicit substances and alcohol. As expected, perceived seriousness is related to risk-taking attitudes based on measures that asked if they would ride in a car if the driver was drunk; the extent to which they liked danger; and if they enjoyed taking dangerous risks. These measures of risk-taking were significantly correlated with all dimensions of delinquency.

We also asked parents to estimate the percentage of Amherst youth who never got drunk, smoked pot, used cocaine, or committed theft. The results in Table 7.4 show that parents were generally correct about the extent of alcohol use among Amherst youth. At the same time, they tended to overestimate both youth drug use and incidence of theft. Parents' overestimating drug use by approximately 25 percent for marijuana and 27 percent for cocaine may be related to media attention to the drug problem and to rhetoric like "the war on drugs."

Table 7.4. *Parental Estimates of Adolescent Illicit Substance Use/ Delinquency and Adolescents' Actual Reported Acts (Last 12 Months)*

	Used alcohol	Used marijuana	Used cocaine	Stole
Self-reported rate	62%	24%	4%	43%
Parental estimates	63%	51%	29%	51%

Preventing and Controlling Trouble

Youth Centers and Other Programs for Youth

Amherst youth and their parents are well aware of the services that the Town of Amherst provides. They are most aware of its four youth centers located throughout the town (Clearfield, Harlem Road, Ellicott Creek, and Williamsville). These centers are not just places of recreational activity; they are also places of adult professional assistance. The centers are operated by youth service workers whose task is to assist youth in a variety of activities, including homework. Both youth and their parents are in agreement about the extent to which they participate (25 percent of the youth population).

The Youth Board Centers operate with a professional staff funded by the Town of Amherst. Based on 1993 interviews with parents and youth about their participation in the youth centers, we found considerable parental interest in maintaining the youth centers. Parents know about the youth centers through their child's friends, school, and advertisements. Parents said they were willing to expend a considerable amount of time driving their younger adolescents to various youth centers. According to our 1993 survey of youth center participation, 70 percent were driven to the center by their parents; the remaining percent arrived on foot, by bicycle, or were dropped off by a school bus. Less than 1 percent of those surveyed said they had difficulty getting to the centers.

The stated reasons for attendance are diverse. According to parents, the most frequently mentioned reason for encouraging their child to attend a youth center was that the youth liked the activities (90 percent) and because the youth wanted to be with friends (76 percent). About 40 percent said they sent their child to improve their socialization skills. Another 20 percent of parents said they sent their children to the center because they were working, and another 13 percent said their children needed another activity. Surveyed youth reported multiple reasons for attending. Most (over 80 percent) said they attended because it was fun and their best friends also attended. Only 15 percent said they came to youth centers because their parents made them.

Generally, Amherst youth and their parents indicated that they were satisfied with the youth center programs and staff. Parents responded on a 10-point scale of overall satisfaction with higher numbers indicating greater satisfaction. Parents indicated that they were very satisfied with the youth center programs. A large majority (69 percent) gave the centers a 9 or a 10 on the 10-point scale. Only about 5 percent of parents gave the centers an unsatisfactory rating (5 or below). Parents showed their approval of center activities in their views of center staff. Almost all agreed that center staff were friendly. Most (74 percent) said it was easy to talk with staff, further indicating that they saw the staff as "professional." Most (82 percent) said center staff members were involved and interested in their children. In other words, the youth center staff contributed to parents feeling that their adolescents were in a caring community.

One question asked of the teenagers was whether having a youth center shows that adults care about kids. The vast majority (73 percent) answered "Yes" to that question. Another 25 percent answered "Sort of." Only 2.5 percent said "No." A second question asked adolescents to say whether youth centers are good activities for the Town of Amherst to provide. An overwhelming (94 percent) said "Yes." Less than 1 percent said "No." A third question asked whether they would vote in an election to have a youth center. Again, an overwhelming majority (93 percent) said "Yes," they would vote to have a center. Less than 1 percent said "No." Moreover, the survey showed favorable attitudes toward youth center staff. Most (74 percent) said they would talk to a staff member if they were having a problem that worried them.

I draw on the 1990 youth and parent surveys to mention other programs sponsored by Amherst. The YES (Youth Engaged in Service) Volunteer Program was especially popular with adolescents once they reached high school. More parents indicated that their children participated than children who said they actually participated, 30 percent compared to 24 percent. The YES program coordinates opportunities for youth to volunteer with persons who are handicapped, senior citizens, and children in a variety of settings. The Amherst YES Volunteer Program was much better known among Amherst adolescents than their parents (70 percent versus 50 percent).

Fifteen percent of youth reported utilizing the Youth Employment Service; 12 percent of parents thought their children had used it. Eighty-eight percent of participants characterized the program as "excellent" or "good." Ninety-two percent of parents rated it "excellent" (50 percent) or "good" (42 percent), and only 4 percent said the program was "fair" and 4 percent "poor." Seven percent of youth reported having taken part in the Summer Musical Theater, which is the same percent that parents indicated.

Other Amherst-sponsored programs focused on treatment and court diversionary options for youth. Approximately 9 percent of youth reported participating in Amherst Y-U (Why You) programs, which provide education and free information on drug and alcohol abuse. (This may have been the school program that Luke referred to as having no effect on his drug use.) In addition, the program provides parents with centralized treatment referrals. Of those who answered the evaluated component of the survey, the vast majority said the program was either excellent or very good.

As mentioned earlier, when Amherst youth are arrested and charged with an offense, they have options in Amherst that they might not have in less affluent cities. These include the town's First Offender Program, which youth can enter upon being referred by the Amherst courts. Adolescents who participated in this program rated it either excellent (20 percent) or good (80 percent). The First Offender program illustrates options that many inner-city teenagers do not have, as previously indicated in the cited government report on disproportionate minority confinement.

The Amherst Youth Board and school boards coordinate one another's prevention programs through their Drop-Out and Early School Intervention programs. As indicated in Figure 7.2, few youth are actually in these programs, which are directed at youth who are identified as being at risk. Other delinquency control programs that are not directly supported by the town, but are available to youth, are: SARAH (Serving at Risk Adolescent Homes), RAP (Responsible Adolescent Parenting), and the nationally recognized Tough Love program.

Recreational Programs

Places to swim, play ball, and to pursue a range of fun activities are enabling features of a safe city. In addition to a wealth of youth programs, the Town of Amherst has two major recreational centers with

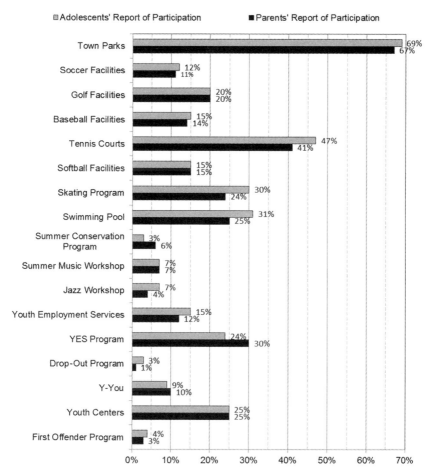

Figure 7.2. Percentage of adolescents and parents indicating youth participation in Amherst programs and facilities

ice-skating rinks and swimming pools. There are many town parks and ball fields. About two-thirds of youth and their parents reported use of the town's parks. Nearly one half of youth (47 percent) said they used the town's tennis courts. A slightly lower percentage of parents (42 percent) said their children used the tennis courts. Based on responses by both adolescents and their parents, the next most common recreational facility utilized by youth was the town's swimming pool; 31 percent of youth and 25 percent of their parents indicated use of the pool. The ice-skating and hockey programs were utilized by 30 percent of youth; 24

percent of parents said their child had used the skating programs. The other town recreational programs such as baseball, golf, soccer, and softball were utilized by 20 percent or less of adolescents according to youth and their parents.

Last but not least, there is a range of programs and recreational activities available to Amherst adolescents through the YMCA and Jewish Center. Both of these facilities have extensive recreational programs that provide their youth members with choices of activities. In this regard, it should be noted that at the time of the youth surveys, there were forty houses of worship operating with their own religious youth groups. In 1987, we asked several questions on religiosity, such as church attendance and beliefs. The vast majority of youth said they attended religious services: 46 percent indicated once or more a week, while 14 percent said they never attended. Moreover, half the Amherst youth population said they participated in some religious youth program. Most said that religion helped them to deal with their problems and that their religious faith helped them.

However, the religiosity of a large segment of youth cannot be determined from the survey data. Attending services and believing are two different matters. Plus the high rate of adolescent offending would suggest that the internalization of religious beliefs does not automatically mean the internalization of legal norms. Recall that Karen's evangelical-fundamentalist beliefs were coupled with her self-reported delinquencies, although at the low end of the spectrum of offending.

Update on Amherst Youth Programs

Since the time of the surveys, Amherst has maintained all the listed programs. One additional diversion program was added in 2001, the Amherst Youth Court. This is an alternative to the juvenile court and most frequently leads to community service. Amherst youth are selected to act as court officials and as jurors. It is diversionary in that no formal charge and no formal adjudication occur. In this sense it is inclusionary, resembling other popular models of community justice.[3]

In total, the reviewed prevention, recreation, and diversionary programs illustrate the capital investments that affluent families and their city governments are willing to expend on their youth. They do so not just to respond to delinquency, although that too is part of their stated objectives. The impact of community programs on offending will be further examined when I turn to my multivariate models of analysis.

Victimization

As previously noted, safe-city youth may be just as troubled as those in the impoverished inner city. They may be subject to acts of crime that place them in the role of victims. Bullying among middle-class youth and college students has lately received considerable media attention. The surveys reveal that a large segment of Amherst youth self-report having been the victim of a crime (Table 7.5). Nearly half of youth (47 percent) indicated that they were threatened; about 14 percent said they were beaten up, with 4 percent indicating so severely that they required medical attention.

When asked if they were "ever" sexually assaulted or raped, 6 percent of Amherst youth said they were. Nine Amherst youth said they were raped, eight of them girls. When asked about sexual assault that included threats, 10 percent of girls said they were sexually victimized compared to 1 percent of boys.

Personal theft is more prevalent for offenses involving amounts of less than $5. Approximately 28 percent of youth indicated that they were victimized by this type of offense. This figure drops to 22 percent for amounts between $5 and $50 and to 12 percent for amounts over $50. This inverse relationship between the frequency and seriousness of victimization is often found in victimization surveys.

Table 7.5. Percentage of Amherst Youth Indicating an Act of Victimization by Type of Offense (Lifetime)

Type of victimization	Percent
Threatened with physical harm	47%
Beaten up (no medical attention)	14%
Seriously assaulted (medical attention)	4%
Sexually assaulted	6%
Raped	1%
Robbed (of less than $5)	27%
Robbed (of $5 to $50)	22%
Robbed (of over $50)	12%

As research on the overlap of victimization and offending has shown,[4] the relationship between victimization and offending is significant. Illicit substance use is more strongly correlated to victimization for girls than it is for boys. In the personal interviews discussed in the previous chapter, girls more often than boys related their drug and alcohol use to sexual assaults.

Parental Troubles

Acts of personal victimization are just one potential source of serious trouble. Recall Kim's fear that her father might sexually abuse her. Not only is a segment of Amherst youth troubled, but their parents are troubled as well. Some parents have addictions to drugs and alcohol, and a few are even in prison. We asked youth about a range of potential familial difficulties. One question was whether they experienced difficulty because of their parents' drinking behavior. We found that youth whose parents drank heavily were significantly more likely to report emotional difficulties than those who said their parents' drinking was not a problem. Fifty-seven percent of youth who said they had difficulties with their parents because of parental drinking behavior reported three or more incidents of emotional difficulties, compared to 36 percent of youth who indicated their parents' drinking did not cause problems.

Responding to Trouble

A theory of relational modernity suggests that the youth of Amherst should have others besides their parents who can assist them in confronting their troubles. We asked them to whom they might turn in case they wished to talk to someone about a range of troubling issues. In figure 7.3, I list individuals to whom they might turn if they had difficulties with alcohol or drugs. According to the youth survey data, the vast majority (94 percent) said they would turn to a friend if they had questions or problems concerning alcohol or drugs. The next most frequent source of assistance would be their mothers or brothers and sisters. Sixty percent said they would turn to their mothers. In contrast, less than half (46 percent) said they would turn to their fathers. A little

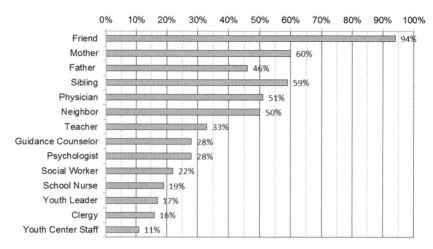

Figure 7.3. Percentage indicating whom they would turn to if troubled by their drug and alcohol use

more than half (51 percent) said they would seek the advice of a doctor. Among school officials the most likely source of help was a teacher, with 33 percent saying they would seek the advice of a teacher. A less frequent source was a guidance counselor or a school social worker, represented by 28 percent and 22 percent, respectively.

A Multivariate Analysis of Relational Modernity

I now move beyond univariate and bivariate statistics to describe the multivariate effects of a set of identified social settings on various dimensions of offending. My objective is to see how well relational indicators influence delinquencies. Relational indicators are the responses of surveyed youth to questions about their emotional attachment to their familial, educational, and peer-group settings. In addition, I consider the effects of community indicators based on attachment to and involvement in Amherst's community-based programs. Several of these indicators I referred to in the previous chapter when I discussed parental trust and empathetic identification. My indicators of offending are the frequency of the previously discussed dimensions of offending. The more specific questions relate to how relational modernity compares to more physical dimensions of supervision and involvement, as they may take place in familial, educational, and peer-group settings, as well as in various community-based programs.

I hypothesize survey indicators of relational control to be significantly related to the frequency of each offending dimension. Moreover, I hypothesize that relational indicators are not only directly related to offending dimensions, but also indirectly linked through instrumental indicators of control, such as parental supervision. Several of these measures were mentioned in the previous chapter when relating the interviewed subjects' responses as well as those of their parents.

My models of relational and instrumental forms of control are based on confirmatory factor analysis techniques. Structural Equation Modeling (SEM) allows for multiple indicators of a single dimension, such as parental attachment. Separate questions about parent trust and empathetic identification can be tested through the confirmatory factor analysis technique. An advantage of the SEM models is their allowing for testing the significance of direct and indirect effects. SEM is similar to path analysis in providing a model of how a set of variables relate to one another. As previously discussed, the dimensions of offending I draw on are common acts of delinquency (theft, property damage, and assault), illicit substance use (drugs and alcohol), cheating, and emotional troubles (attempted acts of running away and suicide). The determinants of the frequency of offending in its various dimensions are, as I have suggested, relational. As adolescents traverse from one field of action to the next, they are impacted by their familial, educational, peer-group, and community settings.

The reliability of the delinquency dimensions has already been mentioned. The confirmatory factor analysis aspect of SEM allows for multiple indicators of the unobservable, such as the relational effect of attachment. Attachment measures vary based on the type of adolescent setting that I analyze. For instance, the relational dimension of parental attachment is based on questions about parental trust, empathy, and identity. The SEM models require me to define the items in each factor so that the relationships among "factors are specified *a priori* rather than letting the factor analytic methods define factors."[5]

The presented models were generated through the Analysis of Moment Structures (AMOS) program and are based on a graphic representation of how relational (exogenous) latent variables interact with one another and with the dependent (endogenous) dimensions of offending. In the presented models, relational attachments predict the more instrumental shape of control. That is, I agree with Travis Hirschi when he states "that the child is less likely to commit delinquent acts not because his parents actually restrict his activities, but because he shares his activities with them; not because his parents actually know where he is, but because he perceives them as aware of his location."[6] Based on this line of reasoning, relational measures not only have an independent direct effect on offending, but also an indirect effect on more instrumental physical dimensions, such as letting parents honestly know where they hang out. I discuss the models' direct and total effects. The presented models provide an adequate fit to the observed data.[7]

Following a theory that I have advocated in the previous chapters, I see relational factors as social/psychological indicators of attachment and support. In the model that includes parental attachment, I draw on multiple indicators of trust, empathy, and identity. Non-relational measures I consider instrumental in that they are less abstract sources of control, such as the physical supervision that parents provide their adolescent children. The instrumental may also be viewed as current in that it requires youth telling their parents where they are going and when they will be returning. Hagan notes this distinction between relational forms of control that stem from emotional affects, while instrumental ones relate to the physical dimensions of control.[8] I extend this model to incorporate instrumental controls as they may vary by setting.

I refer to the family, school, peers, and community as social settings with their own fields of action.[9] Each of these fields has its own set of emotional affects; that is, adolescents may express profound dislike for their school, but may see their parents as a source of relational support. In each social setting, relational dimensions should predict instrumental factors and together explain the frequency of offending.

Parenting

My first set of relational indicators of modernity is based on parental relationships. Michael Gottfredson and Travis Hirschi, who emphasize the importance of parenting,[10] argue that if parents lack the skills to discipline their children, their adolescents will lack self-control. The data for 1990 reveal that all aspects of parental relationships are statistically significant. Figure 7.4 presents the basic model of parental relationships as determinants of offending. Descriptive statistics indicate significant differences in the incidence of offending by all measures of parental relationships. These differences are in the expected direction; that is, youth who perceive their parents as less trusting, empathetic, and less able to identify with them offend with greater frequency. The difference holds not only for 1990 data but also for 1987 survey data. The question remains, however, how these significant bivariate relationships hold once other factors such as parental supervision and permissiveness are taken into account.

The parental relationship model includes attachment, knowledge, support, and permissiveness as latent factors. The parental attachment measure is composed of nine questions that form the relational dimension of parental attachments. Although five measures are indicated, four of those measures combine questions asked about their mothers and fathers. Similarly, parental knowledge is based on four questions asking if their parents knew where they were going and with whom. The parental support factor is based on three separate questions that ask about familial decision-making, fun, and dinner. The parental permissiveness measure is another indicator of physical control. It is based on responses to a question posed to youth about whether their parents would allow them to attend a house party where alcohol would be present and parents were away. The offending dimensions were previously defined: indexed acts of delinquency, illicit substance use (which includes alcohol consumption), cheating in school, and emotional troubles. When the relational indicator of attachment is divided by its mean value into a low and high category, I find statistically significant differences in all offense dimensions. For example, for those who fall into the high category of parental attachment (relational control), the mean rate of delinquency is 9.8 compared to 4.3 for those in the low category.

The question that remains is how relational measures stack up against other indictors of parental relationships, such as those that reflect parental knowledge or supervision. I present the standardized effect parameters based on the SEM model since they take into account differences in the measured scale of the variables. The direct, indirect, and

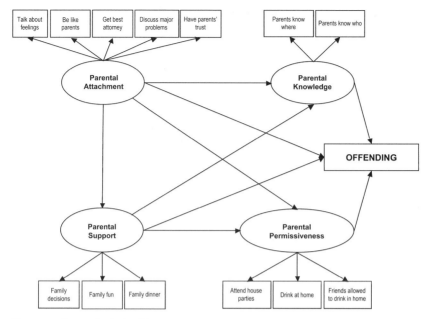

Figure 7.4. Parental relationships

total effects of all four parental factors are significant in their effects on each of the delinquency dimensions. In the appendix, I present tables for this model and subsequent ones. Here, I confine my analysis to a graphic representation of the data, as in Figure 7.4. Included in the appendix are tables with goodness of fit measures and the standardized direct effects for the parental and subsequent SEM relational models.

The results from Figure 7.4 indicate that parental knowledge is significant for three of the four dimensions of offending. When the combined direct and indirect effects of our parental factors are taken into account, however, parental relational attachment is significant for indexed delinquency, substance use, and emotional deviance. The relational offense of running away or suicide is strongly associated with the parental attachment and support factors; the total effect is −.37 for attachment and −.34 for support. As might be expected, adolescents who report thoughts and acts of suicide and running away are troubled by their family situation.

The multivariate effect parameters support the bivariate relationship between the permissive variable and substance use. As might be expected, 87 percent of youth who said their parents were always willing to let them go to house parties indicated alcohol/drug use compared to 54 percent of youth who said their parents were never willing to allow them to attend such parties. Similarly, these differences in permissiveness are significantly related to the frequency of cheating and emotional deviance. The permissive measure is an extreme one, and runs contrary to a theory of relational modernity that suggests maximum tolerance. A curvilinear association may more accurately define how permissiveness relates to offending.

Schooling

I think it starts with school and then that's what gets the parents mad, and that causes a lot of tension, and a lot of families, and then there is a lot of yelling. A lot of time, they will drink or do things because they are so mad.
—Amherst Middle-School Youth

A major reason parents choose to live in affluent suburbs like Amherst is the reputation of their public school systems. That reputation is partially built on the fact that most students are white and middle class. While the importance of school cannot be denied based on the surveyed responses of adolescents and their parents, the extent to which it was stressed varied among those personally interviewed. Recall how Joan thought she could have performed better in school if her parents had pushed her more. Generally, parents know that the school is the place of learning how to be modern. Most of those interviewed complained about too much pressure to succeed in school.

I consider a school attachment factor based on the responses to questions that asked youth how well they liked their school; how well they were able to get along with their teachers; how hard they tried in school; if they would like to have taken fewer courses; and time spent on homework. School frustration is measured based on the disparity between their goals and their beliefs in their ability to meet those goals. The variables in this factor refer to doing well in school, having high grades, and completing school. Grades were based on self-reported estimates of an overall average. Willingness to talk to various school officials was based on eight questions that asked respondents to indicate if they would trust school officials to discuss problems with drugs or problems related to sex. Many of our school indicator measures were significant. For example, 56 percent of youth who said they did their homework often reported an act of delinquency, compared to 75 percent indicating that they rarely did their homework. The difference is even more extreme for youth who said they had trouble in school; 90 percent who said they often had trouble with teachers reported an act of delinquency, compared to 50 percent who said they never had trouble. I also wanted to find out whether there is a difference between private- and public-school youth. Private schools report significantly lower levels of indexed delinquency, but this difference is not significant once school attachment is taken into account. Thus, the private-school effect makes sense if these youth are more connected to their schools; their attachment to school accounts for their lower levels of delinquency.

Figure 7.5 presents the basic model for the multivariate effects of school-related factors. Both attachment and frustration dimensions are significant in their direct effects on indexed delinquency. The more attached to their school, the fewer acts of offending youth reported. Similarly, the more frustration youth expressed, the higher their delinquency rate. Yet much of the relationship between frustration and delinquency is reduced through the negative correlation between frustration and grades. The total effect of frustration on delinquency is reduced from the total effect of .13 to .08. Moreover, the total effect of attachment is reduced from its direct effect values of −.53 to −.35. What appears to matter less once attachments are taken into account is the impact of grades on indexed delinquency.

When we shift to substance use, a slightly different pattern emerges. School frustration matters less as a direct effect on substance use. Grades and willingness to talk to school officials even when drugs are involved have no significant effect on the frequency of drug use. Only the relational dimension of attachment to school is significantly related to the frequency of substance use.

School attachment is equally significant for cheating. School grades are also a predictor of cheating, but in the direction of higher grades leading to reports of more cheating. Personal interviews with several Amherst honor students indicate that a few of teachers were known to

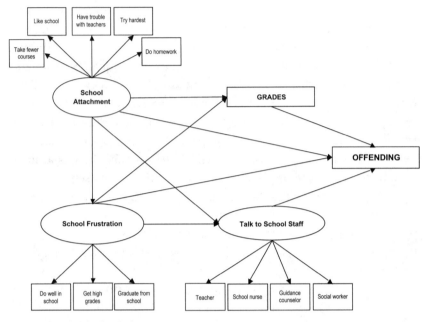

Figure 7.5. School relationships

look the other way so that their students could score exceptionally well on their tests. The case in New Hampshire of honor students burglarizing their school supports the point; that is, some students who have good grades cheat.

The last offending dimension I referred to is emotional troubles. In predicting the extent to which adolescents express emotional trouble, the school attachment measure is the only dimension to have a significant effect. Grades, school frustration, and the willingness to talk to school officials mattered little compared to school attachment. Based on these data, the impact of grades on offending is overrated.

Peers

The Amherst surveys confirm that adolescent peer groups matter. In 1987 we asked youth if the delinquent act they reported was committed with a friend. Of the 401 youth who reported an indexed delinquent act, 76 percent said it was committed in the company of a friend. Usually, their friends were no strangers to trouble. In both 1987 and 1990, youth who said they associated with peers who were often in trouble or who were picked up by the police reported significantly more delinquent acts than those who did not. For instance, among youth who disagreed with the statement "*my friends rarely get into trouble*," 79 percent reported delinquent acts, compared to 49 percent who agreed with the statement. The group context of delinquency has long been noted[11] and is cited as an important reason for considering adolescents to be legally different from adults.[12] The current research literature continues to relate how peers matter.[13] The question that remains is how peer attachments relate to four dimensions of offending when considering delinquent and non-delinquent peer-group relationships.

Relying on friends, identifying with friends, and wanting to stick by them are the measures that produced the factor referred to as "friend attachment." Attachment to friends is further related to the extent that delinquent friends matter. Having positive friends refers to having friends who are rarely in trouble, are not picked up by the police, and are frequently involved in extra-curricular school activities. The willingness to talk to friends about problems they might have in regards to drugs and sex is another peer-setting relational measure. Last but not least, there is the absolute number of friends inside and outside of school that can be expected to make a difference. I suggest that the larger an adolescent's group of friends, the less frequent are his or her acts of offending as measured by its various dimensions.

As indicated in Figure 7.6, the direct and all the indirect effects indicate that friends matter. The largest effect is having a non-delinquent peer group—that is, positive friends. For indexed delinquency and substance use, the standardized effect parameters are -.59 and -.74 respectively. Cheating and emotional troubles are equally significant, although the standardized coefficients are substantially less, -.26 and -.33. The direct effects of peer attachments matter for substance use and emotional difficulties, but not in the expected direction. That is, those youth who are more emotionally dependent on their friends are more likely to report substance abuse and emotional troubles, .29 and .16. For substance abuse this would support the notion that the use of alcohol and drugs has a social bonding effect.[14] A .16 direct effect for peer attachment on emotional difficulties would initially seem to make less sense.

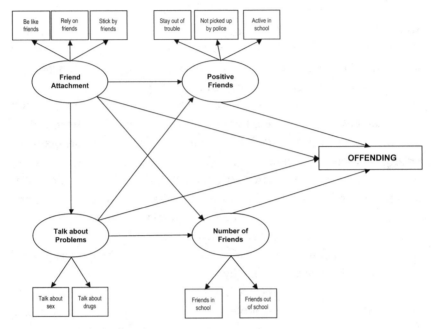

Figure 7.6. Peer relationships

However, the emotional attachments of adolescents may place them in relationships that may at various times be more or less troubling. A better indicator may be the number of friends; those youth who reported fewer friends expressed significantly more thoughts of and attempts at running away and suicide, but the number of friends youth reported was not significantly related to delinquency.

Unlike in the previously presented models, gender appears to be related to the influence of peers on dimensions of delinquency. The effect of positive friends was significantly larger for boys than it was for girls. For emotional troubles, number of friends made a significant difference for girls but not for boys. Also significant is that girls had fewer delinquent friends than boys.

The effects of peers were further examined based on subcultural affiliations. When we asked adolescents to indicate which groups they identified with—namely, burnout, hood, punk, rebel, head-banger, and pot-head, the self-identified group of pot-head had the highest rate of delinquency, substance use, cheating, and emotional deviance.

Community

The resources of an affluent suburb as embodied in the concept of a safe city include more than just good schools and good housing. Although some of the interviewed adolescents reported significant discontents about their community, others reported that Amherst was a good place to be raised. We asked youth specifically about how well they liked living in Amherst, and how they felt about the town's programs and opportunities. We also calculated their participation in youth programs as well as surveyed recreational programs. Last but not least, we wanted a sense of how willing they were to talk to professionals in Amherst. Recall that for youth to make it in a relationally modern world they must *trust* more than just their family members. They require a thin layer of trust to participate in all sorts of programs, including those that would enable troubled adolescents to obtain available assistance.

As Figure 7.7 illustrates, community relationships are important in connection to delinquency. But the results are mixed. For delinquency offenses, participation in programs and recreational activities has significant effects. Participation in programs reduced the rate of delinquency by .12, while involvement in recreational activities increased it by .08. Upon closer examination, the type of recreational programs mattered. I found that for both delinquency and substance abuse, there was a positive sports team effect for boys; that is, the more team sports, the higher the rate of delinquency. This was not the case for girls who reported participating in figure-skating competitions, as opposed to the more competitive team sports that would become subsequently more available to girls. Still, program participation in activities like those offered by youth centers reduced the incidence of delinquency independent of any other effects.

The effects of youth board programs and town recreational programs as well as willingness to talk to officials were not significant for other dimensions of delinquency. No community factors could account for cheating. Substance use and emotional deviance were significant for community attachments. Drug and alcohol use suggests that community matters; the reports of discontent about living in Amherst—that there is little to do and that suburbia is a boring place—expressed a lack of community attachments.

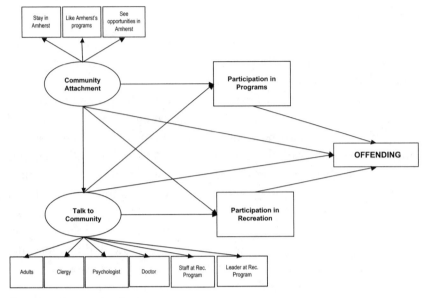

Figure 7.7. Community attachment

We also looked at the religiosity of Amherst youth. Recall the personal interview with Karen and how she related the ways that her religious education sheltered her from delinquent activity. The questions that we asked about religiosity covered only 1987 survey data and were limited in that we asked only about index delinquency and substance use. Religious attendance as previously mentioned is quite prevalent in Amherst. Our religious attachment measure asked how the youth's faith guided their behavior and helped them to confront their problems. Questions of attendance and participation in religious programs were included as well as willingness to talk to clergy about problems. As expected, religious beliefs were significantly related to indexed delinquency and substance use; that is, the higher the levels of expressed religious beliefs, the lower the levels of indexed delinquency and substance use. Willingness to talk to clergy about problems was also significantly associated with delinquency, but in the direction that the more willing to talk corresponded with the more delinquency. This may reflect the need that higher offending youth have to discuss their problems.

One indication of the impact of community that is not reflected in Figure 7.7 is the influence of social science on individual attitudes and beliefs.[15] Critical to the concept of relational modernity is the on-going impact of information on such topics as the proper way to parent or to educate. A theory of relational modernity emphasizes that behavior can be influenced by the on-going events in everyday life. In 1987, we publicly presented the results of our survey. The Amherst Youth Board in conjunction with each of Amherst three school districts developed a campaign to reduce the incidence of alcohol use among high-school youth. The campaign was intended to make parents, youth, and officials more aware of the prevalence of alcohol use among Amherst youth. It was also used as a basis for community discussion. In addition, articles were presented in the local papers, further heightening town-wide awareness about the problem of alcohol abuse.

According to exactly the same methodological procedures and precise set of questions, alcohol use had declined sharply by 1990; in 1987, 28 percent of youth reported they were not drunk or high on alcohol within the last year compared to 1990 survey data which shows the proportion of abstaining from getting drunk increased to 41 percent. Moreover, the drop in alcohol use was specific to the population targeted by alcohol prevention programs—namely, youth who say they drank every week. In 1987, 22 percent of the youth population reported that they got drunk or high every week. In 1990, the percent reporting weekly drinking was cut in half to 11 percent. However, there was no decline in the proportion who reported drinking once every other month or less than twice a year; these occasional drinkers constituted about 31 percent of the population in both 1987 and 1990.

Table 7.6. Percentage of Amherst Youth Reporting Having Been Drunk on Alcohol in 1987 and 1990

	1987	1990
Never	27.9%	40.7%
Once or twice	21.1%	21.9%
Once every other month	9.5%	9.5%
Once a month	18.9%	16.4%
Every week	21.9%	11.2%
Nearly every day	0.7%	0.3%

Social-Psychological Anomie

I now turn to the anomic sense of feeling socially and psychologically lost. My indicators of anomie are based on responses to the following: "there is nothing to do," "feeling useless and unneeded," "hopeless about the future," "rarely thinking of the future," and "to get ahead you have to do bad things." Responses to these prompts provided a good fit for the offending dimensions. The direct effect of this anomie measure of adolescent feelings is significant for delinquency (.24), cheating (.16), and emotional deviance (.58). Not surprisingly, the largest direct effect is between anomie as a predictor of emotional deviance. In a cross-sectional snapshot, the prompts would seem too closely tied to the offense; the large effect size may be partially attributed to several prompts that are indicative of depression (feeling useless and unneeded; and hopeless about the future).

Gender is significant in its influence on the relationship between the anomic dimension and delinquency as well as emotional deviance. Anomie was a better predictor of delinquency for boys, and it was more highly correlated with emotional trouble for girls.

The Follow-Up: Amherst Youth as Young Adults

In 2000, we conducted 340 phone and mail surveys of parents about their children who were interviewed in the 1987 and 1990 surveys, including 250 parents from the 1990 survey. The age range of adult children at the time was between twenty-four and thirty-two. In total, the youth of America's safest city reproduced the social and economic capital of their parents. They were largely enabled by all that modernity has to offer them in the shape of good schools, safe neighborhoods, and lots of recreational activities. Delinquency was controlled. Moreover, the low rate of serious and frequent delinquency correlates with relatively high rates of achievement of educational and occupational status.

Nearly one-third of parents reported that their adult child had achieved a graduate degree; only 12 percent said their adult child did not complete a college degree. Current employment rates were relatively high, with 87 percent indicating full-time employment. Similarly, 86 percent said their adult children were self-supporting. Of those employed, 67 percent were in professional or managerial positions. In terms of living circumstance, 85 percent were still single. Only 37 percent still lived in the greater Buffalo area. The rest moved out of town, again reproducing a condition of modernity that I have previously identified—the willingness to move, particularly for educational and occupational pursuits.

We asked parents not only about their adult child's economic and occupational status but also about how they felt their child was doing emotionally. Only a small proportion indicated any problems; 8 percent said that they were struggling emotionally, and 3 percent said their adult child had problems with substances. The majority of parents (68 percent) felt they had a close relationship with their adult child. We also asked if they would assist their adult child who needed money, and 95 percent said they would.

I next examined the impact of dimensions of offending in adolescence on adult status attainment. Status attainment is measured by parental reports of their child's occupational and educational position. I found no effect of delinquency, substance use, cheating, and emotional troubles on subsequent educational and occupational attainment. It seems that Amherst youth were mainly able to mature into adulthood and reproduce the largely middle-class lives of their parents. Of course, as I moved into the follow-up samples, the data became more selective. The parents who cared to respond to our survey may have been more willing than those whose children were more deeply troubled.

Affluence and Offending

It is not clear if affluence leads to more or less delinquency. Hagan and associates found that those youth who resided in households where parents were in professional positions of occupational authority were more delinquent than those who lacked occupational authority as reflected in their employee status.[16] An assessed housing value is an archival indicator of wealth and income. I assume that people live in houses and subdivision neighborhoods that they can afford. The higher priced neighborhoods of Amherst were not significantly correlated with any of the delinquency measures. There were no neighborhood effects when I look at the data in the aggregate. When I considered several measures of affluence, they were all highly correlated with one another. However, indicators of social class were not correlated with any of the substance abuse, emotional, or cheating dimensions of offending. Nonetheless, there was a statistically significant inverse relationship between assessed housing value and frequency of delinquency (–.11); that is, those youth who lived in higher priced homes with families who could presumably afford them reported more delinquencies than those who resided in lower priced homes.

When I mapped neighborhoods by rate of self-reported offending, subdivisions at the lower assessed end of housing tracts tended to have higher rates of self-reported index delinquency. Only two northwest neighborhoods have low average rates of property values and relatively high rates of delinquency. These are also sections of Amherst that border on a less affluent suburban town where community and recreational programs are not as accessible. Youth who resided in the more expensive subdivisions, however, were just as likely to be delinquent, use drugs, cheat, and have emotional difficulties as those in less expensive subdivisions. I could not detect any observable difference in the frequency of substance use, emotional troubles, and cheating based on subdivision housing.

Official Arrests

Although a considerable number of Amherst youth reported having committed an act of delinquency, few youth were arrested and adjudicated for their delinquency. According to the official court data for 1990, 375 were adjudicated delinquent in juvenile court. Based on the proportion of self-reported delinquency for the previous year (.64) and a youth population of 4,738 persons aged eighteen and younger, I estimate that the possible number of official arrests could have been 3,032. Moreover, based on the youth surveyed self-reports, 22 percent indicated that they were at some point picked up or stopped by the police for their offense. Yet only 10 percent of those stopped indicated that they were adjudicated (47 youth). When this proportion of surveyed youth is projected onto the total population of Amherst youth, the estimated total of 349 adjudicated delinquent is remarkably close to the actual number of the 375 officially recorded delinquent youth. The lower number of surveyed adjudicated delinquent youth may reflect the possibility that these youth were less likely to consent to the surveys, thereby suggesting that the proportion delinquent may be even higher than the self-reported amount.

The risks of Amherst's adolescents facing arrest were relatively low compared to, say, those of Philadelphia youth, 32 percent of whom experienced a recorded police contact by their eighteenth birthday, according to one of the first cohort studies.[17] I referred to the higher rates of arrest and lower rates of diversion in the first chapter when citing a government report on diversion in the Buffalo area. A further look at arrest data provided by the Amherst police supports a maximum-tolerance rather than a zero-tolerance view of adolescent offending. The available official police data for 1998 and 2001 tell a familiar story about the incidence of arrest. Figure 7.8 shows that the most common arrest is for shoplifting offenses. Of the 137 arrests in 2001 (the last year in which confidential juvenile data were made available), 40 involved shoplifting. The next most common offenses were burglary, narcotics, and harassment.

Figure 7.9 shows the expected age and arrest curve for 1998 and 2001. The upper end is fifteen because New York considers adolescents

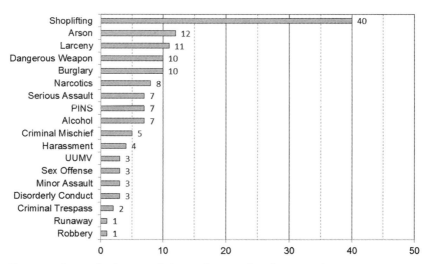

Figure 7.8. Count of police-recorded juvenile arrests by offense type for 2001. *Note:* Juvenile arrests until age sixteen. In New York, eligibility for juvenile court ends at age sixteen.

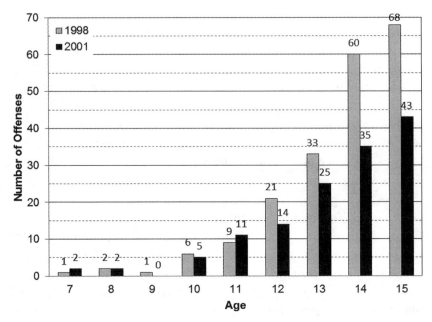

Figure 7.9. Count of arrests by juvenile's age for 1998 and 2001

sixteen and over to be no longer eligible for juvenile justice. However, they can receive youthful offender status until the age of twenty-one. The peak age of arrest is fifteen, confirming the age-crime curve noted in other studies.[18] From age twelve, arrests seem to have declined substantially between 1998 and 2001. This drop in official arrest I attribute to the availability of more diversionary programs, such as the Amherst Youth Court.

Table 7.7 displays the gender of those arrested, confirming the self-report data that shows boys are more involved in offending. But there is also some evidence that during this short period of time an increased proportion of girls are facing arrest. In 1998, boys made up 82 percent of all arrests. That figure declined to 67 percent in 2001. Gender is also related to the arrest charges. In 2001, 60 percent of girls' arrests were for shoplifting compared to 14 percent of boys' arrests. Boys were more often charged with index offenses, such as those involving arson, weapons, burglary, and narcotics.

Race is also related to type of arrest. Black youth make up only 5 percent of the Amherst population yet in 1998 and 2001 represented 15 percent and 28 percent of arrests. A closer look at these data reveal that black boys were more likely to be arrested for shoplifting than white boys. Based on the available data I am unable to tell if the difference in arrest rates by race in Amherst can be attributed to differences in the actual incidence of offending, or variation in how the offenses of black youth (in contrast to white youth) are perceived.

Table 7.8 shows that a little over a third of Amherst youth are referred to juvenile court (family court). Most adolescents are returned to their parents with only a warning. Thus, the point about diversion repeats itself: The youth of a safe city are more likely to be diverted, and many of their potentially frequent and serious delinquencies prevented.

Conclusion

The self-report data confirms the findings of countless studies of self-reported delinquency: There is more offending than is officially recorded, and that the frequency of offending relates to the extent that youth are relationally attached in more than one social setting. Amherst

Table 7.7. Officially Recorded Juvenile Arrests by Gender

	1998	2001	Total
Male	165 (82%)	92 (67%)	257 (76%)
Female	36 (18%)	45 (33%)	81 (24%)
Total arrests	201	137	338

Table 7.8. Dispositions of Juvenile Arrests for 2001 (N = 137)

Disposition	Percentage	Number of arrests
Turned over to parents	43.8%	60
Family court	35.8%	49
Youth court	8.0%	11
Firestarters	6.6%	9
Detention	2.2%	3
Gateway	1.5%	2
School suspension	0.7%	1
Hospitalization	0.7%	1
Turned over to school	0.7%	1
Total	100%	137

remains relatively safe based on official reports about crime despite high rates of self-reported delinquency. Even for those adolescents who are arrested, the chances of ending up in juvenile court are relatively small. The most frequent disposition is for adolescents to be turned over to their parents.

The rate of offending might seem inordinately high given that about 70 percent of youth could have been brought to juvenile court and adjudicated delinquent. But it may not be as high as it could be given the fact that the vast majority of Amherst youth are only occasional delinquents. Their lack of high-offending status indicates that the relational force of modernity largely enables delinquencies to be non-consequential, or part of a learner's permit that goes along with being an adolescent. But this learner's permit is for minor acts of delinquency that are viewed as largely insignificant and worthy of diversion. As I noted, there is a continuum of harm scale that Amherst youth, their parents, and officials operate under to distinguish categories of offending from one another; along this continuum, we find general ambivalence about illicit substance use and a range of status offenses, such as skipping school and cheating in school.

Surveyed youth and their parents acknowledged the benefits of Amherst programs. Youth centers and other programs enabled the kinds of activities that make Amherst a desirable place to reside. Recreational facilities like swimming pools, ice-skating rinks, and numerous ball fields appear to be well supported economically and to provide the quality of life that middle-class residents are willing to support with their local tax dollars. The side benefit is that these activities and programs enable adolescents to transition into more than one social setting.

The multivariate analysis of delinquencies revealed that relational contexts matter. Parenting relationships are more relevant for explaining emotional troubles than they are for delinquency, though both their direct and indirect effects are significant. The roles of school, peers, and the community in the lives of adolescents further predict offending. The relational is consistently significant in substance use and emotional deviance, but less so for offenses that involve common delinquencies and cheating.

Another important conclusion is that adolescent delinquency appeared to have no significant effect on subsequent adult status attainment. There was no significant difference between delinquents and non-delinquents based on the larger set of survey data in educational and occupational pursuits. This partially confirms the qualitative data, which indicates that the offending of Amherst youth did not seriously impede their ability to mature into law abiding adults.

So the police may have the right idea in returning the adolescents they pick up to their parents or to a diversionary youth court. Diversion is alive and well in Amherst as the arrest data illustrates. Despite the high rate of self-reported delinquency, the risk of arrest and referral to juvenile court is quite low. The adolescents of Amherst are fortunate to receive a second and, often, third chance. They are also fortunate to live in an affluent suburb where there are plenty of choices for diversionary programs.

But there is a proportion of youth who do face arrest and adjudication as delinquents or criminals. They may have had one too many chances, or the seriousness of their offenses may have precluded them from any possibility of diversion, or for that matter juvenile justice. If they seriously injured their victims, they may have been punished as if they were adults, and their adolescence would have been subsequently denied. Their safe city would not seem so safe, even if they happen to reside in a relationally modern world.

As proudly displayed on a pool and recreational center gate, Amherst, New York, has been rated as one of America's best communities for young people.

8

Safe Cities and the Struggle to Be Relationally Modern

I began this book by wondering about the safety of city life. I observed that there was more than one type of city to consider in a large metropolitan area. I argued that the suburban city is the latest city to emerge in a globalized information economy. It has become the preferred place to live for most Americans, and the preferred place to create large office parks and university campuses. The suburban city fits a post-industrial economy—one that has less of a need for the centrally located downtown of an earlier era. It exists as a city because of its own government, subdivisions, housing, schools, shopping malls, office parks, high-tech industrial zones, and system of juvenile justice.

The safe city's subdivisions are many. In each of its familial, social, or legal systems, there are opportunities to respond to adolescent offending in a manner that includes rather than excludes. To be relationally attuned to adolescents means to recognize modernity's need for its enabling places. Yet the school, sports field, advanced math club, music and dance classes are more enabling for some than for others. So parents like Terribly Young's were fortunate to live in a safe city where there are lots of diversionary programs. They were also fortunate to have the hard cash to pay for an attorney and the health insurance to pay for their son's therapy. But diversion programs are not always successful, as I pointed out in the case of the Columbine youth raised in an affluent suburb by parents who seemed to really care about their sons' troubling behavior. The risks of serious delinquency and crime cannot be totally eliminated even in the safest of cities. There is more of a struggle to be relationally modern for some than for others.

My definition of safety based on police-recorded crime and *Money Magazine's* designation of Amherst as America's safest city summarizes the well-known point that some areas, neighborhoods, streets, or alleyways are less secure than others. Most people know this, and they act cautiously when they enter certain impoverished city neighborhoods, especially late at night. Many of the impoverished who live in high-crime inner- city neighborhoods would prefer to live elsewhere if they could afford to move. No parent that I know would like to expose their child to the dangerous risks of a high crime neighborhood.

Safety as defined by a city's crime rate cannot be separated from other quality-of-life indicators. My metaphoric use of the term "safe city" is intended to indicate more than just crime rates. Good schools, after-school programs, and a range of recreational facilities make Amherst a good and desirable place. These desired aspects of a city are incorporated into *Money Magazine*'s other lists, such as its most recent 2013 list that placed Amherst among America's top 50 best cities to live.

The fact that most Americans today live in suburbia represents more than just a favorable vote for the housing and services of newly built outer cities. It also reflects an on-going struggle to be modern. Yet government services in the shape of highly ranked schools, youth boards, and recreational programs are far from perfect—there is plenty to complain about, as the personally interviewed youth have detailed. Still these services remain relatively desirable—more so than those available (or not available at all) in impoverished inner-city neighborhoods. Those government services include the willingness to divert youth from a formal system of adjudicating an adolescent as a delinquent. As cited in one government report on racial disparities among incarcerated youth, there is more diversion in Buffalo's suburbs than in its inner city. In this sense, a city's safety means not only a lower likelihood of becoming the victim of a personal or property crime, but also a lower probability of seeing your child adjudicated delinquent.

Safety

But all is not well in Amherst, despite its lower rate of victimization. No city is perfectly safe. The residents of Amherst and other safe cities must face occasional reports of violence perpetrated by others and by their own youth. Soon after *Money Magazine* published its safest city list, Amherst received worldwide attention for the murder of a renowned Buffalo area obstetrician. Dr. Barnett Slepian believed in a woman's right to terminate her pregnancy. On October 23, 1998, James Charles Kopp entered the thickly wooded area behind Slepian's home. Kopp hid behind a large tree and aimed his rifle when Slepian became visible in the kitchen window of his large Tudor-style home. Slepian had just returned from Friday night religious services. He was in the midst of preparing with his wife and three children their traditional Shabbat night dinner when Kopp fired the fatal shot that would abruptly end Slepian's life. Offender and victim were far apart in their personal views toward abortion, and how they viewed their place in the modern-day world. Kopp's extreme fundamentalist beliefs led him into the pre-modern woods of a time that had long past. Even those who opposed abortion distanced themselves from his act of violence, and for that matter the kind of terrorism that continues to plague the world, reminding everyone that no place can be completely safe.

Like all metaphors, the term "safe city" exaggerates the true level of safety. Safe-city residents are well aware of suburban youth crime; they know of sensational cases of violence, such as when a neighbor's kid is charged with murder. The point should be repeated: Only relative safety in relation to other places and times produces the programs and risk assessments that I have described as distinctly modern. These risk-assessment lists are not just generated by popular consumer magazines, but also by an army of social scientists who are in the business of predicting delinquency. Parents, teachers, youth service professionals, police and intake officers, prosecutors, and judges of all kinds are relying on these risk-assessment scales. They contribute to a wealth of techniques designed to prevent youth from becoming high-offending delinquents.

At times the perceived risk becomes too large, and the safe city responds with more exclusionary than inclusionary policies. For example, on June 10, 1999, the principle of one Amherst's middle schools, Charles G. Kramir, sent an official letter to parents stating that a handgun was discovered in a student's personal locker. The letter stated that the "[school] district and the Amherst Police Department are taking appropriate legal action." The letter indicated that students were informed and that counselors were on the scene to provide psychological assistance. In a post-Columbine era, Principle Kramir seemed to have acted appropriately; his staff identified the student and inspected his personal locker and that of others as well. The arrested youth was a young adolescent who had not yet entered high school. In the wake of public concern about school violence, school officials acted in his case and in the cases of other threatening acts of school violence in a more guarded manner. A kind of high security school alert system has emerged—one that heightens public awareness of the risks of serious violence.

In an earlier industrial era of modernity, I doubt if all the parents of Heim Middle School students would have been notified. A confidential system of juvenile justice would have taken over, involving a less anxiety-provoking response—one that would not be so quick to announce the risk of serious violence by a middle-school youth. This was the original intent of the creators of a juvenile court—to save the youth from the drama and the potential stigma of a criminal label.

Yet in the risk-assessing world of modernity, the better schools, housing, and greener pastures of suburban living are supposed to prevent serious delinquencies—and that is, indeed, the case. Most adolescents have few major difficulties in navigating their familial conflicts, educational difficulties, peer relationships, and eventual occupational pursuits. They are able to adjust their expectations as needed. Although nearly all the youth surveyed indicated personal difficulties, discontent, and some sort of trouble, very few of them became deep-end, high-offending delinquents. I attribute their low rate of offending to the relational support they received, not just from their parents but from a range of others. The youth who initially had considerable difficulties confronting their troubles were overwhelmed by the demands of their parents, schools, and status-conscious peers. These were the mentioned Lukes, Bills, and Nancys, and from another safe city, the Terribly Youngs.

Sensational rare acts of suburban violence required me to refer to the stories of non-Amherst youth as exemplified in the case of David O, suburban school shooters, and suburban school jocks who raped. Like most surveys of high-school youth, the Amherst surveys missed those who were incarcerated or away in boarding or therapeutic schools. A small proportion of those randomly selected to participate were unwilling to give their active consent. Terribly Young and his parents might have been one of those selected subjects who would refuse consent, perhaps because they felt too anxious about his probation to participate in a study that promised confidentiality but not anonymity.

Despite the fact that I may have missed a small segment of a high-offending adolescents, a considerable number of offenses were uncovered. The Amherst youth surveys revealed that 71 percent of Amherst youth could have been adjudicated delinquent based on their self-reported acts of theft, property damage, and assault. An even larger population indicated they had used drugs or had emotional troubles serious enough to think about killing themselves or running away. When examining all the types of delinquencies mentioned in the previous chapter, including substance abuse, cheating, and emotional troubles, the fact emerges that 97 percent of Amherst youth reported an act that could have landed them in the juvenile justice system, mental health system, or in school detention. As data in the previous chapter show, the vast majority of adolescents have at some point in their young lives committed an act of delinquency or crime in violation of stated legal rules.

But as the data further led me to suggest, Amherst youth were able to avoid serious and frequent offending because they were enabled by a whole host of adults acting in their positional roles. Parents, teachers, coaches, and other youth professionals provided Amherst youth with the capacities to reflect and to graduate into adulthood with few official arrests. But empathy is not evenly distributed. I think Christine was more likely to receive her share of empathy from her guidance counselor than Luke.

At times more than a guidance counselor or parent is required. Of course, it is easier to state after the fact that David O should have been removed from his abusive home environment. He needed other adults to enter into his life to protect him from the terrible thoughts that were entering his mind in response to a horrendous home life. Interventions are required to remove a segment of adolescents from a suburban roadway that is filled with an unusual number of dangerous signs. For example, Luke's residential drug rehabilitation program removed him from a group of friends who were contributing to his addictions. His parents most likely began to recognize his deep-seated troubles and responded accordingly. In turn, he could appreciate his parents' efforts and came to terms with his earlier feelings of rejection. The fact that he recognized those feelings in the personal interview situation suggests that Luke was writing his own narrative and becoming the kind of adult he would like to be thanks to the caring efforts of others in his life.

Relational Modernity

Not everyone can afford to live in a safe city. It takes a decent income to purchase a house in an affluent suburb and to maintain more than one car to commute reliably about town. Those who can afford safe suburban cities most often have high-paying jobs that require a college degree. During their higher educational pursuits, parents might have encountered a social science course or two, sensitizing them to the scholarly literature on adolescence, parenting, and the reasons for delinquency.[1] They have also been exposed to expert knowledge as it may be rather simply reproduced in newspapers, web sites, parenting magazines, and popular books, which provide advice on subjects that many parents care about, such as how best to talk to your kids about drugs.

But one response to all this expertise might be that it is commonsensical and unnecessary. Yet there is little that remains common in a modern-day world. Common sense is more an attribute of pre-modern times when there were no websites, no foundations, no journals on delinquency and juvenile justice, and surely no adolescence to be defined. The common sense among middle- and upper-class families is generated by the fact that they are socially embedded in a style of life that enables them to work and invest physically and emotionally in a way that is common to the times. It has become commonsensically modern to emphasize inclusion instead of exclusion, talking instead of hitting, and maximum tolerance instead of zero tolerance.

The forms of relational modernity advocated in a safe city are grounded in well-funded schools, extra-curricular activities, and a wealth of youth-oriented programs. In advocating for the good in various educational and recreational programs, parents recognize that they cannot be expected to raise their children on their own. They need the assistance of a society that has in place a host of professionals, including therapists usually paid for through their employers' health insurance. The middle class who occupy safe cities rely on trusted adults to say to their child: "*Yes, I know adolescence can be awfully difficult. The road toward adulthood can be difficult. Your teenage years can become overly complex. But we are here to assist you as you develop your own law-abiding pathway toward adulthood.*" In the lives of adolescents, not only are the adults active agents in a relationally modern world, but also their friends are there to assist them in confronting their troubles.

Of course, some difficulties are deep, and the resources of the youth, their parents, friends, and schools may be limited. They may be unable to prevent personal troubles from turning into serious delinquencies, to keep an adolescent's learning disabilities and other mental disorders from becoming overwhelming. At any point in the life of an adolescent, personal difficulties can be transformed into deep-seated discontents. The tolerant parent may adopt a more authoritarian style; school and police officials have warned the adolescent one too many times; exclusion rather than inclusion becomes the preferred response. The point at which the adults in a safe city invoke exclusionary forms of punishment cannot be easily identified. I have suggested that the severity of the offense is one indicator. Yet a few youth reported being punished physically for what many would consider minor offenses. At various times, the positional intervention of youth service professionals is not enough to make a difference. Talk therapy, medication, and a range of therapeutic programs may have little or no impact. Parents need to make a living and may become overwhelmed by their own personal difficulties. A safe city did not prevent David O from committing his brutal act of violence. A good community may not be good enough to make up for parental neglect.

If the concept of relational modernity seems overly abstract, it is because the post-industrial city is not an easily identifiable city. There is no village or street-corner life. As I have indicated, the street-corner metaphor refers to a simpler and more physically visible life. Suburbia's shopping malls may be the place to see others, but again it is more from the distance. People generally go to shopping malls to shop—not to congregate and discuss the day's troubling events. No longer is the composition of neighborhood subdivisions readily identifiable by ethnicity. Instead, income determines who can afford to live in a particular subdivision. Moreover, modernity is fast-moving, virtual in its states of transition. The Relos are transitioning from one suburban neighborhood to the next, and they are encouraging their kids to move as well—first to college and then to desirable occupations that can take them far.

The relational in modernity I have suggested takes place in a multitude of social settings. High on my list is the familial. Parents are supposed to provide the first line of defense. They should provide the love believed to be critical to normal childhood development. My analysis of survey data and personal interviews suggests that indicators of trust, empathy, and identity accounted for a significant proportion of the variation in offending. Those youth who said they were less likely to trust and empathetically identify with their parents, teachers, and others generally had higher rates of delinquency, alcohol/drug use, and emotional troubles. School, community, and peer-group relational measures were significant, and indirectly impacted the more physical, supervisory measures of control. Relational attachments to school were more important than actual grades in accounting for delinquency, substance use, and emotional troubles. As expected, peers were important, but not in a straightforward direction. Although peers provided the setting for frequent substance use, friends reduced the incidence of emotional troubles. Those youth who reported few friends indicated higher rates of thoughts of and attempts at running away or suicide. Community attachments and involvements were equally significant predictors.

The picture pieced together from the survey data and personal interviews reveals how the familial, educational, peer-group settings of adolescents matter. They matter because they are the required places of a modern-day society. The school is important because students must attend school—whether they want to or not. Peer groups are important because adolescents must be isolated with other youth in age-graded classrooms for extended periods of time. Recreational pursuits and community programs are important because parents cannot always be around for their kids when they are away at work. Juvenile justice and its diversionary programs are important because adolescence has extended the age of criminal responsibility. And parents are important because they are being told to play less of an authoritarian role and more of an authoritative one. All that is deemed important to the prevention of delinquency may be viewed as a consequence of modernity.

The contemporary parenting literature may be less clear than the words I recently heard from a close friend's eulogy to his father. At the funeral, he said:

> *The relationship between a son and a father can often be quite complicated. Not so, for my brothers and me. We were blessed to have a rather simple, yet powerful and loving, relationship with our dad. He was a great teacher and role model. There was never a time that we could not talk to him or that he would not offer advice (asked for or not). He always made time to share his insight, help with homework and play with his sons. Whether it was softball games or football, my brothers and I have great memories of classic touch football games mostly played in the street in front of our house. He would tell anyone who would listen how he taught me to swim. He told how he took me to the Y, grabbed me by the ankles, and tossed me into the deep end of the pool. My rejoinder which I routinely uttered when he told this story was I just wish there was water in the pool.*

My friend referred to his father as a wonderful role model—one who supported each of his children's unique educational and professional pursuits. He was idealized as a great teacher. He was not just a pal to his kids, but a father who approached his children through his own authoritative style of parenting. He was self-educated and had the good sense to parent in a way that was different from his own old-world father (my friend's grandfather). That authoritarian, distant parenting style was rejected in favor of a more relational one, which provided each of his children the opportunities to navigate society and its many settings—even if it meant learning how to swim in the deep end of the pool.

Parental modernity continues to evolve. But parents (even great ones) are limited in their capacities to act on their children's difficulties, discontents, and subsequent troubles. They can fail to recognize their child's needs and in the process risk more serious troubles. The struggle to be relationally modern must be considered in the context of modernity's many expectations. The demands on youth in all cities are substantial—more so today than in earlier times, as I have repeatedly suggested. Those demands were summarized in terms of the adolescent's need to grasp societal complexity, autonomy, and rationality.

Complexity

Initially *Money Magazine*'s safest city list made little sense to me. How can rates of crime for sparsely and densely populated cities be comparable? Central cities contain large pockets of impoverished neighborhoods, and their police recorded violent and property crime rates had to be higher. Similarly, how could a popular consumer magazine refer to a suburb like Amherst as a city? The definition of a city as applied to suburban locales means more than just a division between inner and outer cities: It means that the city has become dispersed into a larger metropolitan region of cities. In contrast to more industrial times, the city has become a less identifiable and visible place; it has lost its center, town square, and names that uniquely identify its location. To repeat my initial example: The State University of New York at Buffalo is no longer in the city of Buffalo; its main campus is now in America's safest city. Like many other universities, it can be just about any place. This kind of suburban, post-industrial relocation of place can be more disorienting for some than for others.

For the many youth who can easily adapt to the globalized, digital information economy of a post-industrial modernity the risk of delinquencies would seem minimal. They are performing well enough and are finding the kind of jobs that will allow them to eventually move into their own suburban city. A small segment of youth will become celebrated for becoming teen-age dot com millionaires, such as seventeen-year-old Nick D'Aloisio whose news-reading app was purchased by Yahoo in a multimillion dollar deal. Nick lives in London and was raised in an era of personal computers and smart phones. Nick's grandparents may have read about the lives of the self-made rich, and how they arrived at their wealth after many years working a business into a thriving success. Even the celebrated sports figures and musicians of today are less likely to spend time working the minor leagues or music clubs. Nick's success and fame could be attributed to his good luck, intelligence, and a kind of modernity that allows young adolescents to develop their own complex "automatic summarization algorithm."[2]

Nick's news-reading app is globally produced. There is little that is local about his investors who as far away as China believed in his app. It hardly matters whether Nick was raised in an affluent suburb or in the inner city of London. Nick's sense of place became his computer, Internet connection, and smart phone. He could have been in any city and still could have produced his news reading app. Although Nick might have been one of those youth who could easily learn on his own, he most likely had a teacher he could trust and extra-curricular class time to pursue his own interest, the opportunity that Bill Gates had when he switched to his private school where he was introduced to the personal computer.

There is a price to be paid to the worldwide summary news that Nick's app will be able to provide. Like Nick's wealth, it instantaneously produces abbreviated news stories. They are short and based on key worded terms. Not unlike *Money Magazine*'s list, Nick's app does not produce in-depth analysis. In telling the abbreviated story of Nick, I can imagine that there is little in the way of a street-corner crowd that he had to navigate. Nick is now in a club of fellow high-tech millionaires who communicate from the distance. Obviously, Nick with no college education could successfully adapt to the new digital economy. He trusted his investors, and then they trusted him, positionally again from the distance.

Few are as fortunate as Nick. A larger segment of youth has considerable trouble fitting into a post-industrial world; they may suffer from learning disabilities or other mental disorders. They may not be able to program no matter how hard they try. Their familial and peer-group relationships have become difficult, because of a more demanding and competitive world that requires more from its adolescents. The adolescents of today's cities are expected to grasp all sorts of complex algorithms, and they must do so by relying less on a locally defined place.

So like cities themselves, there is an on-going narrative to adolescents as they transition into modern-day adulthood. Their problems of adjustments must constantly be readjusted to fit into one newly derived social setting after another. As cities are transformed so are its youth. The inner cities of the twenty-first century are not the same as those of the twentieth century. The New York City of my youth is quite different from today. The rougher sections of Manhattan have become gentrified; its low income residents relocated to the city's outer boroughs or less affluent suburbs. My father's shop near the corner of Lenox Avenue and 125th Street in Harlem has been transformed into a Starbucks. The inner-city neighborhood that William Foote Whyte observed in Boston's North End is no longer a slum. Today expensive Italian restaurants and upscale bars attract tourists from all over the world who consider the North End a wonderfully safe place to visit.

Boston, New York City, San Francisco and other top ranked cities are uniquely situated cities, because its residents no longer depend on the low-tech industries that defined its early twentieth century past. These cities have been fortunate to have the money and human capital to adapt to the complexities of their post-industrial economies. Other cities have not been as fortunate (cities like Buffalo, Cleveland, or Worcester just to name a few). They have become smaller cities, reduced in size, losing much of their working and middle-class populations to their surrounding high-tech suburbs. No one is planning to bring back their once magnificent downtown department stores, and the vast majority of middle-class families are not about to give up their three- or four-bedroom house or suburban condo to return to the neighborhoods of their grandparents, at least while the kids are still in school. The numbers indicating this post-industrial transformation, from small town to large suburban city, are significant and worth repeating: Amherst's population rose rapidly from 33,744 in 1950 to 127,748 in 2010, while Buffalo's dropped from 580,132 to 292,648 during this same period. For those who remain in central cities like Buffalo, unemployment, poverty, and school drop-out rates increased along with their city's rate of crime.

The safe city is a metaphor for a city that fits a globalized, high-tech economy. A segment of youth has considerable trouble grasping its complexities; they express their discontents with words like Amherst is too "white-collar" or too "boring." They see their schools, peers, and parents as too competitive, too status conscious, and too distant from their own local sense of community. While they are able to recognize adult values, as in their near unanimous recognition of the importance of school, their ability to perform well in school varies substantially. Their sense of self is not only influenced by their school grades. Recall Tom's struggles with his parents and how they disproved of his decision to pursue a career in theater. Other youth struggled in their familial, educational, or peer group settings. They were able to express their discontents, such as not being able to attend an out-of-the state college because of the conflicting messages they received.

Complicating the picture of Amherst adolescents further is parental modernity. Most of the interviewed adolescents and their parents seemed to benefit from an authoritative style of parenting. However, this was not always the case, even in professional households. Recall Rena's interview relating that her father who worked as a psychiatrist had hit her repeatedly. She attributed his authoritarian style of parenting to traditional India dictums. Others related how their parents were too permissive, or did not provide enough structure to perform well in school. For another segment of adolescents, parents provided considerable support for the troubles that their adolescents faced; such as, in the case of Patty who told how her teacher touched her in a sexually inappropriate way. Still serious familial troubles were revealed in the case of Kim who related how her father was accused of having sexually abused her sister. Kim, like Tom, was able to survive her familial troubles through her school's theater program.

So too are peer-group relationships increasingly complex. The division between college and corner boys does not exist in Amherst; there are more divisions than those that have been used to describe inner-city youth. There is no simple divide between street and decent families. These are not terms that are used within the boundaries of an affluent suburb. Instead, there are parenting, teaching, coaching, and adolescent styles. There are preferences for certain kinds of music, dress, tattoos, and piercings as ways of uniquely identifying with more than one set of peers. This unique way of belonging falls under the general societal expectation for autonomy.

Autonomy

More so today than in earlier times, there is an expectation that adolescents will develop the capacities to think on their own. Autonomy is a neglected topic in a criminological literature that emphasizes conformity to familial, educational, and societal rules. The delinquent as an artist, innovator, and creator was imagined in a few scholarly renditions, such as in David Matza's book on *Becoming Deviant*.[3] The appreciative mode of thinking about delinquency would seem to have less credence in homogenous, upper-middle-class, white suburbs (like Amherst). Yet the suburban city developed its own set of diversities, wherein a considerable proportion of its population has room to be on its own through choices that only money can provide.

Relo families exemplify only one subdivision within a larger set of suburban subdivisions. They express their choice of places to live and occupations to pursue, albeit through their move from one affluent suburb to the next. They have opportunities to pursue their own suburban roadways as they are disconnected from extended family relationships. In the larger spaces of suburbia, adolescents must grasp the fact that the safe city is a function of people's willingness to move for their educational and occupational pursuits. Few are encouraged to stay local even if they attend local universities or colleges. Their houses, schools, and recreational activities are transportable. Autonomy is expressed through an adolescent's ability to manage despite these transitions. To do otherwise would produce a street-corner mentality that has long passed— one that is contrary to the demands of a larger globalized world.

Not all middle-class families and their youth are able or willing to move beyond their local neighborhoods. They have difficulty buying into globalization; they miss their earlier rural-village life, ethnic enclaves, and past street-corner neighborhoods. Some youth may require more structure, more face-to-face contact, and more personal rather than positional relationships. They need structure, routine, and the security of a tightly knit place. Like Whyte's street-corner boys, they are less prepared to buy into complex educational or occupational pursuits.

The double-edged sword of modernity is that all this movement has positive and negative effects. As noted, the freedom to move negatively impacted inner-city life. White middle-class flight from the inner city left the inner city more segregated. Suburban school districts could avoid the federal court-ordered desegregation plans that affected cities like Buffalo because of their autonomous, local governmental structures. As previously mentioned, the 1974 U.S. Supreme Court Milliken decision allowed suburban school districts to remain their own entities. They could be viewed as private schools, having a select population of students whose parents could afford the higher school property tax. Suburban school districts could both avoid the city and demands for integration and provide youth with their own extra services and extracurricular activities. Youth could be shaped by middle-class desires without having to confront less fortunate families.

The choice of school programs and extra-curricular activities generates opportunities for autonomy. As I have indicated, individual choice is enhanced through a spectrum of safe-city recreational and youth board programs. For-profit and not-for-profit organizations cater to a dense population of middle- and upper-class families who can afford their services. Dance studios, music schools and lessons, private sports clubs, and tutoring centers provide a choice of dance styles, musical instruments, athletic activities, and extra help tailored to a variety of learning styles. Thanks to their affluent parents, the adolescents of a safe city have choices and more ways of expressing their autonomy in a legitimate, law-abiding manner.

For a segment of surveyed Amherst youth, the choices of activities are more than enough to avoid frequent delinquencies. Recall Christine who was enrolled in math club and was taking music lessons as well. The same could be said about other youth who were involved in theater or sports. They could find their niche within a range of available activities that worked to enhance their law-abiding sense of self. But not every youth has the capacity to be part of a math club or can play the piano. Similarly, not every youth is coordinated enough to feel good about his or her performance on the playing field. In other words, a true appreciation of autonomy requires recognition of individual capacities. Yet limited capacities to meet the high standards of an extra-curricular club or a team sport often mean classifying adolescents as disabled, because of their inability to meet the expectations of a highly competitive society.[4]

In a post-industrial age of modernity, a focus on the self can lead to rethinking common definitions of success. It can lead to questioning middle-class life and parental expectations for highly valued educational and occupational pursuits. Recall Tom's resistance to his parents' demands. In turn, parents eventually must recognize their youths' desires and capacities—that is, exercise a form of recognition that can take into account the adolescent's right to be different. This kind of recognition of human difference is incorporated in my use of the term "parental modernity." It places parents in a double bind: They wish to appreciate their child's difference and ability to decide their appropriate course of action, but at the same time parents recognize the necessity for their adolescent to compete successfully. Amherst youth recognize this double bind, too; it is expressed in their discontents.

But autonomy can lead a segment of adolescents to become lost socially and psychologically. When parents tell their troubled adolescents they must work out their own difficulties and face the consequences of their troubling behaviors, they are expressing a kind of social Darwinist approach to their kids' serious, deep-end troubles, such as drug addiction.[5] They are emphasizing their adolescent's need to take responsibility—a kind of responsibility that can lead them to become even more lost in the social and physical spaces of suburbia. The downside to the larger physical spaces of suburbia is that there are fewer adults watching over each other's kids. As previously mentioned, the Glen Ridge Jocks who raped were on their own in their suburban basement when they attacked their mentally handicapped victim. David O could commit his offense in a heavily wooded area that adjoined his house and that of his victim's. These offenses could have also occurred in densely packed cities, as in the famous case of Kitty Genovese who was brutally murdered in a New York City neighborhood where her screams for help were allegedly ignored. The blasé attitude attributed to the autonomous behavior of city residents in an industrial era persists in suburbia. Too few adults are in positions of authority to assist the deeply troubled youth—the less desirable ones whose difficulties seem too overwhelming.

Rationalities

Why would today's adolescents desire to return to a time when they were hanging out on their local street corners or confined to their village squares? Why would they wish to reside in an impoverished, congested inner-city neighborhood when they could have their own room, computer, Internet connection, and smart phone? All these devices are part of a long list of technological advances that have enabled modernity's youth to be in more than one place. Today's affluent youth can choose among numerous possibilities. They can advocate for their own kind of music, styles of dress, and sexual orientation. Many are able to move on a suburban roadway filled with a range of possible directions that previously did not exist.

But my imaginary suburban roadway can be quite rocky for some youth. Most adolescents perform well enough. They perform well enough in school and on the athletic field. Most are not high performers like Christine, who graduated from an Ivy League college and was on her way to medical school. Their suburbanized pathways may be just good enough for them to find the kind of full-time work that will eventually land them in the middle class. Although many adolescents fall into the category of delinquent, they often settle down, managing quite well to avoid the illicit drugs of their younger days. Recall the case of Bill and how in the midst of his college years he decided that he had to reduce his consumption of alcohol and use of drugs. Other youth had difficulties that extended into college; they had trouble and dropped out, and planned to return later once they could find themselves as adults. Some youth had to escape their familial setting. They were enabled by a variety of pursuits, including the arts, even if those pursuits did not involve the high paying jobs that their parents would have preferred. Recall the case of Tom and his decision to become a theater major despite his parents' objections. The youth of Amherst were generally able to become law-abiding adults despite their share of personal difficulties.

Yet modernity's road toward adulthood favors some adolescents more than others. As mentioned, the deep-end youth were not well represented in the presented data; some refused to participate or were away in correctional or mental health facilities. Serious delinquents lacked the trust and empathetic identification that could develop even from a distance—through therapists, school guidance counselors, and other officials. But not all are equally good at changing human behavior; some difficulties are too deep and disturbing. A local parish priest might have sexually abused a youth, as David O revealed. Alternatively, familial, juvenile justice, or mental health systems might not have cared enough to make a difference in their lives, as in the case of Willie Bosket.

There is no shortage of hypotheses to distinguish the advantaged over the disadvantaged in a relationally modern world. Stanley Cohen refers to those who are more inclined to receive the second chance, treatment, or care that can make a difference by the acronym "YARVIS," for "Young," "Attractive," "Rich," "Verbal," "Intelligent," and "Successful."[6] These characteristics are not mutually exclusive of one another; they are meant to convey a certain advantage. Race could be added to the mix. But in largely white middle-class communities, differences emerge. Younger adolescents are more likely to receive a second chance than older adolescents. Those adolescents who look more like a treatment provider's own kids are more likely to find an empathetic response. As the stories of Terribly Young and the Hanover honor students revealed, the rich have options that impoverished youth lack—like the ability to afford a private attorney to navigate the juvenile and criminal justice systems. Just as important is their ability to articulate their intelligence, as William Chambliss observed in describing middle-class delinquents who could explain to the police why that beer bottle happened to be in their hands. Travis Hirschi reminded us that it is not the class of the parent that matters *per se*, but the class of the adolescent.

All the attributes that Cohen views as critical to why treatment providers prefer to treat some more than others could apply to how parents, teachers, and others view the behavior of children from an early age. The division between who is more or less told that they are capable of suburbia's better roadways can begin early in life. Ross Matsueda and Karen Heimer make the point that deviant identities become affixed early in life based on a set of early indicators. They state that the "labeling of children does not occur in a vacuum but reflects objective characteristics of children, like abilities, temperaments, and constitutions." They note that "intelligent, sociable preschoolers tend to have more positive interactions."[7] It is these intelligent and sociable children who have an easier time in a culture that values the bright, attractive, and articulate.

But why are the less intelligent and less sociable unable to have positive interactions? Why would they be condemned so quickly at an early age? To move beyond this street-corner view of youth, adults need to recognize their responsibilities to assist youth in their struggles to fit into the modern-day world. As noted, parents cannot be expected to respond on their own. Extended familial relationships may not be enough. A lot is expected of today's adolescents, especially when compared to all those high performing upper-middle-class youth.

Franklin Zimring's legal scholarship over several decades has repeatedly recognized the need for juvenile justice to be adjusted in the wake of modernity's demands. He writes:

During a period of legal semiautonomy, young persons are progressively given opportunities to make a variety of decisions for themselves, even though it is understood that their relative lack of maturity will lead to a number of errors. This process is justified because trial and error in decision-making constitutes one necessary part of learning adult competencies in any society where the freedom of choosing the path of one's own life is the hallmark of legal adulthood.[8]

Juveniles should be subject to juvenile justice not criminal justice because they lack the maturity to think fully on their own. Although some adults lack this kind of maturity as well, the courts have recognized that adolescents should have their responsibilities mitigated. Other distinguished legal scholars have used the term "youth discount" to suggest why adolescents should not be subject to the same set of punishments that are present for adults.[9] Zimring extends the point when he states why modernity should matter:

The absolute advantage of the modern adolescent over young people in earlier generations is an argument for earlier exercise of some privileges that depend on minimum competence. However on a relative basis, intellectual and social development among today's 18-year-olds is certainly closer to the completed process of adult development in 2005 than was the case in the 1920s or earlier. Young people may have come further, but they also have further to go. The gap that still exists between the equipment for choice possessed by a modern adolescent and what we expect for contemporary adulthood is particularly problematic when we consider those decisions made in adolescence that will have substantial and permanent effect on the life opportunity of young people.[10]

More is indeed expected of adolescents. That is why a substantial proportion of middle- and upper-class families want their kids to stay in school longer. Middle-class youth are discouraged from marrying and working until they have achieved a desired educational and occupational status.

Yet for those adolescents in a safe city, juvenile justice is still there, although the precise form that it takes cannot be easily identified. Recall the cited programs of diversion, the case of Terribly Young, and the context in which Luke eventually could obtain drug rehabilitation. For a large segment of youth, juvenile justice in its more inclusionary form appears to have made a difference. For another segment, it matters little given that they are low-offending youth like Christine or Karen, who reported few personal difficulties. For both good and not-so-good segments of youth, juvenile justice is there in the form of few arrests, a mere warning.

An inclusionary, informal system of juvenile justice has its own set of rationalities that enable knowledgeable parents and their youth. At times, it has redefined illegal acts as problems of mental health. The middle-class parents are enabled by their ability to afford legal assistance, as in the case of Terribly Young and as recommended by the National Institue of Health website cited in chapter 1. The safety of a city reflects its tolerance for delinquencies that are seen as having few long-term consequences. This group is represented by the Toms, Bills and Nancys among those personally interviewed. For a small segment of the frequently delinquent, a different story emerges; Luke and David O illustrated the dangerous risks that this group faced.

One set of legal rationalities denies the adolescence of younger juveniles. If David O had committed his offense just several years prior to New York's passage of its 1978 Juvenile Offender law, he would not have been sentenced in criminal court. He and thousands of other youth would not be serving life sentences in the United States and a few other civilized, economically advanced societies that have moved into a set of legal rationalities that has abolished their possibility for juvenile justice.

The Struggle to Be Relationally Modern

I repeatedly mentioned the case of David O because he lacked that essential element of trust in another adult that could have prevented him from committing his brutal crime. He lacked an adult who could recognize his emotional troubles and the secure setting that he needed to confront his personal difficulties. David O was lost both socially and psychologically. Like many other youth who have committed lethal acts of violence, he was lost in one of modernity's suburban middle-class cities. He lacked the capacity to manage his rejections, beatings, and humiliations. No survey, personal interview, or twenty-four-hour police interrogation could possibly uncover the deep-seated motivations for his crime. A level of analysis is required that moves beyond the legal assignment of criminal responsibility to understanding the reasons that lead youth like David O to suddenly commit a horrendous crime.

Although repeated offending in a safe city may seem more like a mental health problem than a problem of criminal justice, the means for achieving effective treatment is in recognizing the struggle to be relationally modern. For instance, the youths responsible for the Columbine tragedy were subject to their suburban city's court-ordered diversion program. Treatment providers, therapists, and parents who seemed to care were not able to make a difference. There are risks and limits to treatment as well. Not all therapists are able to prevent their patients from committing suicide. Drug rehabilitation programs are effective only some of the time. For a segment of youth, the thin positional role of professionals is not enough; they are missing the deeply personal relationships that simply cannot be provided in the bureaucracies of systems of mental health and juvenile justice. Willie Bosket and the street-corner men that Liebow studied were missing love, or the relational sort of modernity that was briefly described in my friend's eulogy for his father.

Bosket and street-corner men fall into the category of the impoverished whose lives have been wasted by a society that has little room for those who are deemed unemployable. A well-known fork in the road is noted by Zygmunt Bauman when he describes individuals based on their capacities to move about in modernity's many places. The manner in which they move places them in the category of tourist or vagabond. The vagabonds lack the self-control, discipline, resources, or social capital that will enable them to reach the status of a tourist. In contrast to the vagabond, the tourist is affluent and a well-respected consumer of modernity's many products. According to Bauman, "The vagabonds are not really able to afford the kind of sophisticated choices in which the consumers are expected to excel; their potential for consumption is as limited as their resources. This fault makes their position in society precarious."[11] Indeed, the homeless and those on public assistance live highly insecure lives. If imprisoned, they have even fewer choices of where to reside. The tourists live in the larger world—but that world is known from the distance, superficially through relationships that could hardly be considered long-standing. In an effort to produce a safer city, municipalities have created their territories of exclusion. The banished are the vagabonds—the homeless, drug addicted or mentally ill, who are relegated to undesirable sections of a city. Civility laws have justified these zones of safety that are no longer zones of transition, but places where the impoverished are to be kept separated from the affluent.[12]

But the poor always resided in places that were different from middle-class and upper-class locales. The difference is that whereas before, they resided in separate neighborhoods that were in closer proximity to one another, often several blocks or an easy bus ride away, today, the distance as exemplified by modernity's rise of the safe suburban city has become greater, and in turn the problems of youth in isolated suburbs have become more complex.

The reasons for serious delinquencies among affluent suburban youth have been examined by others. Suniya Luthar has recently studied delinquency, drug and alcohol abuse, and the emotional troubles of youth in wealthy suburbs.[13] She reports that affluent youth indicate "significantly higher levels of anxiety across several domains, and greater depression."[14] She attributes these higher levels of anxiety and depression to the intense pressure of "highly affluent" parents. Presumably, the inability to meet parental demands is overwhelming, leading adolescents to the abuse of drugs. Luthar concludes: "It is only when individuals become disproportionately invested in extrinsic rewards, concomitantly neglecting intrinsic rewards such as closeness in relationships, that there are likely to be ill effects on their mental health outcomes."[15]

"Ill effects" are not easily avoided in an achievement-oriented society. Highly affluent parents are affluent because they learned to compete successfully; they achieved their occupational status by graduating from one place of honor to the next. They continue to be driven by the demands of their professions. They live in an era when their status cannot be inherited; they expect their children to achieve repeatedly in a highly competitive society. To deny this kind of globalized, achievement-oriented world is to turn back the calendar to a time that has long past.

Yet as far as I know, no one has figured out how to make everyone feel like a winner in a modern-day society. Luthar is not clear on the exact composition of the intrinsic rewards to which she refers. I interpret them to mean the ability to recognize individual difference and the unique capacities of youth. This requires the sort of empathetic identification that, as I have argued, is not easy to secure, especially for those youth who lack YARVIS qualities: It is easier to bond with an adolescent who is performing well. Yet the relational in modernity requires recognition and trusting adults to enable adolescents to survive more than one kind of trouble. That misfortunes, depression, illness, and a range of other troubles can happen to anyone at any time should heighten sensitivity to some of the struggles that I have identified in adolescence.

I agree with Luthar that adults in society have to deemphasize the extrinsic rewards of modernity's many demands. The positional, professional, or organizational trust that a segment of troubled adolescents requires needs to be affirmed. A truly safe city is one that emphasizes a community where difference is recognized through basic commonalities, such as simply being a human being in a large all-encompassing community. In this larger community, not only would adolescent troubles be recognized, but the trouble that youth service professionals and juvenile justice officials have in acknowledging and confronting their difficulties would be better recognized, too.

To deny the serious struggles that youth face in finding their place in a complex society transitioning rapidly is to deny adolescence and modernity. I have pointed to evidence of these struggles. Authoritarian styles of parenting still persist among the educated and middle class; some parents resort to physical punishment, as Karen, Bill, and Rena revealed. Others noted that their parents had their own set of troubles, such as facing accusations of sexual abuse. The survey data showed a segment of adolescents who were upset at their parents' use of alcohol, as well.

Clearly a proportion of safe-city youth are seriously discontented for reasons that I have related to their personal difficulties. They are deeply troubled by their inability to meet the expectations of those in their familial, educational, and peer-group settings. Some dislike Amherst and others like it as the place of their childhood and adolescence. In all cases, the personally interviewed youth were able to reflect back on their adolescence—on sources of discontent and on how they were able to avoid the more serious troubles that could have led them into juvenile court or criminal court. They could find their own legitimate suburban pathway because they were enabled by their familial, educational, recreational, and occupational pursuits. To repeat, modernity in all its force resides in a multitude of places. I leave it to others to document how cyberspace should also be recognized as another place of activity.

So there is just one more story to tell of the serious trouble that has plagued Amherst and many other affluent suburbs. It is the story of a fourteen-year-old Amherst youth, Jamey Rodemeyer, who committed suicide on September 18, 2011.[16] His suicide may have been the consequence of online and in-person bullying. He felt tormented for being openly gay.[17] The police investigated and concluded that they lacked the necessary evidence to prosecute several of his accused classmates. Although the suspected youth were subsequently suspended from school, the reason for Jamey's suicide appeared more complex, and responsibility for his suicide could not easily be determined. The torments that Rodemeyer faced did not occur in one singular setting. One online commentator noted,

> If you read his blog he actually talks about how the kids at his high school were more accepting of his sexuality than they had been in middle school, but he had been having problems with his parents. He actually said, "My parents just said they never wanted me to be born." I don't think this is a simple case of school bullies.[18]

Again, we have complexity on top of complexity, one division in society after another. Could Jamey's familial, educational, and peer-group settings have been more accepting and sensitive to his personal struggles? It is easy to answer "yes" from the distance, after the fact, without fully knowing the intimate details. In either case, Jamey lacked the relational modernity that would have allowed him to confront his difficulties. These difficulties are not easily visible; a good therapist who could delve into the troubles in his life may have made a difference. There were no guarantees in the cities of the past, and there can be no guarantees in the post-industrial suburban cities of today. For youth like Jamey, the difficulties of meeting parental, peer-group, and societal demands can become so unbearable that self-punishment takes the form of delinquency, suicide, or drugs. They need assistance at the first sign of trouble.

So I close this book with the hope that the structure of a relationally modern world will be examined not only in safe affluent cities but also in unsafe impoverished inner cities. I have highlighted some of the many consequences of modernity as exemplified by the incidence of delinquencies among youth living in a safe suburban city. The reasons for high and low rates of adolescent offending should be examined in other suburban cities. If we can recognize the struggles that affluent as well as impoverished adolescents face, we might be better able to prevent serious delinquencies, such as, the taking of one's own life or that of another's. We might be in a better position to advocate policies, programs, and parenting techniques that include rather than exclude, and that are equally available to impoverished as well as affluent youth.

Structural Equation Model Fits and Coefficient Estimates

Structural equation model fits and coefficient estimates as well as variables and related survey questions for Figures 7.4 through 7.7 appear below. The CMIN/DF (Chi Square/Degree of Freedom ratio) and RMSEA (Root Mean Square Error of Approximation) refer to the model fit. As indicated, all the models produced acceptable levels of statistical fit.

Figure 7.4. Parental Relationships

	Indexed delinquency	Substance use	Cheating	Emotional deviance
CMIN/DF	3.64	3.75	3.45	3.63
RMSEA	.064	.066	.062	.064

COEFFICIENT ESTIMATES

	Indexed delinquency	Substance use	Cheating	Emotional deviance
Attachment	−.08	.00	.12	−.12
Knowledge	−.25*	−.26*	−.18*	−.07
Support	.02	−.14	−.14	−.29*
Permissive	.06	.20*	.16*	.11*

* p < .05

Figure 7.5. School Relationships

	Indexed delinquency	Substance use	Cheating	Emotional deviance
CMIN/DF	2.70	2.78	2.63	2.87
RMSEA	.052	.053	.051	.054

COEFFICIENT ESTIMATES

	Indexed delinquency	Substance use	Cheating	Emotional deviance
Attachment	−.53*	−.44*	−.42*	−.33*
Grades	.07	−.04	.14*	−.02
Frustration	.13*	.04	.06	.02
Talk	−.04	−.04	−.02	.07

* p < .05

Figure 7.6. Peer Relationships

	Indexed delinquency	Substance use	Cheating	Emotional deviance
CMIN/DF	4.80	5.21	4.70	4.92
RMSEA	.077	.081	.077	.078

COEFFICIENT ESTIMATES

	Indexed delinquency	Substance use	Cheating	Emotional deviance
Attachment	.01	.29*	−.02	.16*
Positive	−.59*	−.74*	−.26*	−.33*
Talk	−.11*	−.11	.05	−.08
Number	.11	.17*	.04	−.23*

* p < .05

Figure 7.7. Community Attachment

	Indexed delinquency	Substance use	Cheating	Emotional deviance
CMIN/DF	3.52	3.60	3.35	3.52
RMSEA	.063	.064	.061	.063

COEFFICIENT ESTIMATES

	Indexed delinquency	Substance use	Cheating	Emotional deviance
Attachment	−.01	−.26*	−.02	−.29*
Programs	−.12*	.02	.06	.01
Talk	−.02	−.06	−.05	.02
Recreation	.08*	.00	−.06	.02

* p < .05

Variables and Related Survey Questions

Figure 7.4. Parental Relationships

PARENTAL ATTACHMENT

Talk about feelings: Do you talk with your mother/father about your thoughts and feelings?

Be like parents: Would like to be the kind of person your mother/father is?

Get best attorney: If you were arrested for stealing something that didn't belong to you, would your parents get the best possible attorney?

Discuss major problems: If you had a major personal problem, would you discuss it with your mother/father?

Have parents' trust: Does your mother/father trust you?

PARENTAL KNOWLEDGE

Parents know where: Does your mother/father know where you are when you are not at home?

Parents know who: Does your mother/father know who you are with when you are not at home?

PARENTAL SUPPORT

Family decisions: How much do you contribute to family decisions?

Family fun: How often do you and your family have fun together?

Family dinner: During the average week, how often do you and your family have dinner together?

PARENTAL PERMISSIVENESS

Attend house parties: Would your parent(s) let you go to a "house party" at night if the host parents were away on vacation?

Drink at home: Do your parents allow you to drink alcohol in your home?

Friends allowed to drink in home: Do your parents allow your friends (who are under legal drinking age) to drink alcohol in your home?

Figure 7.5. School Relationships

SCHOOL ATTACHMENT

Take fewer courses: Would you take fewer courses in school now if you could?

Like school: How often do you find that you like school?

Have trouble with teachers: How often do you have trouble with your teachers?

Try hardest: In school, do you try your hardest?

Do homework: How often do you do homework, school projects, etc., after school?

GRADES

My overall average in school is at least . . . (Responses categories: 90–100, 80–90, 70–80, 65–70, below 65)

SCHOOL FRUSTRATION

Based on questions that asked:

How important is it to you to do well in school/get high grades/graduate from school? (Scaled Likert responses: Very Important/Not Very Important)

How good are your chances for achieving this goal? (Scaled Likert responses: Very Good/Very Poor)

TALK TO SCHOOL STAFF

Based on eight questions that asked:

If you had questions or problems concerning, alcohol or other drugs/pregnancy or sexuality would you ever talk with a school teacher/nurse/guidance counselor/social worker? (Scaled response: Yes/No)

Figure 7.6. Peer Relationships

FRIEND ATTACHMENT

Be like friends: Would you like to be the kind of person your best friend is?

Rely on friends: When you are having trouble, can you rely on your best friend?

Stick by friends: Would you stick by your best friend if he or she got into a lot of trouble?

POSITIVE FRIENDS

Stay out of trouble: My friends rarely get into trouble. (Scaled Likert response: Strongly Agree/Strongly Disagree)

Not picked up by police: How many of your best friends have ever been picked up by the police?

Active in school: Are your friends at school active in extra-curricular activities (e.g., sports, clubs, etc.)?

TALK ABOUT PROBLEMS

Based on two questions that asked:

If you had questions or problems concerning alcohol or other drugs/pregnancy or sexuality would you ever talk about them with a friend? (Response: Yes/No)

NUMBER OF FRIENDS

Friends in school: Have you many friends from school?

Friends out of school: Have you many friends outside of school?

Figure 7.7. Community Attachment

COMMUNITY ATTACHMENT

Stay in Amherst: I will probably live in this area when I am an adult. (Scaled Likert response: Strongly Agree/Strongly Disagree)

Like Amherst's programs: I feel the town of Amherst provides the kinds of programs that I like to get involved in. (Scaled Likert response: Strongly Agree/Strongly Disagree)

See opportunities in Amherst: I feel there are lots of opportunities for me in Amherst. (Scaled Likert response: Strongly Agree/Strongly Disagree)

TALK TO COMMUNITY

Based on twelve questions that asked:

If you had questions or problems concerning alcohol or other drugs/pregnancy or sexuality would you ever talk with clergy/psychologist/physician/other adults/recreational and religious staff? (Response: Yes/No)

NOTES

All the photographs in this book are of Amherst, New York. They were taken by long-time Buffalo resident Ginny Stewart and by Craig Ceremuga of Rochester, New York, between 2012 and 2013. I provided Ginny and Craig with a list of shopping malls, high schools, and the university where I worked for nearly twenty years. Despite the fact that Amherst is a suburban city of over 100,000 residents, the photos show few faces in order to protect confidentiality. Moreover, I also selected these photos to emphasize the anonymity of suburban living. So where are the people? Some of them are inside one of Amherst's several shopping malls; others are in their homes or cars. On a nice day, they might be gardening, at a garage sale, or a town event, such as a parade along Main Street. They might also be out playing golf at one of the town's private or public golf clubs, or playing some other sport in a town recreational facility. They might also be walking in one of Amherst's many parks.

NOTES TO THE INTRODUCTION

1. The murder of Chester Solinsky made the local television news and the front page of New York City's newspapers. The most extensive and lengthy coverage appeared in Mark Rose, "Time to Kill? Good Kids in Bad Trouble," *Village Voice*, December 6, 1983. The title of the article is deceiving. They were white kids from a lower-income neighborhood of Queens. I was Chester's only friend to have been interviewed and quoted in the article.

2. I will repeatedly refer to a "Broken Windows" theory of crime, which was developed by James Q. Wilson and George Kelling in "The Police and Neighborhood Safety: Broken Windows," *Atlantic*, March 1982, 29–38. It is one of the most popular and accessible theories of criminal justice to appear in the later part of the twentieth century and has revitalized the notion of community policing. For a review and critical assessment, see Bernard E. Harcourt, *Illusion of Order: The False Promise of Broken Windows Policing* (Cambridge: Harvard University Press, 2001).

3. Claude S. Fischer, Michael Hout, and Jon Stiles, *Century of Difference: How America Changed in the Last One Hundred Years* (New York: Russell Sage Foundation, 2006).

NOTES TO CHAPTER 1

1. Carla Fried, "America's Safest City: Amherst, N.Y.; The Most Dangerous: New-ark, N.J.," CNN Money Magazine, November 27, 2006, http://money.cnn.com/magazines/moneymag/moneymag_archive/1996/11/27/219684/index.htm.

2. In 2010 the Buffalo News reported: "Once again, it's time to acknowledge Amherst, N.Y., as one of the safest communities in America. 'City Crime Rankings 2009-2010,' an annual publication from CQ [Congressional Quarterly Press], ranked Amherst first for the lowest crime rate ranking among municipalities with a population from 100,000 to 499,000." http://www.buffalonews.com/article/20100703/CITYANDREGION/307039951. Steve Brachmann, "Town Again First for Lowest Crime Rate," Buffalo News, August 21, 2010.

3. "Best Places to Live 2012—Top 100," Money Magazine, September 2012, http://money.cnn.com/magazines/moneymag/best-places/2012/top100/index2.html

4. The FBI's Uniform Crime Report index includes larceny and arson. These offenses were not included in Money Magazine's calculation of a city's crime rate.

5. Carla Fried, "America's Safest City: Amherst, N.Y.; The Most Dangerous: New-ark, N.J.," CNN Money Magazine, November 27, 2006, http://money.cnn.com/magazines/moneymag/moneymag_archive/1996/11/27/219684/index.htm.

6. The President's Commission on Law Enforcement and Administration of Justice, The Challenge of Crime in a Free Society (Washington, DC: US Department of Justice, 1967).

7. See generally, Marvin E. Wolfgang, Robert M. Figlio, Paul E. Tracy, and Simon I. Singer, The National Survey of Crime Severity. (Washington, DC: U.S. Department of Justice, 1985).

8. Wendy Ruderman and Joseph Goldstein, "Lawsuit Accuses Police of Ignoring Directive on Marijuana Arrests," New York Times, June 23, 2012, A15.

9. Travis Hirschi, Causes of Delinquency (Berkeley: University of California Press, 1969).

10. Travis Hirschi, Causes of Delinquency (Berkeley: University of California Press, 1969), 82.

11. See for example: Pamela Richards, Richard A. Berk, and Brenda Forster, Crime as Play: Delinquency in a Middle Class Suburb (Cambridge, MA: Ballinger Publishing Company, 1979); Herman Schwendinger and Julia Siegel Schwendinger, Adolescent Subcultures and Delinquency (New York: Praeger, 1985).

12. William J. Chambliss, "The Saints and the Roughnecks." Society (November/December 1973): 24–31.

13. The classic statement on how the police are more likely to arrest those who show less deference to their authority is contained in Donald J. Black and Albert J. Reiss, Jr., "Police Control of Juveniles," American Sociological Review 35 (1970): 63–77.

14. Labeling theory supports an inclusionary, restorative form of justice that avoids

stigmatizing offenders. See John Braithwaite, *Crime, Shame, and Reintegration* (Cambridge: Cambridge University Press, 1989).

15. Gerald D. Suttles, *The Social Order of the Slum: Ethnicity and Territory in the Inner City* (Chicago: University of Chicago Press, 1968), 35.

16. Mary P. Baumgartner, *The Moral Order of a Suburb* (New York: Oxford University Press, 1988), 10–11.

17. Aaron Cicourel, *The Social Organization of Juvenile Justice* (New York: Wiley, 1968), 32.

18. Jonathan Simon, *Governing through Crime: How the War on Crime Transformed American Democracy and Created a Culture of Fear* (New York: Oxford University Press, 2007), 277.

19. Margaret K. Nelson, *Parenting out of Control: Anxious Parents in Uncertain Times* (New York: New York University Press, 2010), 17.

20. National Drug Control Policy advertisement, *New York Times*, September 8, 2006, A21. See also http://www.theantidrug.com.

21. "Adolescent Depression," National Institutes of Health, July 27, 2012, http://www.nlm.nih.gov/medlineplus/ency/article/001518.htm.

22. A Google search of "at home Drug Test" produced 1,150,000 results. All the major drug store chains advertise variations of this kind of home drug-testing product. The advertisement I refer to appeared in the *Boston Globe*, October 24, 2012, A8.

23. Anthony Giddens, *The Consequences of Modernity* (Stanford, CA: Stanford University Press, 1990), 100.

24. Adam Phillips, *Going Sane: Maps of Happiness* (New York: Fourth Estate, 2005), 97.

25. Robert Sampson, *Great American City: Chicago and the Enduring Neighborhood Effect* (Chicago: University of Chicago Press, 2011).

26. Robert Sampson, *Great American City: Chicago and the Enduring Neighborhood Effect* (Chicago: University of Chicago Press, 2011), 216–19; Just as critical to Sampson's analysis of collective efficacy and crime is the impact of poverty, race, and inequality. See Robert J. Sampson and William J. Wilson, "Toward a Theory of Race, Crime, and Urban Inequality," in *Race, Crime, and Justice: A Reader,* eds. S. Gabbidon and H. Taylor (New York: Routledge, 2005), 177–80.

27. Erik Erikson, *Childhood and Society* (New York: Norton, 1963).

28. These and other statistics on Amherst and on population growth in Amherst and its neighboring city of Buffalo are contained in the "Town of Amherst: Demographic Analysis 2000–2010," Planning Department (Amherst, NY, 2012).

29. Claude S. Fischer, Michael Hout, and Jon Stiles, *Century of Difference: How America Changed in the Last One Hundred Years* (New York: Russell Sage Foundation, 2006).

30. Claude S. Fischer, Michael Hout, and Jon Stiles, *Century of Difference: How*

America Changed in the Last One Hundred Years (New York: Russell Sage Foundation, 2006), 173.

31. U.S. Census Bureau, *Census 2000 Data for the State of New York*, http://www.census.gov/census2000/states/ny.html.

32. I draw on statistics presented by David Harvey, *The Condition of Postmodernity: An Enquiry into the Origins of Cultural Change* (New York: Oxford Blackwell, 1989).

33. Probably still the best introduction to suburban development is Kenneth Jackson, *Crabgrass Frontier: The Suburbanization of the United States* (New York: Oxford University Press, 1985).

34. Mark Gottdiener and Joe R. Feaggin, "The Paradigm Shift in Urban Sociology," *Urban Affairs Quarterly* 24 (1988): 163–87; Mark Gottdiener, *The New Urban Sociology* (New York: McGraw, 1994), 24.

35. *See Milliken v. Bradley*, 418 U.S. 717 (1974).

36. Jane Jacobs, *The Death and Life of Great American Cities* (New York: Random House, 1961). Lewis Mumford, "The Culture of Cities," *Metropolis: Centre and Symbol of Our Times* (New York: New York University Press, 1995). Richard Sennett, *The Uses of Disorder: Personal Identity and City Life* (New York: Alfred A. Knopf, 1970).

37. Richard Sennett, *The Uses of Disorder: Personal Identity and City Life* (New York: Alfred A. Knopf, 1970), 108.

38. Saul Bellow, *Seize the Day* (New York: Viking Press, 1956), 115.

39. I have chosen 1990 census data because it is the point that is closest to the first set of surveys when youth were still in their high-school years.

40. Alfred Blumstein, "Making Rationality Relevant," *Criminology* 31 (1993): 1–16.

41. Bruce Western, *Punishment and Inequality in America* (New York: Sage Foundation, 2006), 47.

42. John Hagan, *Who Are the Criminals? The Politics of Crime Policy from the Age of Roosevelt to the Age of Reagan* (Princeton: Princeton University Press, 2010), 64–65.

43. James F. Nelson and Sharon E. Lansing, "Disproportionate Minority Confinement in New York State," New York State Division of Criminal Justice Services (1997), 86.

NOTES TO CHAPTER 2

1. Kevin M. Kruse and Thomas J Sugrue, *The New Suburban History* (University of Chicago Press, 2006), 2.

2. Fox Butterfield, *All God's Children: The Bosket Family and the American Tradition of Violence* (New York: Knopf, 1995), 142.

3. Simon I. Singer, *Recriminalizing Delinquency: Violent Juvenile Crime and Juvenile Justice Reform* (New York: Cambridge University Press, 1996).

4. Fox Butterfield, *All God's Children: The Bosket Family and the American Tradition of Violence* (New York: Knopf, 1995), 159.

5. Fox Butterfield, *All God's Children: The Bosket Family and the American Tradition of Violence* (New York: Knopf, 1995), 142.

6. Fox Butterfield, *All God's Children: The Bosket Family and the American Tradition of Violence* (New York: Knopf, 1995), 149.

7. I am referring specifically to the impoverished black juveniles (known as the Central Park Five) who confessed to crimes they did not commit. See Sarah Burns, *The Central Park Five: A Chronicle of a City Wilding* (New York: Alfred A. Knopf, 2011).

8. Jason Horowitz, "Mitt Romney's Prep School Classmates Recall Pranks, but also Troubling Incidents," *Washington Post*, May 11, 2012, http://www.washingtonpost .com/politics/mitt-romneys-prep-school-classmates-recall-pranks-but-also -troublingincidents/2012/05/10/gIQA3WOKFU_story.html.

9. Robert A. Guth, "Raising Bill Gates," *Wall Street Journal*, April 25, 2009.

10. David Matza, *Delinquency and Drift* (New York: John Wiley, 1964).

11. Barack Obama, *Dreams from My Father: A Story of Race and Inheritance* (New York: Crown, 1995, 2004), 93.

12. Barack Obama, *Dreams from My Father: A Story of Race and Inheritance* (New York: Crown, 1995, 2004), 95.

13. Barack Obama, *Dreams from My Father: A Story of Race and Inheritance* (New York: Crown, 1995, 2004), 95.

14. Elizabeth S. Scott and Laurence Steinberg, *Rethinking Juvenile Justice* (Cambridge: Harvard University Press, 2008).

15. Elizabeth S. Scott and Laurence Steinberg, *Rethinking Juvenile Justice* (Cambridge: Harvard University Press, 2008), 32.

16. *Miller v. Alabama*, 567 U.S. 8-9 (2012).

17. Anthony Giddens, *The Consequences of Modernity* (Stanford, CA: Stanford University Press, 1990), 18–19.

18. Peter T. Kilborn, "The Five-Bedroom, Six-Figure Rootless Life," *New York Times*, June 1, 2005, A12.

19. Basil B. Bernstein, *Class, Codes and Control* (London: Routledge and K. Paul, 1971).

20. Erving Goffman refers to social control as entailing front- and backstage performances. The backstage I picture as including the amount of time that is spent transporting adolescents from one activity to another. Erving Goffman, *Behavior in Public Places: Notes on the Social Organization of Gathering* (New York: Free Press, 1963).

21. Robert Sampson, *Great American City: Chicago and the Enduring Neighborhood Effect* (Chicago: University of Chicago Press, 2011), 152.

22. Robert Sampson, *Great American City: Chicago and the Enduring Neighborhood Effect* (Chicago: University of Chicago Press, 2011), 151.

23. George Simmel, "The Metropolis and Mental Life," in *Metropolis: Center and Symbol of Our Times*, ed. P. Kasinitz (New York: New York University Press, 1995), 17.

24. William I. Thomas, *The Unadjusted Girl: With Cases and Standpoint for Behavior Analysis* (Boston: Harper Torchbooks, 1923).

25. William I. Thomas, *The Unadjusted Girl: With Cases and Standpoint for Behavior Analysis* (Boston: Harper Torchbooks, 1923), 78.

26. William I. Thomas, *The Unadjusted Girl: With Cases and Standpoint for Behavior Analysis* (Boston: Harper Torchbooks, 1923), 80.

27. Lewis Mumford, "The Culture of Cities," in *Metropolis: Center and Symbol of Our Times*, ed. P. Kasinitz (New York: New York University Press), 24.

28. Abraham Maslow, *Motivation and Personality* (New York: Harper and Row, 1970), 70.

29. Abraham Maslow, *Motivation and Personality* (New York: Harper and Row, 1970).

30. Lee G. Bolman and Terrence E. Deal, *Reframing Organizations: Artistry, Choice, and Leadership* (San Francisco: Jossey-Bass, 2003), 118.

31. David O lacked the basics. He lacked emotional security that would have enabled him to proceed normally into adolescence. He lacked the basics in that hierarchy of emotional needs.

32. Mark Warr, *Companions in Crime: The Social Aspects of Criminal Conduct* (Cambridge University Press, 2002).

33. Emile Durkheim, John A. Spaulding, and George Simpson, *Suicide: A Study in Sociology* (New York: Free Press, 2010), 248.

34. Steven F. Messner and Richard Rosenfeld, *Crime and the American Dream* (Belmont, CA: Wadsworth Publishing Company, 1994), 2.

35. There are a number of theories to draw on to explain America's high crime rate. The heightened frustration that a segment of Americans can feel by their impoverished circumstances or the bad things that may have happened to them may fall under the general category of strain theory, as articulated by Robert Agnew in "A Revised Strain Theory of Delinquency," 64 *Social Forces* (1985): 151–66.

36. Kenneth T. Jackson, *Crabgrass Frontier: The Suburbanization of the United States* (New York: Oxford University Press, 1985), 50.

37. H. L. A. Hart divides rules into those that are internalized and those that are externalized. Internalized rules would be comparable to moral rules, and they require no external legal threats to ensure compliance. H. L. A. Hart, *The Concept of Law* (New York: Oxford University Press, 1972).

38. Emile Durkheim, *The Division of Labor in Society* (New York: The Free Press, 1933), 296.

39. Peter Gay, *Schnitzler's Century: The Making of Middle-Class Culture, 1815–1914* (New York: W. W. Norton & Company, 2002).

40. Max Weber, "Law, Rationalism and Capitalism," in *Law and Society*, ed. C. E. Campbell and Paul Wiles (Oxford: Martin Robertson, 1979), 51–73. In contrast to Max Weber's iron cage image of bureaucracies, see Peter Manning, *The Technology of Policing: Crime Mapping, Information Technology, and The Rationality of Crime Control* (New York: New York University Press, 2008).

41. Karl E. Weick, *Sensemaking in Organizations* (Thousand Oaks, CA: Sage Publications, 1995).

42. *Dusky v. United States*, 362 U.S. 402 (1960).

43. Barry Feld, "A Slower Form of Death: Implications of *Roper v. Simmons* for Juveniles Sentenced to Life without Parole," *Notre Dame Journal of Law, Ethics & Public Policy* 22 (2008): 9. Elizabeth S. Scott and Laurence Steinberg, *Rethinking Juvenile Justice* (Cambridge: Harvard University Press, 2008).

44. Warren G. Bennis and Philip E. Slater, *The Temporary Society* (New York: Harper & Row, 1968): 75.

NOTES TO CHAPTER 3

1. Katherine S. Newman, *Rampage: The Social Roots of School Shootings: Why Violence Erupts in Close-Knit Communities—And What Can Be Done to Stop It* (New York: Basic Books, 2004), 138.

2. There is no shortage of articles and books to explain Columbine. Dave Cullen, *Columbine* (New York: Twelve / Hachette Book Group, 2009). His website provides commentary and interviews with the parents of Dylan and Eric: http://www.columbine-online.com/columbine-parents-killers-eric-harris-dylan-klebold.htm; Arrest and diversion reports for both youth can be found at: http://acolumbinesite.com/report.html

3. Bernard Lefkowitz, *Our Guys* (Berkeley: University of California Press, 1997), 422.

4. Bernard Lefkowitz, *Our Guys* (Berkeley: University of California Press, 1997), 423.

5. I use the term "honor students" with caution. They stole exams for advanced honor classes that they were taking. Sarah Schweitzer, "School Cheating Scandal Divides N.H. Town; Criminal Charges too Harsh, Some Say," *Boston Globe*, September 19, 2007, A1.

6. *Money Magazine*'s best small city list can be located at the following website: http://money.cnn.com/magazines/moneymag/bplive/2007/top100.

7. Andrea Seabrook, "New Hampshire Split over High School Cheating," National Public Radio, September 29, 2007, http://www.npr.org/templates/story/story.php?storyId=14811147.

8. Norbert Elias, *The Civilizing Process* (Oxford: Blackwell, 1994), 53–54.

9. Michael R. Gottfredson and Travis Hirschi, *A General Theory of Crime* (Stanford: Stanford University Press, 1990).

10. Rogers Brubaker and Frederick Cooper, "Beyond 'Identity,'" *Theory and Society* 29 (2000): 1–47.

11. Pierre Bourdieu, "Social Space and Symbolic Power," *Sociological Theory* 7 (1989): 14–25.

12. Marcel Danesi, *Cool: The Signs and Meanings of Adolescence* (Toronto: University of Toronto Press, 1994); Dick Hebdige, *Subculture, The Meaning of Style* (London:

Methuen, 1979); Ali Rattansi and Ann Phoenix, "Rethinking Youth Identities: Modernist and Postmodernist Frameworks," *Identity* 5 (2005): 97–123.

13. Elizabeth S. Scott and Laurence Steinberg, *Rethinking Juvenile Justice* (Cambridge: Harvard University Press, 2008), 41.

14. Elizabeth S. Scott and Laurence Steinberg, *Rethinking Juvenile Justice* (Cambridge: Harvard University Press, 2008), 57.

15. John Stuart Mill, *On Liberty* (Boston, MA: Ticknor and Fields, 1863), 28–29.

16. Travis Hirschi, *Causes of Delinquency* (Berkeley: University of California Press, 1969), 5.

17. Michael R. Gottfredson and Travis Hirschi, *A General Theory of Crime* (Stanford: Stanford University Press, 1990).

18. Charles Tittle, *Control Balance Theory* (Boulder: Westview Press, 1995), 147.

19. Emile Durkheim, *Moral Education: A Study in the Theory and Application of the Sociology of Education* (New York: Free Press, 1973), 148.

20. Herbert Spencer, *Essays on Education and Kindred Subjects* (London: J.M. Dent & Sons), 113.

21. Albert Bandura, *Self-Efficacy: The Exercise of Control* (New York: Worth, 1997).

22. Albert Bandura, *Self-Efficacy: The Exercise of Control* (New York: Worth, 1997), 3.

23. Richard Sennett, *The Uses of Disorder: Personal Identity and City Life* (New York: Alfred A. Knopf, 1970), 119–20.

24. Simon Baron-Cohen, *The Essential Difference: The Truth about the Male and Female Brain* (New York: Basic Books, 2003), 26.

25. Simon Baron-Cohen, *The Essential Difference: The Truth about the Male and Female Brain* (New York: Basic Books, 2003), 26.

26. Richard Sennett, *The Uses of Disorder: Personal Identity and City Life* (New York: Alfred A. Knopf, 1970), 60.

27. Murray Levine and Adeline Levine, *Helping Children: A Social History* (New York: Oxford University Press, 1992).

28. Ernest W. Burgess, in Clifford R Shaw, *The Jack-Roller: A Delinquent Boy's Own Story* (Chicago: University of Chicago Press, 1966), 194–95.

29. According to David Matza, juvenile justice officials are conflicted by more than one set of organizational objectives. On the one hand, their stated mission is to treat and rehabilitate the adolescent so that more serious acts of delinquency can be averted. On the other hand, there are too many cases and too little time to spend on each adolescent who appears before the juvenile court. As a consequence, officials are not able to understand (empathize with) the delinquents they are asked to judge "for if they could they would in that measure no longer be able to render routine judgment." In other words, the relational as defined by empathetic identification with one another is limited in a complex society where routine decision-making is required. David Matza, *Delinquency and Drift* (New York: John Wiley, 1964), 159.

30. Markus D. Dubber, "The Right to Be Punished: Autonomy and Its Demise in Modern Penal Thought," *Law and History Review* 16 (1998):113–46.

31. Elizabeth S. Scott and Laurence Steinberg, *Rethinking Juvenile Justice* (Cambridge: Harvard University Press, 2008), 56.
32. Modernity requires trust in "abstract systems of knowledge." Anthony Giddens defines trust as "confidence in the reliability of a person or system, regarding a given set of outcomes or events, where that confidence expresses a faith in the probity or love of another, or in the correctness of abstract principles (technical knowledge)." Anthony Giddens, *The Consequences of Modernity* (Stanford, CA: Stanford University Press, 1990), 37.

    How adolescents are able to trust the complex and abstract in society is not easily addressed. Karen S. Cook and Alexandra Gerasi refer to "relational trust" as grounded in beliefs about the appropriateness of relationships based on an identifiable set of interests. They define this thin, modern-day level of trust as "when one party to the relation believes the other party has incentive to act in his or her interest or to take his or her interests to heart." Cook and Gerasi, "Trust," in *The Oxford Handbook of Analytical Sociology*, eds. Peter Hedström and Peter Bearman (New York: Oxford University Press, 2009), 218–41. Although trust involves reliability of the people who occupy modern-day organizations, it is closely related to an individual's ability to empathetically identify with another.
33. Diana Baumrind, "Effects of Authoritative Parental Control on Child Behavior," *Child Development* 37 (1966): 887–907; Diana Baumrind, "The Influence of Parenting Style on Adolescent Competence and Substance Use," *Journal of Early Adolescence* 11 (1991): 56–95; Diana Baumrind, "The Discipline Controversy Revisited," *Family Relations* 45 (1996): 405–14.
34. Carter Hay, "Parenting, Self-Control, and Delinquency: A Test of Self-Control Theory," *Criminology* 39 (2001): 707–36.
35. See, for example: Laurence D. Steinberg, Julie D. Elmen, and Nina S. Mounts, "Authoritative Parenting, Psychosocial Maturity, and Academic Success among Adolescents," *Child Development* 60 (1989): 1424–36; Laurence D. Steinberg, Susie D. Lamborn, Sanford M. Dornbusch, and Nancy Darling, "Impact of Parenting Practices on Adolescent Achievement: Authoritative Parenting, School Involvement, and Encouragement to Succeed," *Child Development* 63 (1992): 1266–81; Laurence D. Steinberg, Nina S. Mounts, Susie D. Lamborn, and Sanford M. Dornbusch, "Authoritative Parenting and Adolescent Adjustment across Varied Ecological Niches," *Journal of Research on Adolescents* 1 (1991): 19–36.
36. Laurence D. Steinberg, *Adolescence* (Boston: McGraw-Hill Higher Education, 2002), 141.
37. Laurence D. Steinberg, *Adolescence* (Boston: McGraw-Hill Higher Education, 2002), 141.
38. Duane Alwin, "Parenting Practices," in *The Blackwell Companion to the Sociology of Families*, eds. Jacqueline Scott, Judith Treas, and Martin Richards (Malden, MA: Blackwell, 2004), 142–58.

39. Duane Alwin, "Parenting Practices," in *The Blackwell Companion to the Sociology of Families*, eds. Jacqueline Scott, Judith Treas, and Martin Richards (Malden, MA: Wiley-Blackwell, 2004), 142.

40. Duane Alwin, "Parental Values, Beliefs, and Behavior: A Review and Promulga for Research into a New Century," in *Children at the Millenium: Where Have We Come from, Where Are We Going?*, eds. S. L. Hofferth and T. J. Owens, (Amsterdam: JAI, 2010), 97–139.

41. David Popenoe, *Disturbing the Nest: Family Change and Decline in Modern Societies* (Aldine: Transaction Publishers, 1988), 8–9.

42. Mark Colvin and John Pauly, "A Critique of Criminology: Toward an Integrated Structural-Marxist Theory of Delinquency Production," *American Journal of Sociology* 89 (1983): 516–51; Melvin L. Kohn, "Social Class and Parental Values," *American Journal of Sociology* 64 (1959): 337–51; Melvin L. Kohn, "Social Class and Parent-Child Relationships: An Interpretation," *American Journal of Sociology* 68 (1963): 471–80; Melvin L. Kohn, "Social Class and Parental Values: Another Confirmation of the Relationship," *American Sociological Review* 41 (1976): 538–45.

NOTES TO CHAPTER 4

1. Clifford R. Shaw and Henry D. McKay, *Juvenile Delinquency in Urban Areas* (Chicago: University of Chicago Press, 1942).

2. William Foote Whyte, *Street Corner Society* (Chicago: University of Chicago Press, 1948).

3. Robert E. Park, Ernest W. Burgess, and Roderick D. McKenzie, *The City: Suggestions for the Study of Human Nature in the Urban Environment* (Chicago: University of Chicago Press, 1925).

4. Elliot Liebow, *Tally's Corner: A Study of Negro Streetcorner Men* (Boston: Little, Brown, & Co., 1967).

5. Elijah Anderson, *A Place on the Corner* (Chicago: University of Chicago Press, 1978); Elijah Anderson, *Street Wise: Race, Class, and Change in an Urban Community* (Chicago: University of Chicago Press, 1990); Elijah Anderson, *Code of the Street: Decency, Violence, and the Moral Life of the Inner City* (New York: W. W. Norton, 1999).

6. William Foote Whyte, *Street Corner Society* (Chicago: University of Chicago Press, 1948), xv.

7. William Foote Whyte, *Street Corner Society* (Chicago: University of Chicago Press, 1948), 106.

8. William Foote Whyte, *Street Corner Society* (Chicago: University of Chicago Press, 1948), 95.

9. William Foote Whyte, *Street Corner Society* (Chicago: University of Chicago Press, 1948), 96.

10. William Foote Whyte, *Street Corner Society* (Chicago: University of Chicago Press, 1948), 96.

11. William Foote Whyte, *Street Corner Society* (Chicago: University of Chicago Press, 1948), 105.

12. William Foote Whyte, *Street Corner Society* (Chicago: University of Chicago Press, 1948), 106.

13. William Foote Whyte, *Street Corner Society* (Chicago: University of Chicago Press, 1948), 96.

14. William Foote Whyte, *Street Corner Society* (Chicago: University of Chicago Press, 1948), 255.

15. William Foote Whyte, *Street Corner Society* (Chicago: University of Chicago Press, 1948), 276.

16. Darrell Steffensmeier and Jeffery T. Ulmer, "Black and White Control of Numbers Gambling: A Cultural Assets–Social Capital View," *American Sociological Review* 71 (2006):123–56.

17. Elliot Liebow, *Tally's Corner: A Study of Negro Streetcorner Men* (Boston: Little, Brown, & Co., 1967), xxvii.

18. Elliot Liebow, *Tally's Corner: A Study of Negro Streetcorner Men* (Boston: Little, Brown, & Co., 1967), 34.

19. Elliot Liebow, *Tally's Corner: A Study of Negro Streetcorner Men* (Boston: Little, Brown, & Co., 1967), 55.

20. Elliot Liebow, *Tally's Corner: A Study of Negro Streetcorner Men* (Boston: Little, Brown, & Co., 1967), 55.

21. According to psychoanalytical theory, being unrealistic with oneself is a reason for all sorts of deep-seated problems. The point is further made that a sense of facticity is crucial to integrative accounts of sociological motivation. Johnathan H. Turner, "Toward a Sociological Theory of Motivation," *American Sociological Review* 52 (1987):15–27.

22. Elliot Liebow, *Tally's Corner: A Study of Negro Streetcorner Men* (Boston: Little, Brown, & Co., 1967), 65.

23. Elijah Anderson, *A Place on the Corner* (Chicago: University of Chicago Press, 1978); Elijah Anderson, *Street Wise: Race, Class, and Change in an Urban Community* (Chicago: University of Chicago Press, 1990); Elijah Anderson, *Code of the Street: Decency, Violence, and the Moral Life of the Inner City* (New York: W. W. Norton, 1999).

24. Elijah Anderson, *Code of the Street: Decency, Violence, and the Moral Life of the Inner City* (New York: W. W. Norton, 1999).

25. William J. Wilson, *The Truly Disadvantaged* (Chicago: University of Chicago Press, 1987).

26. Elijah Anderson, *Code of the Street: Decency, Violence, and the Moral Life of the Inner City* (New York: W. W. Norton, 1999).

27. Elijah Anderson, *Code of the Street: Decency, Violence, and the Moral Life of the Inner City* (New York: W. W. Norton, 1999), 36.

28. Philippe Bourgois, *In Search of Respect: Selling Crack in El Barrio* (Cambridge: Cambridge University Press, 2003).

29. Philippe Bourgois, *In Search of Respect: Selling Crack in El Barrio* (Cambridge: Cambridge University Press, 2003), 145.

30. Philippe Bourgois, *In Search of Respect: Selling Crack in El Barrio* (Cambridge: Cambridge University Press, 2003), 146.

31. Loic Wacquant, "Scrutinizing the Street: Poverty, Morality, and the Pitfalls of Urban Ethnography," *American Journal of Sociology* 107 (2002): 1468–1532.

32. Beckett, Katherine, and Steve Herbert, *Banished: The New Social Control in Urban America* (New York: Oxford University Press, 2009).

33. The reference to "spokes" comes from Bernice A. Pescosolido and Beth A. Rubin, "The Web of Group Affiliations Revisited: Social Life, Postmodernism, and Sociology," *American Sociological Review* 65 (2000): 52–76.

34. Jack Katz, *Seductions of Crime: Moral and Sensual Attractions in Doing Evil* (New York: Basic Books, 1988).

35. Jack Katz, *Seductions of Crime: Moral and Sensual Attractions in Doing Evil* (New York: Basic Books, 1988), 52.

36. John Hagan, *Structural Criminology* (New Brunswick, NJ: Rutgers University Press, 1989); John Hagan, A. R. Gillis, and John Simpson. "The Class Structure of Gender and Delinquency: Toward a Power-Control Theory of Common Delinquent Behavior," *American Journal of Sociology* 90 (1985): 1151–78.

37. Nancy Chodorow, *The Reproduction of Mothering: Psychoanalysis and the Sociology of Gender* (Berkeley: University of California Press, 1978).

38. John Hagan, John Simpson, and A. R. Gillis, "Feminist Scholarship, Relational and Instrumental Control, and a Power-Control Theory of Gender and Delinquency," *British Journal of Sociology* (1988): 303.

39. Max Weber, *The Theory of Social and Economic Organization* (Glencoe, IL: Free Press, 1957).

40. Danah Boyd, "Why Youth ♥ Social Network Sites: The Role of Networked Publics in Teenage Social Life," in *MacArthur Foundation Series on Digital Media and Learning—Youth, Identity, and Digital Media,* ed. David Buckingham (Cambridge: MIT Press, 2007), 119–42.

41. Albert K Cohen, *Delinquent Boys* (New York: The Free Press, 1955).

42. Talcott Parsons, *Essays in Sociological Theory* (New York: The Free Press, 1954).

43. Albert K Cohen, *Delinquent Boys* (New York: The Free Press, 1955), 168.

44. Travis Hirschi, *Causes of Delinquency* (Berkeley: University of California Press, 1969), 89–90.

45. James F. Short and Fred L. Strodtbeck, *Group Process and Gang Delinquency* (Chicago: University of Chicago Press, 1965), 264.

46. James F. Short and Fred L. Strodtbeck, *Group Process and Gang Delinquency* (Chicago: University of Chicago Press, 1965), 276.

47. Robert J. Sampson and John H. Laub, *Crime in the Making: Pathways and Turning Points through Life* (Cambridge: Harvard University Press, 1993).

48. Anthony Giddens, *Modernity and Self-Identity* (Cambridge: Polity Press, 1991).

49. Anthony Giddens, *Modernity and Self-Identity* (Cambridge: Polity Press, 1991), 14.

NOTES TO CHAPTER 5

1. Murray Levine and I conducted several of the interviews referred to in this chapter. Several graduate students assisted in collecting personal interview and survey data. Timothy McCorry conducted the vast majority of young-adult interviews referred to in this chapter. Susyan Jou was the project director for the 1990 survey.

2. Parent-adolescent attachment measures indicate the capacities of parents to monitor their adolescent's activities and to remain close to them. "Parental control" is the phrase that repeats itself in the literature. But attachments are a two-way street. Parental control suggests that the adolescent is an object rather than independent person. Both must be mutually attached to one another if they are to claim the controls that are necessary to prevent delinquency.

3. I have changed a few non-consequential facts about their stories to preserve the confidentiality of my subjects. There is a risk when working with a relatively small number of subjects that certain attributes will be associated with certain individuals. Of course all names have been changed.

4. I later divide parental relationship questions into those that are considered relational or instrumental. The instrumental questions refer to parental monitoring. They refer to questions that ask: Does your mother (father) know where you are when you are not at home? Does your mother (father) know who you are with when you are not at home? The scaled possible responses for these questions are: always, usually, sometimes, never, can't answer. Relational measures are based on a series of ten questions that ask about child-parent feelings of trust, empathy, and identification.

5. The consistency of self-control from childhood to adolescence and then adulthood is disputed in Jackie's narrative. Although criminologists have long noted the importance of self-control, where it comes from and how it is maintained are subject to considerable debate. For a discussion of how self-control is believed to be stable through the life course, see Michael R. Gottfredson and Travis Hirschi, *A General Theory of Crime* (Stanford, CA: Stanford University Press, 1990).

6. Elijah Anderson, *Street Wise: Race, Class, and Change in an Urban Community* (Chicago: University of Chicago Press, 1990).

7. The violent father is part of the David O narrative and is a story that I have heard about from other middle-class youth who have killed. The extent to which this is the case cannot be easily verified. Bill's outlet was drugs and alcohol and their anesthetizing effect may have served him well, especially in preventing him from responding to violence with even more violence.

8. Laurence D. Steinberg, *The Ten Basic Principles of Good Parenting* (New York: Simon & Schuster, 2004), 148.

NOTES TO CHAPTER 6

1. My use of the term "typification" draws on Alfred Schutz, *On Phenomenology and Social Relations; Selected Writings* (Chicago: University of Chicago Press,

1970), 111–22. For an example of its application to juvenile justice, see Aaron Cicourel, *The Social Organization of Juvenile Justice* (New York: Wiley, 1968). How officials typify adolescents is also illustrated in George Bridges and Sara Steen, "Racial Disparities in Official Assessments of Juvenile Offenders: Attributional Stereotypes as Mediating Mechanisms," *American Sociological Review* 63 (1998): 554–70.

2. David Matza, *Delinquency and Drift* (New York: John Wiley, 1964), 28.
3. David Matza, *Delinquency and Drift* (New York: John Wiley, 1964), 69.
4. Elliot Curie, *The Road to Whatever: Middle-Class Culture and the Crisis of Adolescence* (New York: Metropolitan Books, 2004).
5. Elliot Curie, *The Road to Whatever: Middle-Class Culture and the Crisis of Adolescence* (New York: Metropolitan Books, 2004), 121.

NOTES TO CHAPTER 7

1. Even Christine had her share of parental conflict and emotional difficulties as she related in her personal interview. Few youth are in the category of having performed as well she, as indicated by her educational attainments, few acts of offending, and her parental attachment scores.
2. "Developmental Assets: A Profile of Your Youth," Report Prepared for the Town of Amherst, New York (Minneapolis, MN: Search Institute, 2010).
3. John Braithwaite, *Crime, Shame, and Reintegration* (Cambridge: Cambridge University Press, 1989).
4. See Janet L. Lauritsen and Kenna F. Quinet, "Repeat Victimization among Adolescents and Young Adults," *Journal of Quantitative Criminology* 11 (1995): 143–65.
5. Geoffrey M. Maruyama. *Basics of Structural Equation Modeling* (Thousand Oaks, CA: Sage Publications, 1997), 131.
6. Travis Hirschi, *Causes of Delinquency* (Berkeley: University of California Press, 1969), 89–90.
7. The models had acceptable levels of fit based on their Chi-square to degrees of freedom ratio of less than 5. They also had Root Mean Square Error of Approximation (RMSEA) indicators of below .10. See Rex B. Kline, *Principles and Practice of Structural Equation Modeling* (New York: Guilford Press, 2011); L. Hu and P. M. Bentler, "Fit Indices in Covariance Structure Modeling: Sensitivity to Underparameterized Model Misspecification," *Psychological Methods*, 3, 4 (December 1998): 424–53.
8. John Hagan, *Structural Criminology* (New Brunswick: Rutgers University Press, 1989).
9. My use of the term "field of action" draws on contemporary sociological theory to suggest a social setting with its own set of interests and concerns. Each social setting can be recognized as having its hierarchal source of power, such as the authority of a parent, and misrecognized in terms of the impact that power has on desired attributes, such as the autonomy of the adolescent. The relational is critical in Pierre Bourdieu, "Social Space and Symbolic Power," *Sociological*

Theory 7 (1989): 14–25. Also see Mustafa Emirbayer, "Manifesto for a Relational Sociology," *The American Journal of Sociology* 103 (1997): 281–317.

10. Michael R. Gottfredson and Travis Hirschi, *A General Theory of Crime* (Stanford, CA: Stanford University Press, 1990).

11. Edwin Hardin Sutherland, *Principles of Criminology* (Philadelphia: Lippincott, 1955); Frederic M. Thrasher, *The Gang: A Study of 1,313 Gangs in Chicago* (Chicago: University of Chicago Press, 1963).

12. Elizabeth S. Scott and Laurence Steinberg, *Rethinking Juvenile Justice* (Cambridge: Harvard University Press, 2008); Franklin E. Zimring, *The Changing Legal World of Adolescence* (New York: Free Press, 1982).

13. Dana L. Haynie and D. Wayne Osgood, "Reconsidering Peers and Delinquency: How Do Peers Matter?" *Social Forces* 84 (2005): 1109–30.

14. John Hagan, "Destiny and Drift: Subcultural Preferences, Status Attainment, and the Risks and Rewards of Youth," *American Sociological Review* 56 (1991): 567–86.

15. Anthony Giddens, *The Consequences of Modernity* (Stanford, CA: Stanford University Press, 1990).

16. John Hagan, A. R. Gillis, and John Simpson, "The Class Structure of Gender and Delinquency: Toward a Power-Control Theory of Common Delinquent Behavior," *American Journal of Sociology* 90 (1985): 1151–78.

17. Marvin Wolfgang, Robert Figlio, and Thorsten Sellin, *Delinquency in a Birth Cohort* (Chicago: University of Chicago Press, 1972).

18. Offending peaks in the teenage years and then subsequently declines. Rolf Loeber and David P Farrington, "Age-Crime Curve," in *Encyclopedia of Criminology and Criminal Justice* (New York: Springer, 2014), 12–18.

NOTES TO CHAPTER 8

1. Giddens refers to the double hermeneutic of social science. The first is the scholarly publication and its interpretation by the social scientists. The second is the public's internalization of those findings as it might appear in the popular press or even in college courses. Anthony Giddens, *The Consequences of Modernity* (Stanford, CA: Stanford University Press, 1990), 16.

2. Brian Stelter, "Nick D'Aloisio, 17, of Britain, Developed His News-Reading App when He Was only 15";actual *New York Times* title is "He Has Millions and a New Job at Yahoo. Soon, He'll Be 18," March 25, 2013, http://www.nytimes.com/2013/03/26/business/media/nick-daloisio-17-sells-summly-app-to-yahoo.html?_r=0.

3. David Matza, *Becoming Deviant* (Englewood Cliffs, NJ: Prentice-Hall, 1969).

4. A description of a society that focuses solely on economic rewards is contained in Steven F. Messner and Richard Rosenfeld, *Crime and the American Dream* (Belmont, CA: Sage, 2007).

5. Elliot Curie, *The Road to Whatever: Middle-Class Culture and the Crisis of Adolescence* (New York: Metropolitan Books, 2004).

6. Stanley Cohen, *Visions of Social Control.* (Oxford, UK: Polity Press, 1985), 152–55.

7. Ross L. Matsueda and Karen Heimer, "A Symbolic Interactionist Theory of Role Transitions, Role Commitments, and Delinquency," in *Advances in Criminological Theory: Developmental Theories of Crime and Delinquency*, vol. 7, ed. T. Thornberry (New Brunswick, NJ: Transaction, 1997): 185.

8. Franklin E. Zimring, *American Juvenile Justice* (New York: Oxford University Press, 2005), 126.

9. Barry Feld, "A Slower Form of Death: Implications of *Roper v. Simmons* for Juveniles Sentenced to Life without Parole," *Notre Dame Journal of Law, Ethics, & Public Policy* 22 (2008): 58.

10. Franklin E. Zimring, *American Juvenile Justice* (New York: Oxford University Press, 2005), 126-127.

11. Zygmunt Bauman, *Globalization: The Human Consequences* (New York: Columbia University Press, 1998), 96.

12. Katherine Beckett and Steve Herbert, *Banished: The New Social Control in Urban America* (New York: Oxford University Press, 2009).

13. Suniya S. Luthar, "The Culture of Affluence: Psychological Costs of Material Wealth," *Child Development* 74 (2003): 1581–93.

14. Suniya S. Luthar, "The Culture of Affluence: Psychological Costs of Material Wealth," *Child Development* 74 (2003): 1582.

15. Suniya S. Luthar, "The Culture of Affluence: Psychological Costs of Material Wealth," *Child Development* 74 (2003): 1592.

16. Sarah Anne Hughes, "Jamey Rodemeyer, Bullied Teen Who Made 'It Gets Better' Video, Commits Suicide," *Washington Post*, September 21, 2011.

17. Anahad O'Connor, "Suicide Draws Attention to Gay Bullying," *New York Times*, September 21, 2011; "Jamey T. RODEMEYER Obituary," *Buffalo News*, September 21, 2011.

18. Sandra Tan, "Police Close Rodemeyer Case: Fail to Find Sufficient Evidence." *Buffalo News*, November 23, 2011;comment to article at www.buffalonews.com/article/20111123/CITYANDREGION/311239919.

INDEX

Italicized page numbers specify a table or illustration on a page, or its caption.

actualized self, 73–74, 124

adolescence, 92–107; biology of, 94–95; definition, 64; emotional security, 32–33; extra-familial adult relationships, 32; impulsivity, 95; in New York State, 82; as a period in life, 64; relational capacities for recognizing, 92–107; self-reliance, 32; transition to adulthood, 43, 47–49, 65, 83, 141, 175, 180, 242–243; transitional nature, 11; U.S. Supreme Court, 64–65

adolescents, 257–264; arrests, 22; autonomy, 74, 257–260, 290n9; decision-making, trial and error in, 263; depression, 28–29; expectations of, 257, 262–263, 267; freedom, 95–96; friendships, 109; "half a brain," 94–95; one trusted adult, need for, 103; parents, 134–135, 199, 200–201, 252, 289n2; rationality, 64–65, 260–264; responsibility assigned to, 48–49; second chances, 262; settings for, important, 252; values, their, 181; verbal abilities, 23; "youth discount," 263. *See also* youth

adulthood: achieving an adult identity, 175–176; Amherst youth as young adults, 236–237; delinquency, 242–243; transition from adolescence, 43, 47–49, 65, 83, 141, 175, 180, 242–243

affluence: Amherst, New York, 18; anxiety, 266; capital investments in youth, 220–221; Columbine, Colorado, 88; crime rate, 41, 43; delinquency, 237–238, 266; depression, 266; egalitarianism, 106; expertise, trust in professional, 70–72; levels of, 131–132; power, 132; safe cities, 17–18, 40–43, 74, 250; suburbs, 75; theft, thrill of, 131

affluent youth: juvenile justice, 25–26; offending among, 21–22; relational

modernity, 10; second and third chances, 45

Alwin, Duane, 105–106

American Builder (magazine), 77–78

American Dream, 76

Amherst, New York: affluence, 18; Boulevard Mall, *14*; census classification, 34; crime in, 182; crime rate, 19; density, *70*; educational attainment, 42; high schools, *46, 138*; home ownership rate, 43; houses of worship, number of, 220; housing, government-subsidized low-income, 41, 42, *108*; income, 42–43; juvenile court, youth referred to, 241; juvenile diversionary programs, 243; library, *84*; *Money Magazine*, 15, 34, *35*; Newark, New Jersey, compared to, 41–42; office parks, *18, 39, 178*; parks, 219; policing, 6–7, 239, 250; population, 15, 36, 41, 42, 256; recreational centers, 218–220, 233, 242, *244*; signage, *178*; subdivisions, *70, 75, 93, 108*; unemployment rate, 42; University of Buffalo campus, *xiv, 5, 41*, 254; woods, *75*; youth programs and facilities, *202, 216*–220, 242; youth studies of, 205–209

Amherst Central High School, *138*

Amherst Youth Board, 68, 205, 214, 218, 235

Amherst Youth Board Centers, 216

Amherst Youth Court, 220, 240

Analysis of Moment Structures (AMOS), 224–225

Anderson, Elijah, 113, 114, 124–128

anomie, 75–76, 236

anxiety, 266

arrests: of adolescents, 22; black *vs.* white, 23; gender, 240; inner cities, 21; official arrests, 238–239; peak age of, 240; race,

Simon I. Singer is Professor of Criminology and Criminal Justice at Northeastern University. Previously, he was Professor of Sociology at the University of Buffalo, SUNY. He is the author of *Recriminalizing Delinquency: Violent Juvenile Crime and Juvenile Justice Reform* (1996), winner of the American Sociological Association's 1999 Distinguished Scholar Award in Crime, Law, and Deviance.